3/2/3

Hannah Senesh

OTHER JEWISH LIGHTS
BOOKS OF INTEREST

I Am Jewish: Personal Reflections Inspired
by the Last Words of Daniel Pearl
Edited by Judea and Ruth Pearl

The Ethiopian Jews of Israel:
Personal Stories of Life in the Promised Land
By Len Lyons, PhD
Foreword by Alan Dershowitz
Photographs by Ilan Ossendryver

A Dream of Zion: American Jews Reflect
on Why Israel Matters to Them
Edited by Rabbi Jeffrey K. Salkin

Hannah Senesh

Her Life and Diary
The First Complete Edition

Foreword by **Marge Piercy**
Preface by **Eitan Senesh**
Afterword by **Roberta Grossman**

For People of All Faiths, All Backgrounds

JEWISH LIGHTS Publishing
Woodstock, Vermont

Hannah Senesh: Her Life and Diary, the First Complete Edition

2010 Quality Paperback Edition, Third Printing

Library of Congress Cataloging-in-Publication Data
Senesh, Hannah, 1921–1944.
Hannah Senesh : her life and diary / by Hannah Senesh ; foreword by Marge Piercy ; preface by Eitan Senesh.—1st complete ed.
p. cm.
ISBN-13: 978-1-58023-212-8 (hardcover)
ISBN-10: 1-58023-212-4 (hardcover)
1. Senesh, Hannah, 1921–1944. 2. Jews—Palestine—Biography. 3.Holocaust, Jewish (1939–1945)—Hungary. 4. World War, 1939–1945—Jewish resistance—Hungary. 5. Senesh, Hannah, 1921–1944—Diaries. I. Title.
CT1919.P38S3668 2004
940.53'18'092—dc22

2004014535

ISBN-13: 978-1-58023-342-2 (quality pbk.)
ISBN-10: 1-58023-342-2 (quality pbk.)

10 9 8 7 6 5 4 3

Parts of this book were published as *Hannah Senesh: Her Life and Diary* by Schocken Books, New York, 1972.

Cover design: Tim Holtz
Manufactured in the United States of America

Published by Jewish Lights Publishing
A Division of LongHill Partners, Inc.
Sunset Farm Offices, Route 4, P.O. Box 237
Woodstock, VT 05091
Tel: (802) 457-4000 Fax: (802) 457-4004
www.jewishlights.com

CONTENTS

Foreword   vii
   Marge Piercy

Preface   xi
   Eitan Senesh

Translator's Preface   xiii
   Marta Cohn

Memories of Hannah's Childhood   xvii
   Catherine Senesh

The Diary   1

The Letters   167

The Mission

   The Last Border   223
     Reuven Dafne

   How She Fell   231
     Yoel Palgi

   Meeting in Budapest   253
     Catherine Senesh

Selected Poems   295

Afterword   309
   Roberta Grossman

Reader's Guide   313

Historical Note   317

Notes   321

Foreword:
The Enigma of Hannah Senesh

For many years, after the lighting of the candles at my seder, as we begin the haggadah, we have recited Hannah Senesh's poem "Blessed Is the Match." I first ran across the story of Hannah Senesh in 1984, when I was researching and writing *Gone to Soldiers,* my novel about World War II. I did not use her in the novel, but her life and death deeply impressed me and I have never forgotten her.

I asked, as many have, why did a young girl from a relatively privileged background who was safely out of the war become a heroine? We have had in English only a few brief and poignant poems. What possessed her to fling herself back into danger? Why did she leave Palestine, enlist in the British army, train for clandestine activity behind enemy lines?

When we look at what she did, a young woman with the foresight to leave Hungary in 1939 and move to what was then Palestine, alone at eighteen, we are astonished. No one in her family or their circle were Zionists. They were not religious and she had never learned Hebrew until she chose to study it, with the aim of emigrating. They were assimilated Jews—her father had been a successful writer of comedies that were quite popular and was also a columnist for a paper. Her early diaries reveal a girl with the usual interests: She worried about doing well in school, wanted to be a writer, flirted with boys, adored her grandma, was teased by her brother. Only prescience adds meaning to the diaries of her early high school years.

Then in the midst of the early repression of Jews, her sense of that injustice awakened. She began to explore her identity as a Jew. Swiftly, that search became the core of her identity. She decided to prepare herself to go to Eretz Israel, and with little support of anyone close to her and to the dismay of her family, she persevered and was accepted to an agricultural school in Palestine.

This section of her diaries might be particularly useful to those too young to have any memory of the context in which the State of Israel was founded. Hannah, of course, died before Israel existed, but her reasons for becoming a Zionist should interest many to whom the word is almost a curse these days. Her diaries once she came to Palestine give us insight into what it was like under British rule.

She threw herself into whatever labor was assigned her—planting and harvesting in the fields, carpentry, poultry husbandry (her chosen field of interest), laundering, baking—no matter how boring she sometimes found the work. Her diaries from the moment she began to explore her Jewish identity gain in interest. She was honest about her occasional feelings that doing physical labor and menial work might not prove the best use of her talents. Yet her excitement and commitment continued to build. She was confident in her choice.

Her leadership emerged early in the kibbutz where she lived after agricultural school. Then, when a chance arose for her to return to Hungary to try to save Jews from the Holocaust, she again moved swiftly, this time to enlist under British control. That ability to imagine something and the moment it became possible to force it into reality was one of her outstanding traits. She was aware the British were only interested in rescuing their downed pilots, but nothing interfered with her sense of her true mission.

Somehow, she managed to escape the constricting effect of gender roles that hamper the full development of so many women. She never fell in love and her flirtations were minor. False modesty never compelled her to pretend she could not do what she could succeed at. She assumed leadership and it seemed to feel natural to those around her as well as to her. She was not particularly concerned with her appearance and her self-critical faculties were focused on her character and her actions, not on her face or her hair or her body. Every Yom Kippur, she took stock and found herself falling short of her ideals and intentions. She exuded charisma and vitality. Although introspective and judgmental toward herself, she was a cheerful person, energetic and able to enjoy whatever she could, even in prison, even in the shadow of the death we know from her last poem she expected.

Her bravery seemed natural and unforced, and yet almost blinding to those around her—whether she was learning to parachute, fighting with the partisans in what was then Yugoslavia, or refusing to talk under torture. The accounts from that last period of her life, from a fellow soldier, from her mother in the same prison, are particularly moving. The Nazis seemed puzzled by her, this young woman who was so proud to be a Jew, but they solved their discomfort by shooting her.

For us, she is also a puzzle, this short life that became so supercharged in her last years. Extraordinary courage is never quite explicable. But her later diaries, letters from Palestine, and the memories of those who knew her help us approach her far more closely than even her few beautiful unembellished poems. There is a directness and powerful simplicity in them that accords with our sense of Hannah Senesh as a woman who saw what she thought was right and should be done time after time, and as soon as she could, went and did it, no matter how difficult or dangerous it might prove to be. Reading those poems has to make a reader wish she had lived to develop her talent fully and to write far more to leave to us. If this collection helps us remember an exemplary and heroic woman, then it will have accomplished much.

Marge Piercy

PREFACE

Sixty years have passed since the death of my aunt, Hannah Senesh, who has become a symbol of Jewish heroism in the modern era. Many know the story of her mission and her murder, but few are familiar with the story of her life. I was born five years after her death—I got to "know" my aunt by reading her diaries and letters, and from stories that my grandmother Catherine and my father, Hannah's brother George, told me.

After my grandmother's death in 1992 at the age of ninety-six and my father's death in 1995, I began to receive letters from people who saw me as one of the last links to my aunt's legacy. When I visited the Holocaust Museum and Memorial in Washington, DC, in 1998, I spoke to Jewish educators from all over the world. Their continuing interest in Hannah catalyzed my decision to do as much as I could to keep her memory alive. Upon my return to Israel I worked with friends of my aunt's from Kibbutz Sdot Yam to launch a nonprofit foundation whose mission is to commemorate my aunt's life and values. Hannah Senesh exemplifies the Jewish—indeed, the universal—virtue of taking personal responsibility for general suffering. She never hesitated to sacrifice her own needs and comforts to serve others.

As someone who was born, educated, and raised in the sovereign state of Israel, I believe that Hannah's story, the values she embodied, and her way of life should be brought to the attention of young people throughout the world. I extend my thanks to Jewish Lights and its publisher, Stuart M. Matlins, for this newly expanded edition of my aunt's diaries, letters, and poems; and to my editor, Arthur Goldwag. I see this book as a blessed match and a flame, which fires the imagination, brings people closer to one another, and embodies the universal prayer for peace in this world.

Eitan Senesh
Haifa, Israel

TRANSLATOR'S PREFACE

In the national military cemetery, situated on top of the highest of the Judean Hills overlooking Jerusalem, there is a small circle set apart; within it are seven graves in the shape of a V, the outline of a parachute carved on each headstone. Buried in that circle are seven of the thirty-two Palestinian-Jewish parachutists, members of the British Armed Forces, who were dropped into Nazi-occupied Balkan countries during World War II in an effort to save their people from the Nazi Holocaust. Of the thirty-two sent, seven fell. One of the seven was Hannah Senesh, aged twenty-three and the only one of the seven about whom there is clear, definite testimony regarding her fate from the time of her capture until her execution.

Hannah Senesh has been called the Joan of Arc of Israel; she is a national heroine who has inspired books and plays. There are few in Israel who have not read her diary and poems, which have been translated into many languages. A ship, a forest, and two farming settlements have been named after her; thirty-two streets in Israel bear her name. The leading members of the government of Israel saluted her memory when she was buried with highest military honors among thousands of Israeli soldiers, her body having been brought from the Martyrs' Section of Budapest's Jewish cemetery, where she was buried by unknown hands after her execution in 1944.

Hannah Senesh was born on July 17, 1921, and began her diary when she was thirteen. It opens the door to a surprising Jewish world that continued to exist, relatively normally, while the rest of Europe's Jewry was being decimated. At the same time it explains why the talented daughter of a distinguished, assimilated Hungarian family chose to leave home, friends, and country to become a pioneering farm worker in Palestine.

When Hungary joined the Axis, Hannah, long since in Palestine, noted in her diary, "Sometimes I feel like one who has been sent ...

xiii

to perform a mission. What this mission is, is not clear to me...."
Although by then Palestinian Jews were fighting together with the
Free French, the British, and Tito's partisans, and operating in the
vast European underground, it was not until August 16, 1942, when
a group of Polish women arrived in Palestine and brought positive
and shattering reports of the systematic decimation of European
Jewry, that a decision was made by the Palestinians to attempt to rescue their brethren.

In January 1943, Hannah wrote in her diary, "I have had the sudden idea of going to Hungary.... Regardless of how clearly I see the
absurdity of this idea, it still seems possible and necessary to me." And
at that very moment a group in Palestine was making plans to reach
the remaining Jews in the Balkans and in Hungary—by parachute—
in order to help them flee for their lives. Hannah Senesh immediately volunteered for this mission. It was a military operation
without precedent, a crusade in which each member was a novice as
well as his or her own commanding officer. None had been drafted;
all had begged and demanded to be chosen. They had been selected
with infinite care. Each had outstanding physical and mental attributes; each required special linguistic qualifications. They had to be
parachutists, secret agents, and saboteurs. And they had to have that
special brand of courage possessed only by those who are willing to
die for a cause.

Their first objective, and the sole condition upon which the
British military granted approval and cooperation, was the liberation
of Allied pilots shot down behind Nazi lines and the organization of
resistance in all occupied countries. Only after this mission was completed were they free to attempt rescuing, via the underground in
partisan territory, the million and a quarter Jews still believed to be
alive in Rumania, Hungary, and Czechoslovakia.

The parachutists, among them Hannah, took off on their mission
from Brindisi, Italy, on March 13, 1944, and were dropped into
Yugoslavia. Reuven Dafne, a fellow parachutist whose account
appears in this volume, said during a conversation: "We parachutists
were not supermen—nor superwomen. Supermen exist only on tel-
evision. We were small, frail, inexperienced romantic people with all

the shortcomings of the average person. None of us was unique—excepting perhaps Hannah. She was different ... a spiritual girl guided almost by mysticism. Perhaps one can say she had charisma.... She was fearless, dauntless, stubborn. Despite her extraordinary intelligence and prescience, she was a kind of tomboy—a poet-tomboy—which sounds rather odd, I know. A girl who dreamed of being a heroine—and who was a heroine."

Dafne parted from Hannah on June 9, 1944, at a village near the Hungarian border, just before she crossed into Nazi-occupied territory. "When we said good-bye she pressed a piece of paper into my hand saying, 'If I don't return, give this to our people.' I was amazed by her attitude. It was so unlike her. I looked at the piece of paper and was even more surprised. At a time like that she had written a poem. I had had no idea she even wrote poetry. I almost threw it away. It was 'Blessed Is the Match,' the poem every Israeli, young or old, can now recite from memory."

Marta Cohn

Hannah Senesh, three years old, with her brother Gyuri,
four years old.

Memories of Hannah's Childhood

The deepest pain a mother can experience is to outlive her child—perhaps because it is so alien to nature. It is also unusual, and an emotional contradiction, for a bereaved parent to step out of retirement and make public her most treasured and painful memories. But I have been haunted by the idea of chronicling my memories of Hannah for years, not because I want to call attention to myself, but because her life now belongs to posterity. Whether what she did was the consequence of circumstances, early environment, or a specific feeling of mission, she herself answers in her diary and other writings. There were, however, certain events in her richly endowed and tragically curtailed life to which I was the most intimate witness, and thus it is probably right that I should record them.

From earliest childhood Hannah's environment was warm and cheerful. With her brother, Gyuri, a year her senior, the question of a playmate was completely solved, and the gay, cheerful nursery, filled with joyous laughter, was not only their domain but a wellspring of happiness for my husband and myself, and for "Fini Mama"—my mother—who lived with us.

Hannah's father was an author and playwright. He used to work mainly in the evening and often late into the night, and because of this, as well as a serious heart condition caused by an illness he suffered in early youth, he would stay in bed most of the morning. Thus, unless rehearsals or the heat of work drove him to bed at dawn, the children were part of his morning routine. They would sit on his bed while he bantered with them and told them a wealth of stories that were born in his fertile imagination and created solely for their pleasure. It turned out later that all these stories lived on in Hannah's memory.

I so clearly recall a morning when Hannah was five years old. She sat on her father's bed and reenacted the entire holiday program given by her brother's first grade. She recited from beginning to end, almost word for word, the legend of the christening of the heathen Vajk, who was baptized as Saint Stephan by Bishop Gellert, as well as the story of the growth of Christianity in Hungary. She gave exact dates and names without skipping a single one. My husband motioned me to listen, and he later noted that Hannah's comprehension seemed to him extraordinary. When we were about to celebrate Hannah's fourth birthday, her father sat her on his knee and told her that as she was such a good, obedient child and gave us so much joy and happiness, we wanted to give her a gift that would really please her. Would she tell us what she really wanted, what would give her the greatest joy? She gave this amazing answer: "I'd like just one single thing, Daddy ... I know every child is supposed to love her parents best. But if you'll both let me, I'd like to love Fini Mama best of all." Of course her father was delighted by this answer. He hugged and kissed her, and happily consented to this "birthday gift."

And who could have been more pleased than Fini Mama, her grandmother? She was extremely close to the children, as we were often away for weeks at a time, secure in the knowledge that they were being thoughtfully supervised and receiving the most loving care. No matter where we were, my mother's detailed accounts of their welfare reached us punctually. One summer, after a particularly lengthy absence, we reached home to find the children dressed in their best clothes, flowers clasped in their hands. As I hugged Hannah, who must have been about three, I felt that she was unusually warm. "Is anything the matter?" I asked my mother. "Hannah seems feverish." In fact, she was ill, but she had begged to be allowed to get up and dress for our arrival, "So Mommie won't be frightened." She was singularly gentle, sensitive, good-natured, and compliant, but at the same time independent—and, even as a small child, extremely self-assured.

Foreseeing that his sick heart would rob him from us at an early age, my husband attempted to provide the children with as many rich and happy memories as possible. There were all sorts of excursions, visits to the amusement park and the delightful Budapest Zoo, and innumerable "story-telling" afternoons for the children and their friends. All of this was surpassed by the joy of having their father come to the nursery to play with them, which he often did. But their uninterruptedly happy childhood ended cruelly and suddenly in May of 1927, when a heart attack, suffered in his sleep, snatched their father from them. Gyuri was seven, Hannah barely six. He was only thirty-three. A few days earlier my husband had risen very early, anxious to get to work on a half-finished play that was giving him trouble. I watched him in the mirror opposite my bed as he knotted his tie, and I happily observed how well he looked, tanned from a recent vacation at Lake Balaton. Suddenly he said, "You know, I was just thinking—I actually could end my life now. I've attained everything a Jewish writer possibly can in Hungary. I'm a respected columnist on the foremost newspaper,[1] my plays are performed at the Comedy Theater with casts of my own choosing ... the ink hardly has time to dry before my work is in print. What more can there be? The gates of the National Theatre will never be open to a Jewish writer; but even if I had a choice, I think my plays are really far better suited to the Comedy Theatre. So what more can happen? Success abroad? Films? Money? I've had it all. Really, I could calmly go now."

This was not the first time he had talked of death, and there are many posthumous poems that bear witness to a mood of resignation which—who knows how often?—sometimes engulfed him. But outwardly he seemed so contented, his writing invariably filled with unstinted wit and humor. Forcing back tears, I asked, "And don't you even think of us? What would become of us without you?"

"Naturally, that's the painful part," he answered. "But I entrust the children to you with complete confidence. I know they'll be in the best of hands." (Had he but guessed!) He ended the grimly serious conversation with a humorous remark, and went to his study.

You can see how Hannah's sensitive nature reacted to her loss by the poems she wrote soon afterwards: "Sadness," "Oh, You Happy Children," and "Past Happiness," the first two lines of which read, "I would like to be glad, but don't know how/No matter how I'd like to be, no matter how I want to be...." Since she was only in the first grade and still somewhat uneasy about using pen and ink, she dictated these poems to Fini Mama, who recorded them in her beautiful, symmetrical script. That Hannah inherited her father's talent is beyond dispute. Later—if only from force of habit—Fini Mama recorded all of Hannah's poems in a little copybook, which Hannah took with her to Palestine along with her other most cherished possessions.

In their early childhood, Gyuri and Hannah heard little about religion and Judaism. Though we considered ourselves to be good, steadfast Jews, we did not feel it important to observe the outer formalities of religion. My husband's creed, his guiding principle, was humanism, and he worshiped at its altar with his deeds, in the written word, and in speech. Thus, it was at school that the children were versed in the foundations of religion and religious life. Hannah participated in all Jewish movements from the very beginning—but then she was in the vanguard of all her school activities. From the very first she felt at home in school. Her first-grade teacher once told me that whenever it was necessary to leave the children alone for a while, she had only to tell Hannah to sit at the desk. Hannah would tell the children stories, and hold their attention to such an extent that they listened in utter silence.

A charming childhood episode—somewhere between the ages of eight and ten—was the "Newspaper of the Little Seneshes," which the children published. Readers who paid for it with chocolates passed typewritten copies of its "limited edition" from hand to hand. Gyuri was its "illustrator," and Hannah supplied practically all the copy. Among their circle of little friends a few volunteered as associates, and their writings duly appeared. When the noted Hungarian author Zsolt Harsany heard about the little paper, he sent a charming verse for publication, accompanied by a letter stating that he was making an exception and waiving his usual fee for his contribution. While their father was alive the children didn't see any of his plays. After all, they were written for adults. But after his death I took them to see those still running, to revivals, and to performances of posthumous comedies, so they could retain some memory of their father's theatrical success. However, this actually proved to be unnecessary, since they heard about the plays—still very much alive in people's memories—wherever they went. Thus, they not only guarded his memory with profound love but were also enormously proud of him. At the age of seven, Hannah expressed this pride in a most touching manner. Every evening the children gave me a detailed report of how they had spent their day. Gyuri, who had passed the afternoon with a friend, enthusiastically elaborated on each of the many interesting new toys with which they had played. He finally ended with the sincere, deep sigh of a child and said, "Ivan is really a lucky kid to have so many good toys." Whereupon Hannah, her widened eyes reflecting astonishment, said, "You think Ivan is a lucky boy because he has so many toys? I thought you were going to say he's lucky because his father is alive. But I wouldn't change places with him anyway because no one in the world has the kind of father that we had."

When Hannah was about to enter the fifth grade, the new quarters of a prestigious Protestant girls' school opened in the immediate vicinity of our house. After a great many years of strict segregation, they had started accepting Catholic and Jewish pupils. There was, however, the stipulation that those of Christian faiths other than Protestant had to pay double the normal tuition fees, the Jewish students treble. Nevertheless, I decided to enroll Hannah. At the end of the first year, when she brought home her usual outstanding report, richly annotated with the praise of her teachers, I felt the moral issue of discrimination—quite apart from the financial burden—to be intolerable. I called on the principal and said that whereas in any other school Hannah would have been awarded a scholarship, in this one I was paying a three-fold tuition fee. Because of this, regardless of how much I valued the high academic standards of the school, I said I felt compelled to enroll elsewhere—whereupon the teacher Hannah loved most said, "No, no, we won't allow her to leave. She is our finest student and sets an example to the entire school. There has never been a precedent, but please submit a written request stating your point of view, and we'll bring it up at our next meeting." Considering that, according to the rules formulated by the school's founders, only Protestant girls were permitted to pay the minimum fee, it was some satisfaction—though not very much—that thereafter

Bela and Catherine Senesh, Hannah's parents, in the early 1920s.

Hannah's tuition fees were to be the same as those of the Catholic girls. But whenever they could, Hannah's teachers demonstrated their recognition of her abilities by awarding her prizes for the various scholastic competitions.

At home she was completely involved, and obviously happy, interested in everything that concerned the family. She was considerate, gentle, conscientious, responsible. She managed her time amazingly well, making use of every moment. When she came home from school she spent the half hour before lunch at her desk finishing the day's homework, and apart from that I rarely saw her study. Instead, she tutored others. From the age of eleven on she always had pupils. A marvelous pedagogic sense, coupled with endless patience, seemed to predestine her for teaching.

I was astonished that she found the time to do so many things, and often protested that her days were too crammed with activities. For besides her regular schoolwork she studied languages and music, participated in various sports, was extremely social, went on excursions and to concerts, and was an omnivorous reader. Her levelheaded, accurate judgment surprised us on many occasions, and her exceptional organizational ability manifested itself early. As she matured she enveloped her brother with increasing thoughtfulness, love, and almost maternal solicitude, as if to compensate for the loss of their father. During adolescence they argued a good deal, quarreled, made up. But if we scolded Gyuri because of his passion for sports, or for his occasionally loutish behavior, Hannah invariably defended him. She told my mother and me that we were totally unfamiliar with the psychological factors involved in the development of a growing boy, and unaware what boys his age were generally like. Compared with most boys, she assured us, Gyuri was absolutely angelic.

Not only did Hannah respect her Grandmother Fini, she loved her devotedly. They spent many cozy, intimate hours in Fini Mama's room sewing and discussing the past, the future, the present. Hannah was her favorite of her seven adored grandchildren. But Hannah was also close to her paternal grandmother, who told her stories about her father's childhood. We generally spent the Jewish high holidays with my mother-in-law and the immediate members of her vast family, who, during Hannah's childhood, numbered so many that it was difficult to seat them all around her huge dining room table. In a letter Hannah wrote her from Palestine in 1940, she said that in thought she would still be at the table on the eve of Passover. (By then the table was much smaller, as many of the older members of the family had died, and the younger ones had fled from the dreadful Jewish Laws.)

Her relationship with me can best be gleaned from her diaries, letters, and poems. On school holidays and Sunday mornings we often took long walks together, and although she tended to be reticent, with me she made a conscious attempt to overcome this characteristic. Never, not even during her adolescence, did I feel that I had anything less than her complete confidence. When she was twelve, she wrote a poem that included the following verse:

> Dearest Mother I feel, dearest Mother I know
> That in this big, wide world
> The best friend I have—is you.
> Wherever I will live, wherever I will go,
> A better friend than you I'll not find
> Ever.

Around the time she wrote this, the chief rabbi of our synagogue praised Hannah for her recital of a votive text. "Only one other person has ever recited it more beautifully," he said, "and that was Franceska Gal." To which Gyuri commented, "It's possible Franceska Gal recited it more beautifully, but Hannah will also keep her vows." (The renowned Hungarian actress had converted to Christianity.)

Was Hannah pretty? At first glance, no. But once you knew her, you could see how appealing she was. Her face was dominated by large, expressive eyes, which mirrored her intelligence; sometimes they were green, sometimes blue-green. Her wide forehead was framed by soft, wavy hair; her face was attractively oval; her smile charming; her figure excellent; her manner, behavior, personality, and character in general, winning. When she spoke she was listened to attentively.

Until the age of seventeen Hannah fully enjoyed the delights, pleasures, and amusements of youth, but then her diary reveals a radical change of direction in her life. We had lost our Fini Mama only a year before. Gyuri had gone to France to continue his education instead of to Vienna, as originally planned, because Austria had surrendered to Hitler. We didn't discuss it, but it seemed unlikely that Gyuri would ever return. Hannah knew how upset I was by these partings. Only gradually, over a period of months, did she acquaint me with her plans to emigrate to Palestine. At first I was strongly opposed to her decision, but her many intelligent and convincing arguments weakened my objections. Once she said that even if she had not happened to be born a Jew she would still be on the side of the Jews because one must help, by all possible means, a people who were being treated so unjustly now, and who had been abused so miserably throughout history. On another occasion, when I asked what had become of her ambition to be a professional writer (considering one had but one mother tongue), she answered, "That question is dwarfed by present burning problems." Finally she tackled me with this statement: "Mother, if you don't agree to my going, of course I won't go. But I want you to know I feel miserable in this environment and don't wish to live in it."

I resigned myself to her going, but when she asked me to further her plans by assisting her in obtaining a WIZO (Women's International Zionist Organization) certificate through the good offices of friends, I brushed aside her request, saying, "I won't place any obstacles in your way now that you've made your decision, but don't ask me to help you leave."

So she made her arrangements entirely on her own. She ran back and forth to the secretary of WIZO, repeatedly wrote to the Agricultural School at Nahalal in Palestine concerning admission, went often to the Maccabee Society, diligently studied Hebrew, and read a tremendous number of books—almost all concerning Zionist and Jewish matters. Though she was physically still with me, she was actually already living in another world. Outwardly she appeared controlled, as always, but anyone close to her could sense the excitement and stirrings within her.

I certainly didn't see her prepare for her graduation, and she spent a minimum amount of time with her erstwhile friends and companions. When I asked her why I so rarely saw her with boys, she confessed she had decided to moderate her association with boys so that the pain of her eventual departure would not be compounded by the additional burden of the breakup of a romantic relationship. "As soon as I notice a boy showing particular interest in me, I stop seeing him," she said.

Here I must mention a school incident that occurred in 1937, and which undoubtedly precipitated matters. Hannah was elected to a post in the school's literary society. At the very first meeting she attended, Hannah was told that a new election for the office to which she had been duly elected was already scheduled, because Jewish students were not allowed to hold office. Apparently calm and controlled, she sat through the meeting, and when one of her classmates was elected, and tearfully approached Hannah declaring she would not accept the appointment because she knew she was not deserving of it, Hannah said, "Accept it calmly, and don't think for an instant that I begrudge it to you. Not at all. If you don't accept it, someone else will. After all, it has nothing to do with whether Hannah Senesh or Maria X is more capable of fulfilling the assignment, but whether the person is a Jew or a Gentile." Her teacher vehemently condemned the students' behavior, but obviously she could do nothing about the decision of the self-governing student body. "I hope, Hannah, you'll continue to participate in the activities of the literary society, despite what has happened," she said. "How can you imagine such a thing?" Hannah responded. When she told me of the incident I realized how deeply hurt she had been by the whole affair, though she never spoke of it again.

During the Easter holiday of 1939 we went to visit Gyuri in Lyon. Hannah was delighted to learn that he had also become a dedicated Zionist. I watched them indulgently as they discussed and planned the future with youthful zeal, eyes sparkling. They decided that Hannah would emigrate within a few months and that Gyuri would follow when his studies were completed. Their great concern was for me to join them. I felt then as if a cold hand were gripping my heart: Would we ever again sit together like this, I wondered—the three of us? Where ... when ... ?

When we returned home, the feverish preparations for her departure actually began. She gathered together her most cherished keepsakes—books, letters, photographs—and assembled her thoughtfully and lovingly selected collection of art reproductions. One day she told me that she would like to say farewell to the grave of Fini Mama and asked if my sisters and I would go along with her. My parents were buried in my native town of Janoshaza, where Hannah had never been. The visit was planned for the day before her final exams. When I warned her that the long, tiring journey might have a detrimental effect on her work, she smilingly reassured me that it wouldn't. She wandered all over the little town, determined to see everything—including the house where I was born. She took a great many photographs and interrogated the elderly relatives who still lived there. She had long been planning to assemble a family tree and took advantage of the opportunity to add more data to her growing file. Before she left for Palestine, she actually did prepare a complete family history, including her notes and observations, which she dedicated to the memory of Fini Mama.

After graduating summa cum laude, Hannah said good-bye to the school and to all her teachers. She was extremely pleased to receive the book award from the Jewish Community of Buda "in appreciation of outstanding diligence in Bible Class and work in furthering the advancement of the Jewish Community." By then her plans were general knowledge, but her teachers were reluctant to accept her decision to emigrate. Each in turn tried to prevail upon me to prevent her from taking this step, emphasizing that they would positively guarantee her acceptance by the university. (During those years the numerous clauses that restricted the number of Jewish students permitted to enter university had become increasingly strict.) When I related all this to Hannah, she said, "Perhaps I ought to be impressed that in view of graduating summa cum laude, and with a plethora of recommendations from teachers and friends, I can get into the university, while a Gentile who just barely squeezed through the exams can sail in! Don't they understand that I don't want to be

Gyuri, six years old, and Hannah, five years old.

just a student; that I have plans, dreams, ambitions; and that the road to their fulfillment would only be barred to me here?"

When I brought up the most disputed question between us—that if she must go to Palestine, why to agricultural school, why not to the university, where, according to her talents and capabilities, she actually belonged, and where she would certainly prove more useful and productive than in something so completely alien to her as farm work—I received an answer that had, by then, become customary: "There are already far too many intellectuals in Palestine; the great need is for workers who can help build the country. Who can do the work if not we, the youth?"

That summer we went to Dombóvár, as we always did, for all our vacations. The Sas family, our most beloved relatives, lived there; since the death of my husband, theirs had been my children's second home. Every morning of that vacation found Hannah studying Hebrew, and during the noon hours, when the sun was scorching and everyone tried to remain in the cool indoors, she worked in the big garden in order to accustom herself, she explained, to the torrid climate of Palestine. And every day she expectantly awaited the mail, which finally, in the latter half of July, brought her the long-awaited immigration certificate. The remaining few weeks skipped by with dizzying speed.

At the beginning of September, the time of her expected departure, World War II broke out, and for the moment all roads leading to Palestine were apparently closed. I resigned myself to this new situation, but not she. She ran to various travel agencies, to the official representative of Palestine, to the Jewish Social Aid office—wherever she thought there was a glimmer of hope. One evening she quietly commented, "I know, Mama dear, even if you don't say it, that you would be completely resigned to my remaining here. But look—for me life here has become absolutely meaningless." Finally she succeeded in attaching herself to a group of Palestine-bound Slovaks, and we rushed to the Jewish Social Aid office to arrange her papers. Toward evening we were standing in one of the outer rooms when an official motioned us to follow him to his office. "For whom shall I do this, if not for the daughter of Bela Senesh?" he said. "He was one of

my father's favorite pupils. I'm the son of Chief Rabbi Miksa Weiss."
After making out the required papers, he informed us that departure
would be the next day from the east railway station.

I felt as though ice were flowing through my veins. "Tomorrow?
But she has to get ready, to pack." "Madame, I've done my share," he
replied. "The rest is up to you."

Grandmother Senesh, the closest relatives, a few good friends were
told, and they came to say good-bye. Hannah and I packed all night.
Next morning she still had to run to travel agents and consulates for
visas. On September 13, 1939, at one o'clock, we stepped through
the gate of our little house. We both tried to control our emotions,
but at the last moment, as she put her arms around our faithful
Rosika, Hannah began sobbing and said, "Rosi, take care of Mama."
And the simple peasant girl—goodness personified, in whose eyes
Hannah was the Lord's most perfect creation—fulfilled this request
as faithfully as if it had been God's own command. At the station one
of my sisters saw to the customs and luggage, and we all took final
leave of Hannah. Standing at the train window, she required all her
strength to choke back the sobs. The tensions of the last weeks,
months, the excitement were topped by the parting, the final break,
and the total uncertainty of the future. As the train inched out, it
seemed as if a great shadow were being cast over the entire station.
When I arrived home in the early dusk of that September afternoon,
the melancholy mood of Rosh Hashanah had already settled over
the empty house, and the flickering candles seemed to magnify my
feeling of being utterly spent. Fate had relentlessly intruded upon
our lives, torn our little family apart, scattered us in three directions.

Catherine Senesh

THE DIARY

There are stars whose radiance is visible on earth though they have long been extinct. There are people whose brilliance continues to light the world though they are no longer among the living. These lights are particularly bright when the night is dark. They light the way for Mankind.

—Hannah Senesh

Budapest, aged thirteen, September 7, 1934

This morning we visited Daddy's grave. How sad that we had to become acquainted with the cemetery so early in life. But I feel that even from beyond the grave Daddy is helping us, if in no other way than with his name. I don't think he could have left us a greater legacy.

September 12, 1934

Today was the first day of school. Once again a year has passed. New teachers; everything seems so strange now. I shall miss Aunt Ilona[1] an awful lot, and even though Aunt Boriska seems nice, one can't form an opinion so soon. Our new teacher of Hungarian literature is marvelous, and a distinguished poet as well. His name is Lajos Jékely, but he writes under the name of Lajos Áprily. It is a joy to attend his classes. It's strange to realize that next year I'll be in high school. It's horrible to think how quickly time passes. I hope this school year will be satisfactory too.

September 20, 1934

The other day there was an election in school as to who would keep the Day Book. I got all the votes but two. It was not the appointment that made me so happy, but rather that all the girls in my class like me.

October 7, 1934

Yesterday, and today, Sunday, no school. This morning there was a lovely celebration, and this afternoon I went to synagogue. Those afternoon services are so odd; it seems one does everything but pray. The girls talk and look down at the boys, and the boys talk and look up at the girls[2]—this is what the entire thing consists of.

I'm glad I've grown lately. I'm now five feet tall and weigh 99 pounds. I don't think I'm considered a particularly pretty girl, but I hope I'll improve.

3

October 14, 1934

Today I finally reached an agreement with Marianne's mother. I'm
to tutor Marianne six hours a week. I will be paid 15 *pengö* per
month.[3] It's not as much as Mrs. Erdy paid me, but I am happy about
it just the same. I don't think any other girl in my class earns as
much. Now I can pay for dancing and skating lessons with my own
money. Perhaps I'll even buy a season ticket for the ice rink.

October 20, 1934

Yesterday morning Dalmady, whose father recently died, came back
to school. The poor girl is very sad, naturally. But at least she did have
her father for thirteen years. Something very touching happened
during physics. Dalmady, of course, had not prepared the lesson, and
she wanted to explain why to the teacher. However, you have to stay
at your desk during class, and if you want to say anything you have
to do so from there. The poor dear began crying the moment she
stood up. She remained standing for a few moments, uncertain what
to do, then suddenly walked up to the teacher and whispered that
her father had died. There followed a beautiful scene in which the
old teacher shook hands with the little girl. Written down this way
it isn't moving, but almost the entire class wept.

November 18, 1934

I have not been able to write for a long time, as I've been extremely
busy. Gyuri found my diary not long ago and read the entire thing.
I was furious because he constantly teased me about it. But last night
he took a solemn oath never to mention it again.

Friday was the fifteenth anniversary of Horthy's[4] election. We
went down to the Vérmezö and saw the whole celebration. As I
stood there watching all those soldiers I somehow thought that seeing them on parade was beautiful. But what would become of them
in a war? Mother says that the present atmosphere is very warlike. It's
a good thing Gyuri is still so young. Even so, God protect us from

war. Why, the whole world would be practically wiped out.

But at the moment I have more immediate problems: report time is approaching. It's possible I'll have a bad mark for neatness, but we'll hope for the best. Otherwise I think I'll be all right.

November 27, 1934

All my marks were good, including neatness. But I must improve in French. It's good to think that in less than a month it will be Christmas vacation!

December 25, 1934

Sunday we went to the Opera to hear *The Barber of Seville*. It was a beautiful performance with an exceptionally fine cast. This long vacation is wonderful—from December 22 to January 7. I received a lot of presents too. From Mother, tickets to the Opera; from Fini Mama,[5] two pairs of stockings; from my other grandmother, a lovely little brooch; from Aunt Ilus, fabric for a sweet little summer dress; from Aunt Irma, handkerchiefs and ski socks. Besides all this, three handsome books. I embroidered a bookmark for Mama; I gave Fini Mama stationery, and Gyuri a little savings bank.

January 1, 1935

Again a New Year! How time flies! While awaiting it at midnight such a strange feeling took hold of me. What, I wonder, will the New Year bring? Happiness? Sadness? If it will be only as good as last year, that will be all right too. Yesterday we went to the Opera to hear *Die Fledermaus*. It was very beautiful. What a pity vacation will soon be over.

January 30, 1935

I had a very good time at the Dance Circle. It lasted from six-thirty to ten o'clock. According to Gyuri I looked very well, and I thought

I did too. I danced a lot, not only with Gyuri's friends, but with a lot of older boys as well. This was my first real dance!

Tomorrow distribution of report cards! I think I'll get a B in French. Nevertheless, I think I'm presently the best pupil in my class.

April 7, 1935

Évi[6] is arriving at noon and will stay for a few days. I'm looking forward to seeing her. It's possible that she may come to my school next year, because its standards are much higher than those in Dombóvár. I put up a big fight to get her to transfer, even though this would mean a great responsibility for me. I hope we won't quarrel—though I am a little worried about this. And we will have to be very careful not to become rivals. That would disrupt the peace.

A few days ago we all had quite a fright: Gyuri and I were fighting about my English notebook, and while we were at it he had his fountain pen in his hand—which he probably forgot. In the midst of battle the pen injured me just under my eye. Mother became very frightened and I cried horribly (though it actually didn't hurt much). Gyuri was terrified.

Of course I couldn't tell my teachers or classmates that I was hurt while fighting with my brother, so I said I fell and hurt myself. The iodine is finally beginning to wear off, so I don't look quite so awful.

April 27, 1935

We got our class reunion rings today. We'll meet on May 1, 1945. Ten years from now! What a long time! How many things can happen between now and then.

May 31, 1935

We are going to have a celebration at school and give a performance of Madách's *The Tragedy of Man*.[7] I'm going to take the part of the Angel Michael. It was rumored that boys would be invited and that after the performance there would be a dance. But the rumors proved false. I'm sorry because I do so like to dance.

Things at school look very good, apart from French. I'm really ashamed of myself for having such difficulty improving in the only subject with which I have any trouble. This has nothing to do with grades—I actually got an A in French—but with my lack of self-confidence in the subject. My only consolation is that all the others in my class are being tutored at home, so they have a decided advantage.

Aged fourteen, August 29, 1935

I didn't take my diary along this summer because I didn't expect to have time to write, and also because I was afraid someone might find it. Not that I have any secrets. Even so, I don't think I would like anyone to read it. So I'll have to write everything in retrospect.

School ended on June 15 (my report card was straight A's, as I expected—with the exception of French), and at two o'clock the same afternoon I was on the train. We met Judy and her family at the station, and I said good-bye to Mother. I had not realized until then that I would not see her for a month and a half. I spent seventeen days at Lake Balaton. Considering everything, I must say I enjoyed myself, though I certainly did not feel as much at home as, for example, at Dombóvár. Nor did I achieve a truly warm friendship with Judy. Her little sister was the one, I think, who really was fond of me.

Aunt Ella and Uncle Egon were very nice, and what really made the two weeks most interesting and meaningful were all the new things I heard from Uncle Egon. He opened a whole new world to me, though there are a good many things in that world I don't quite believe in—like whether there really are elves and fairies. However, I think that in astrology, spiritualism, and the development of the soul, there is a lot in which I can believe, and if people believe in some of this they can be greatly comforted.

During the summer I read Maeterlinck's *Blue Bird* and found in it things of great value, such as I've found in no other book I have read so far. For instance, the premise that there are no dead because the dead can be resurrected through memories. I felt an empathy with this great truth, because just by thinking of Daddy I seem able to bring back that time when he was alive. I can't describe exactly what I feel, but one thing is certain: one must be careful with whom one talks about such things, because most people just laugh and poke fun.

From Balaton I went to Dombóvár on July 3. The first few days I missed Balaton a little, it's really wonderfully beautiful. But in Dombóvár I joined in so many interesting and amusing activities that it amply compensated for not having the lake. I got along well with Évi. In fact, we hit it off so perfectly that I felt horrible about her not being accepted by my school. Actually I got the news of her rejection while I was at the lake, and felt so badly about it I went to my room and cried. Of course the others didn't know why I was crying, but they noticed something was bothering me. This I couldn't stand, because if there were anything wrong with me I would rather not mention it, as I can't bear to have people feeling sorry for me.

Now I'm going to answer a question Gyuri has repeatedly asked: Do boys interest me? Well, yes, they interest me more than before, but only in general because I didn't see a single boy I really liked the entire summer. True, I didn't meet very many. This is my idea of the ideal boy: he should be attractive and well dressed, but not a fop; he should be a good sportsman, but interested in other things besides sports; he should be cultured and intelligent, but good-humored and not arrogant; and he should not chase after girls. And so far I have not met a single boy like this.

I wrote two poems during the summer. One is for Mama's birthday; the other I've told no one about, as I'm embarrassed that it's about life again. I guess I was born to be a philosopher because in all things I see life in miniature: in the day (morning, noon, evening), in the river (source, course, outlet), in the seasons (spring, summer, fall, and sleep is winter)—everything is like birth, life, death. This is why I am always thinking of life and death—not the way romantic little girls do who are so sure they will never marry, and die young—but as the great, everlasting laws of nature. This is the poem:

> Life is a brief and hurtling day,
> Pain and striving fill every page.
> Just time enough to glance around,

Register a face or sound
and—life's been around.

This morning we went to the cemetery. As far as I'm concerned,
I can see no point in going such a very long way merely to stand
before Daddy's grave for a few moments when I'm actually with him
in thought every evening, asking whether he is satisfied with me,
whether my behavior pleases him. I can hardly remember Daddy (his
face), but just the same I love him very much and always feel he is
with me. I would like to be worthy of him as a writer, too. I know
I have a little talent, but I don't think it's more than that. Although
the desire to write is constantly alive within me, I still don't consider writing my life's goal or ambition, but rather a way of making
myself and those around me happy. Perhaps, through writing, I will
be able to contribute something toward human happiness. This, in
itself, is a fairly ambitious task, and outside of it I don't really know
what I would like to do or be. On the whole, I would say I would
like to be a teacher, but this, I know, is difficult.

I am reading Harsányi's *Ecce Homo*. It's very interesting.

September 16, 1935

Mama asked whether I would like to take piano lessons again this
year, and I said yes. So I had my first lesson today. Although I know
I haven't got a very good ear, and that I could never consider music
as a profession, I still like to play the piano very much, and really do
enjoy music. Sometimes when Mama plays Chopin I feel like crying. It is so inexplicably beautiful and enjoyable.

In general, I delight in all things beautiful. Last Sunday I went to
the Fine Arts Museum and loved everything, but above all, the paintings of Munkácsy.[8] The most moving of the statues was one of
Strobl's,[9] called "Mothers." Gyuri was not willing to go with me, the
silly. He is more interested in sports.

This year, at least for the time being, we're not fighting nearly as
much, though even now we are not exactly angelically harmonious.

But goodness, this isn't so awful, because I think even so, we love each other very much.

October 4, 1935

Horrible! Yesterday war broke out between Italy and Abyssinia. Almost everyone is frightened the British will intervene and that as a result there will be war in Europe. Just thinking about it is terrible. The papers are already listing the dead. I can't understand people; how quickly they forget. Don't they know that the whole world is still groaning from the curse of the last World War? Why this killing? Why must youth be sacrificed on a bloody scaffold when it could give so much that is good and beautiful to the world if it could just be allowed to tread peaceful roads?

Now there is nothing left to do but pray that this war will remain a local one, and end as quickly as possible. I can understand Mussolini wanting to acquire colonies for Italy, but, after all, the British ought to be satisfied with owning a third of the world—they don't need all of it. It is said, however, that they are frightened of losing their route to India. Truly, politics is the ugliest thing in the world.

But to talk of more specific things: One of Gyuri's friends is courting me. He was bold enough to ask whether I would go walking with him next Sunday. I said I would, if Gyuri went along. If everything he told me is true, then I feel very sorry for him; evidently he doesn't have a decent family life. There is something wrong there, that's for sure.

October 25, 1935

Tuesday, the 22nd, was the première of a film based on Daddy's play *Terminal*. Paul Hörbiger plays the leading role quite charmingly, and his costar is Maria Andergast. The entire film is rather delightful. I was very nervous about it. I don't quite know why, because it would not have been Daddy's fault if it had been a poor film.

I have a new pupil, besides Marika. I can't say she's a great brain, but if she were she wouldn't need me!

November 4, 1935

Tonight I feel as if it's worthwhile being good! Recently I oiled Gyuri's tennis racket, as well as my own, before putting them away for the winter. Since then I've been more or less on hostile terms with Gyuri, so I didn't want to tell him that I had greased his racket. Today Mother warned him that he wouldn't get his new overcoat until he oiled his racket. I spoke up and said he didn't have to, as I already had. Gyuri looked at me, obviously very touched, then went to wash up. When he came back he said, "Hannah, that was really nice of you." I think this little incident has cleared the air and we've made up. The whole thing made me very happy—happy that it pays to be kind!

December 14, 1935

After this long silence I would like to write about two experiences. One, *The Tragedy of Man*, the other, the Bruno Walter concert. The play made a deep impression on me, even though I had already read it. The direction was wonderful; the actors, unfortunately, less so. At any rate, when one sees it as a play it is entirely different than reading it. The eternal history of mankind is so moving and beautiful, and truly gives one much to think about as to the fate of humanity.

Tuesday I went to the Bruno Walter concert. It was magnificent. The first number was the Mozart-Haffner Symphony. It was all lightness and charm, from beginning to end. The second selection was a Brahms symphony—the Fourth, I believe. It was generally praised, but I didn't like it all that much. It was rather long and heavy, and my attention often wandered. I was much more impressed by *Tristan and Isolde* and the overture to *Die Meistersinger*. Even though I'm not very musical, I do enjoy music very much.

January 4, 1936

Before starting to write I turned back the pages to last New Year. I asked myself then what the New Year would bring. Now, as if closing accounts, I've decided that 1935 was all good. I'm satisfied with it. I pray God I can look back next year and feel the same way about 1936.

Wednesday I was at Judy's. We discussed many things, among them our choice of a profession. Uncle Egon joined the conversation and stated that the occult sciences have a great future, particularly graphology. This field doesn't interest me at all. I told him I was much more interested in pedagogy, and besides that, I would like to do organizational work. His response to this was that after graduation I ought to go to Switzerland and work in a hotel, where I could learn all about the organization and management of a hotel. All things in due course!

January 16, 1936

I'm in bed with a slight cold. First of all, I want to write about last Saturday—not because it was so pleasant, but because I hope that after I've written about it I'll think about it less. I was invited to an afternoon dance at Zolya's house, and, but for me, everyone knew everyone else. The only person I knew was Zolya, who certainly did not prove to be the best hostess because all they talked about—at least in the beginning—were things that interested themselves only. This very boring situation lasted from five until seven, after which we had tea, and then the dancing began.

Frankly, I felt rather bad because I noticed how reluctantly most of the boys asked me to dance, and that they left me immediately after the dance was over. As a matter of fact, only one or two of the boys were anything less than rude. It seems boys think all girls are so stupid that they don't even know that the music doesn't end in the middle of a record! However, I don't really mind the fact that I went, because at least it taught me a lesson: I'll never again go where I don't know anyone. The rudest of all was a girl who got up and moved away when I sat down next to her, taking everyone with her, and leaving me stranded. People are really strange!

But I want to write a longer account about a lot of far more interesting and enjoyable things. I went to a Furtwängler concert. It was fabulous! *The Manfred Overture* by Schumann, the Schumann Spring Symphony in B Major, and the Seventh Symphony of Beethoven. It was all simply magnificent!

Yesterday I had a little incident with Mama. I was reading something and Mama took it out of my hand, saying it was not a proper thing for me to read. This hurt me very much, as it was a letter from school addressed to Mama, and I felt I could read it too. Later I thought about it, and wondered what I would do if the same thing happened with a child of mine. I decided that if she already had the letter in her hand I would not take it away, but would, instead, be careful not to leave such a letter lying about. Of course I don't know if I'll still think this way when I'm grown up.

February 8, 1936

We've bought a house! This has been Mother's greatest wish, but now that it's fulfilled she is all doubts, wondering whether she made a wise decision. As far as I'm concerned, I'm very happy about it. It's in a wonderful location and has a beautiful big garden.

April 19, 1936

Today was my first opening. My play is called *Bella Gerant Alii, Tu, Felix Austria, Nube.*[10] We performed it for Aunt B. I wrote and directed it, and it was really an awful lot of work. But I don't feel Aunt B. is capable of properly assessing its worth. They say the play is quite good, but certainly not good enough to lead to anything. As far as a profession is concerned, I still think I ought to attend a hotel school. A more serious and interesting profession which tempts me is one that has to do with children—such as running a boarding school on the lines of a British public school, or something like that.

Of more immediate concern is a school assignment entitled "Do I Know Myself?" On the whole, I think I do know myself, as much as it is possible for a girl my age to know herself. But even so, I find this a difficult assignment. I can't put my finger on my major problem, and still, I would like to write a sincere, honest essay. It is truly a difficult subject.

May 9, 1936

We're here in our new home already. It is such a wonderful feeling to be in our own house. Every day we discover something good and beautiful about it. Of course there is still a great deal to be done, but after all, we only moved in five days ago!

I'm invited out tonight. I hope it will be pleasant. Gyuri is coming too. Now he is rather interested in girls, and he would like me to introduce him to some of my classmates. I must say Gyuri was very dear and decent yesterday. One of the boys said he couldn't understand what G. saw in me, whereupon Gyuri said I was very intelligent, and that even though I never study, all my grades were excellent. Hearing this his friend said, "Well, that's something." But I think that from a boy's point of view, this is really not important. A girl has to have certain other attractions. This is very evident in Thackeray's *Vanity Fair*. I like the book very much; one is constantly reminded of oneself while reading it, or of one's friends. It is quite witty, as well.

May 31, 1936

The G. affair continues: yesterday he "confessed" his love, in the literal sense of the word. True, only in writing. I suppose it's my fate to have boys of my own age confessing their love in writing. We were trying to do our physics assignment together, when suddenly he wrote his "confession" in the notebook. I didn't know what to say and quickly closed the notebook. Later he asked if I had anything to say about it. I said I had not. He is really very silly. A fifteen-year-old boy can't write such things to a girl his own age. It's too ridiculous. I don't think I really like him much, except as a sort of chum.

June 15, 1936

I have had such strange thoughts lately. I would like to be a writer. For the time being I just laugh at myself; I've no idea whether I have any talent. I've been inspired by the success of *Bella Gerant*—everyone likes it. But even so, I don't think I would write plays. I would rather write novels. I have an idea now, but it isn't quite developed: the paralleling lives of two people who are not even aware of each other's existence, and at the same time demonstrate what completely opposite interests interlace them. I know that if I am ever capable of writing such a complex plot it will be much later in life. But even so, I am going to attempt it now—though I don't have much confidence in the thing.

June 18, 1936

I got up at six this morning. It's such beautiful weather that I've no desire to stay in bed. And as Mother is away for a few days, I can get up when I like. Since the 15th I've been living like a fish in water. I go swimming every day and play tennis (though I don't know whether fish play tennis!). I'm not going to Dombóvár until the end of the month.

When I began keeping a diary I decided I would write only about beautiful and serious things, and under no circumstances constantly about boys, as most girls do. But it looks as if it's not possible to exclude boys from the life of a fifteen-year-old girl, and for the sake of accuracy I must record the development of the G. matter.

He was not satisfied with my aforementioned answer, but put into a book I borrowed from him (which, incidentally, is very good and titled *Mirthful Thoughts*) a picture of himself autographed "With Love Forever, G." I didn't say a word about the picture. Ever since, whenever I see him (quite often) he showers me with compliments, which I try to brush off.

Well, a few days ago he was here, and we played ping-pong. I don't even know how we came to discuss it (in any event it was my fault things went as far as they did), but I told him I had already had two proposals of marriage. Of course I presented the entire thing in a sort of jocular way, and even mentioned how terribly embarrassed I was.

In answer to this, the "old man" said he would like to see me get embarrassed, and what would I say if ten years from now he would ask me to marry him, etc., etc. I told him not to be such a

Hannah at fifteen years old.

baby—that this sort of thing made absolutely no sense, since we were both only fifteen, and let's just remain good friends.

Well, now my diary has become like that of any fifteen-year-old girl, with nothing serious in it, and without any individuality.

June 23, 1936

This is my newest poem. I can't judge whether it's any good.

> Slowly descends the quiet night,
> For earth I know that is right:
> It is the order of each evening.
>
> A bird is singing in a tree,
> The eye of God looks down on me
> From somewhere in the dark sky.
>
> How infinite this is and great,
> Bright and mysterious—I am dazed
> By its sweetness and loveliness:
>
> A spirit and great Being
> Guards me through my wanderings
> And forever along my path

I wonder, will I ever become a writer.

Dombóvár, aged fifteen, July 17, 1936

As of today I'm a vegetarian. I am completely in agreement with the Bircher-Benner[11] concept, and will try to convince Mother too. For the time being I am going to give it a six-month trial, and if my views don't change during that time, I think I'll remain a vegetarian.

August 3, 1936

I still long to be a writer. It's my constant wish. I don't know whether it's simply a desire for praise and fame, but I do know it is such a marvelous feeling to write something well that I think it is worth struggling to become a writer. On the whole, the above-average man suffers more, but his joys are greater too, and I would rather be an unusual person than just average. I am not even thinking now of the writing profession, because when I think of an above-average man I don't necessarily think of a famous man, but of a great soul ... a great human being. And I would like to be a great soul. If God will permit!

August 4, 1936

As I reread my last entry I became quite angry with myself. What I wrote seems so terribly conceited. Great soul! I am so far from anything like that. I'm just a struggling fifteen-year-old girl whose principal preoccupation is coping with herself. And this is the most difficult battle. But even these sounds contrived. Whatever I think and feel, however beautiful my thoughts, they sound so different in black and white. For this reason I would rather not write anything.

August 10, 1936

I am really rather homesick, and longing to see Mama. I can hardly wait to discuss this vegetarian business with her, and above all, with my cousin Tibor, who is a doctor. I want to argue the matter with him, and if I can convince him I shall be extremely pleased.

Budapest, August 21, 1936

When I came home and stepped into the garden, into the house, I didn't dare believe this is all really ours. We are enjoying it so very, very much.

G. was here, and he doesn't mean anything more to me now than he did before. Now I realize I really didn't feel anything serious about him, that I just liked him the way I would a girl friend. (This isn't exactly true, because one feels differently about a boy than about a girl.)

My writing activities have come to an absolute standstill. I'm afraid the entire thing was just a silly daydream. Pity, because it would have been so nice to be a respected author. But one doesn't generally "run dry" by fifteen!

August 31, 1936

Not long ago I wrote a letter to Dr. Bircher-Benner to ask him a few questions concerning the vegetarian diet. I received a meaningless reply from his secretary. So I think I'll eat meat a couple of times a week this winter after all; besides, Mother won't allow me to be a vegetarian all the time. Gyuri returned from his summer holiday. We're very good friends now, and I hope we'll stay this way.

September 18, 1936

It's the second day of the Jewish New Year. Yesterday and today we went to synagogue. I am not quite clear just how I stand: synagogue, religion, the question of God. About the last and most difficult question I am the least disturbed. I believe in God—even if I can't express just how. Actually I'm relatively clear on the subject of religion, too, because Judaism fits in best with my way of thinking. But the trouble with the synagogue is that I don't find it at all important, and I don't feel it to be a spiritual necessity; I can pray equally well at home.

September 27, 1936

I'm the treasurer of the Stenographic Circle and secretary of the Bible Society. I'm pleased to be an officer in both, even though it does mean a lot of work.

Miki is coming again today, but it's a bit too much for me. We don't have enough in common, and I find him rather shallow. I'd like to meet a really nice boy, because the old ones bore me.

So this book is filled now. When I started it I thought I would never be able to fill it.

October 10, 1936

This morning we went to Grandma's and from her window saw the funeral of Prime Minister Gömbös. Gyuri and I did not go very willingly. This sort of military pageantry doesn't interest me much. They say I am too blasé, but I don't think it's that at all. After all, the most interesting things were the flowers, and some of the notables, i.e., Goering, Mussolini's son-in-law (Ciano), Austrian Chancellor Schuschnigg. And they don't interest me in the least bit.

October 12, 1936

I have been wondering with what entry to start this new diary. It is so thick I can't imagine how I shall ever fill it. But not a single nice thought comes to my mind. And it isn't really important. I'll try to record all my thoughts and feelings so that I'll see them reflected exactly the way they lived within me. Thereby my diary will be as close to me as a second self.

I know my other diary isn't very substantial, and perhaps this one won't be much better. But I'm fond of it because it is filled with lovely memories. I won't care if this one has things about boys in it, too, like the last part of the first one. After all, that's a small part of my life too—or perhaps not even such a small part.

So I'll start this diary rather ceremoniously with the conviction that by the time I reach the end I shall have grown into a young lady.

The first boy to be mentioned is a carryover from the first diary: Miki has declared that in all his life he has never loved anyone the way he loves me. He was here again today, and after a rather long discussion I told him I don't want to mislead him, that I am not in love with him, but like being with him.

Actually, I don't even find him particularly pleasing, as I expect a boy to be my intellectual superior, and don't think Miki is. But even if we don't take the intellectual superiority into consideration, I don't find him especially attractive. In fact, he no longer appeals to me at all. What a pity I haven't met anyone yet about whom I can say there is a mutual attraction. Perhaps the fault is mine. But it's also possible that I still don't know many boys, and that even those I do know are far from my "ideal."

I had my English lesson today. I would like to take English very seriously this year. Considering how long I've been studying it, my conversation is still weak. But I like the language so very much.

October 19, 1936

I am reading *War and Peace* but nearing the end, and can now understand Tolstoy's ideas quite clearly. This book is among the very best I have ever read. The plot itself is tremendously interesting, but even more fascinating is Tolstoy's views on the historical facts which led to the winter campaign of the War of 1812 and other events, and the way he examines and passes judgments on those events. It is obvious he does not think the roles played by individuals in the enactment of history were nearly as important or decisive as one generally believes. This is particularly so in the case of his principal characters. The part I am reading now is most interesting: he discusses the question of power. That is to say, what exactly prompts or induces the mob to place itself under the domination of a single man, and then turn against that man and drive him to the scaffold? So far Tolstoy has not answered this question, but is content with merely throwing the outdated concepts of historical writers on the rubbish heap. I am curious to see whether, in the end, he will answer it.

October 20, 1936

I finished *War and Peace*. Of course Tolstoy finally did answer the question, but to be honest, I didn't quite understand the answer. I must also confess that toward the end I was counting pages, reading out of duty rather than for pleasure, and eager to finish. Anyway, I'll reread the epilogue—the part that is a remembrance of the past—because it is almost impossible to understand it completely after one reading.

October 25, 1936

I'm so happy! I read one of my poems, "The Ice-Cream Man," to Mother, and she liked it very much. Perhaps I can still hope to become a writer. But so many people write!

November 4, 1936

My happiness was premature. Yesterday there was a conference to discuss the holiday activities for Hanukah. I read my play, *Marriage Proposal in 2036* (I wrote it specifically for school), which I thought might be suitable for the celebration. But judging by the icy silence that followed my reading I could see they didn't like it at all. I think my face must have been very red—at least it was burning—but I think I behaved well enough. Now I'm nervous about having to read it in class tomorrow, and I'm afraid it won't have much success there, either. But in spite of everything I'm going to recite one of my new poems at the Debating and Literary Society. I'll call it "Evening Mood," or "Twilight," or something like that.

November 14, 1936

I read the play in class a while back, and it went down well. I've written another poem. Its title is "The Tear." It came out of a personal experience. I am going to enter it, and "Evening," in the Literary Society competition.

January 1, 1937

The year 1936 has ended. I feel it brought many changes into both my outer and inner life, though the changes are more obvious in the former. First of all, a year ago we had hardly dared hope we would welcome 1937 in our own home. Besides that, dancing school, skiing—all new activities. This past year I also spent a little more time with boys.

My inner life—well, I can't accurately describe the changes I've experienced. My problems have increased, primarily concerning a career (writing!) and boys. As far as improvement goes, I don't think I have improved much; perhaps I'll do better this year. But taking everything into consideration, this year was good and lovely too, and it went by so fast.

February 14, 1937

Except for drawing, I had all A's on my report card. Meanwhile, an important event: I got my first long party dress! It's blue taffeta, and everyone says I look very pretty in it. So far I've worn it only to the Hubermann[12] concert, which was more noteworthy than my dress! The program consisted of Beethoven's Spring Sonata, the Bach sonata, Brahms, and Schubert.

February 25, 1937

I just got back from the Literary Society, where I read "The Ice-Cream Man," which the Society considered good. But I thought Ági's two poems were much better, particularly the first one, "Death of a Teacher," which I thought excellent. It somehow destroyed my confidence and interest in my own poems. Up till now I thought I was quite talented, but Ági is definitely more gifted. Perhaps I have greater potential as a writer of prose. I don't know. In a way I'm afraid to become too involved in writing and in the idea that I am really talented. On the other hand, I can't stop writing, nor do I want to. I just sent two of my poems, "The Tear" and "Dance of the Moments," to a magazine. The second of the two is new, and the best poem I've ever written. At least that's what I think. Now I constantly wonder whether my poems are as good as Ági's. Goodness, it would be wonderful to be truly talented.

For every action there is a reaction. Yesterday I was so happy about my literary activities; today I'm depressed. But I'll continue writing—in spite of everything! This is always my reaction to failure, or to momentary despair.

March 16, 1937

No news, but I have nothing else to do, and the diary happened to be in front of me. As a matter of fact, it's about time for a bit of self-appraisal, though I am not sure it would prove advantageous. What I must be most careful of is not to become conceited. But as a matter of fact, I am far more apt to be self-critical than self-satisfied.

I know I have plenty of faults. I'm supercilious at times, at home even impertinent now and then. But actually I'm not too bad on either count. In the long run I'm always eager and willing to improve, filled with good intentions. At worst I'm somewhat lacking in willpower.

Now I want to study my Italian for a while, and later Mother and I are going to see *Romeo and Juliet*, so I must stop. I enjoyed jotting down these few lines.

March 21, 1937

I have a short new poem, the kind that is really only meant for a diary:

> Spring begins her song,
> My soul has found her voice.
> Sunbeams frolic up above,
> Violets have burst open,
> Imitating my own heart,
> And of a sudden I'm in love
>
> I don't know how this feeling became mine,
> Maybe spring's bound me under her spell,
> I'll never ask since when, or why
> I'm in love—but with love itself.

April 15, 1937

For days I've been experiencing a general dissatisfaction with myself, and I don't know what's causing it. Because actually nothing unusual has happened to me. And I've certainly done nothing wrong. I can't understand myself. Possibly I'm just tired; I've been very busy. I'm doing all sorts of things, and I'm rather sorry I undertook so many school activities. The only thing I don't regret, even for a moment, is the tutoring I do.

I'm bored with the boy situation too. They just keep coming, and I don't really know how I stand with them. I'm afraid I'm a little disappointed in Peter. He is too complicated, a bit pompous, and his manner of speaking is not entirely straightforward. Perhaps after a few more meetings I'll have a more positive opinion of him.

Meanwhile Ági gave me her new poem to read. I am now less impressed by her.

April 25, 1937

The last few days I've been very busy with literary matters. For our Hungarian Literature class we decided to write a trilogy: epic, lyric, drama. I wrote the first two, in verse, and they turned out quite well. I had barely finished when Aunt Judit Kiss[13] asked me to write an introduction for the celebration of the tenth anniversary of her school—an assignment I completed today. I don't like writing things to order, but the important thing is that I did it, and now hope it will be satisfactory.

May 15, 1937

The other morning there was some discussion concerning the election for the secretary of the Literary Society. Aunt Boriska reminded us that we had to keep certain factors in mind, among them that the person elected must be Protestant. This is certainly understandable in a Protestant school, but even so, it's very depressing. Of course it is not certain I would be worthy of the office, but this way I am already excluded from the competition. Now I don't know how to behave toward the Literary Society. Should I put myself out and work for the improvement of the Society's standards, even though I am now aware of the spirit that motivates it, or should I drop the whole thing? But if I drop it, then I am going against the interests of my class. It is extremely difficult to find a way that is not demeaning, proud, or isolationist, and also not forward. One has to be extremely careful before making any kind of move because one individual's faults can be generalized about. To my way of thinking, you have to be someone exceptional to fight anti-Semitism, which is the most difficult kind of fight. Only now am I beginning to see what it really means to be a Jew in a Christian society. But I don't mind at all. It is because we have to struggle, because it is more difficult for us to reach our goal that we develop outstanding qualities.

Had I been born a Christian, every profession would be open to me. I would become a teacher, and that would be the end of it. As it is, perhaps I'll succeed in getting into the profession for which, according to my abilities, I am best suited.

Under no circumstances would I ever convert to Christianity, not only because of myself, but also because of the children I hope one day to have. I would never force them into the ignoble position of having to deny or be ashamed of their origin. Nor would I rob them of their religion, which is what happens to the children of converted parents. I think religion means a great deal in life, and I find the modern concept—that faith in God is only a crutch for the weak—ridiculous. It's exactly that faith which makes one strong, and because of it one does not depend upon other things for support.

En route to Italy, June 18, 1937

I am writing this on the train.

I left South Station at eight-thirty this morning. Mother was extremely nervous and entrusted me to the care of a lady sitting opposite, who is very nice. In fact we have spent so much time chatting I've barely had time to read, particularly as we reached Lake Balaton meanwhile. Each time I see it, it seems to me more beautiful. I stood in the corridor for a while in order to have a better view of the great, fabulous, sparkling inland sea.

A boy of about seventeen came out of the neighboring compartment and with studied carelessness lit a cigarette, while watching my reaction out of the corner of his eye. I laughed to myself.

We are now leaving the principal lake resorts, Siófok, Földvár, etc. Meanwhile I've become quite friendly with my traveling companion. Just before reaching the border there was currency control. I was simply asked how much money I had; it all went very smoothly. At the moment we are at the border station of Murakeresztúr, and there are a great many customs officers on board. Since I am only passing through, they had little to do with me.

This Yugoslav part is very beautiful. We are passing through wonderful areas, the landscape entirely different from that of Hungary. The Drava River runs through relatively high mountains, and little stone houses cling to the sides of the hills, or are wedged between them. Now we're traveling through Laibach (Ljubljana). It's a rather large, attractive city with a lovely residential section. I particularly noted a green tram, and a lovely Greek Orthodox church.

In the meantime the lady in my compartment left, but I was not to enjoy my solitude for long. Before leaving she entrusted me to the care of the people in the neighboring compartment, who immediately moved into mine: a lady with a good-natured seventeen-year-old son, and a young man who turned out to be the brother of one of my classmates. He has a letter of introduction to my relatives in Milan! I'm astonished how small the world is!

The Italian customs inspection took place at about seven in the evening. I could barely wait to put my knowledge of Italian to use, but regardless how much I offered to open my bags for inspection, they were not at all interested, and only superficially inspected the bags of the others.

We arrived in Trieste at nine in the evening, and I broke my promise to Mother about not getting off the train. We spent an hour of the two-hour wait sightseeing. Trieste is quite a large city, but without any Italian characteristics. There are a great many sailors and cafés, and we went to one of the latter and drank a "cappuccino," a sort of warm café au lait. We left Trieste at about eleven and bedded down for the night in the compartment.

I slept for about an hour in all. We arrived at Venice at one in the morning, and of course I looked out of the window; even though I didn't see much, it was interesting to enter a station that was practically in the middle of the sea. We arrived in Ravenna at 3 a.m., and from then on I stood in the corridor and watched the countryside slip by. It was very interesting, typically Italian, the shapes of the trees and houses unusual. The train ran along Lake Garda for a while, and it is truly magnificently situated. It was particularly beautiful when the sun rose behind the mountains.

We cleaned up a bit and arrived in Milan a few minutes before seven. Géza was waiting for me with the car, and in a few minutes we were home in their adorable little flat, which is very near to where Klara and her family live.[14]

Milan, June 20, 1937

This morning we went to Menaggio. There was ample room in the car—the three women in the back, the three men in front, including little Giorgio. The drive was most interesting, the first part because of the houses, all displaying Mussolini's proclamations, the second because of the magnificent landscape, which included Lake Como and its environs. It is truly a remarkable sight, the lake now green, now blue, surrounded by snow-capped mountains. The picture will, I believe, remain deeply engraved in my memory forever.

Menaggio itself, on the shore of Lake Como, is a dear little place. It has a splendid beach, wide lawns, swings, tennis courts, and above all, sun, water, mountains. In one word: magnificent. We bathed, sunbathed, played tennis for an hour and a half, and did not leave for home until after six in the evening. There was an endless line of cars, bumper to bumper (there are an enormous number of cars here), and the roads are superb.

June 21, 1937

The big event of the day was the Duomo. I had seen many pictures of it, knew it was built of white stone, that it had small pinnacles for every day of the week, and great pinnacles for holidays, plus a hundred to spare, that it was decorated with innumerable statues. In fact

I saw it in my mind's eye. And yet, when I stood in the vast square opposite the resplendent, glittering structure, I stared, dumbfounded at the storybook cathedral. Then I walked toward it, and stepped through the embossed bronze portal.

The first few moments in the semidarkness, I saw only the huge pillared outline and the brilliantly colored, huge stained-glass windows. Then slowly my eyes reached the vaulted Gothic ceiling and the tops of the statue-ornamented pillars. There, in the vastness, fluttered the countless lives of human beings whose hopes, fears, dreams, and sorrows had been poured into those statues and pillars and wonderful frets.

I walked around the vast cathedral. Sacrificial candles burned on the altars, and the sun poured through some of the stained-glass windows. Suddenly the interior was both overpowering and exalting, and at the same time beautiful and meaningful. Even so, it was not that which most impressed me.

The hour I spent atop the dome—that, I shall never forget. When I stepped out of the lift, which took me up several hundred feet, my breath caught in my throat. I was dazzled. I moved forward toward the lacy, supple Gothic arches, pinnacles, and pillars, thinking: if this were music it would be trills played on the highest notes of violins. The white marble sparkled under the blue sky, and the entire scene reminded me of half-forgotten childhood fancies. This was how I had imagined fairyland to be: blue sky, white throne, white angels, and tiny windows through which one could look down upon Earth. How distant the feverish commercial city, the noise of cars and trams from up there; how ridiculous the glitter of the shop windows looked compared to the great brilliance of that majestic height.

I reached the bottom of the tower and began climbing the narrow spiral staircase leading to the summit. A new vista at every turn, another statue, another lacy crenellation—like some sort of frost flower, or something equally diaphanous. I stood on the top step for a long while, feeling as if I had climbed there on Jacob's ladder, in a dream.

I looked at my watch. I had to turn back. I said good-bye at every step. It hurt so to leave the brilliance, the height, the peacefulness. I could take none of it with me. But as I walked down I suddenly knew I was actually taking an everlasting memory—a memory of a great longing for light, for height, for peace.

June 26, 1937

Tonight we attended an outdoor performance. The tickets cost 4 *lire,* which is very inexpensive. It is greatly to the credit of Fascism that such performances are arranged for, and placed within the means of, the people. The greater part of the audience of five thousand appeared to be from the lower stratum of society, but despite this they had a better knowledge of music than the elegant audiences that generally attend the monstrously expensive concerts in Budapest.

June 27, 1937

This afternoon we went by car on a wonderful excursion in the direction of Certosa and Pavia. We spent more than an hour in Certosa, where we visited a magnificent church[15] and monastery. The enormous cloister was actually built for the use of just twenty-four people, and there are always twenty-four monks in residence. They live in separate cells, each decorated with frescoes, inlaid marble or embossed altars, icons, and other priceless art treasures. A carved ivory polyptych of intricate workmanship was particularly beautiful.

Each monk has his own quarters. The cells are whitewashed, the workshop and dining room are downstairs, the bedrooms upstairs, and each monk has his own little garden to tend. They live out their lives there without ever talking to anyone, except for one hour each Sunday when they eat together and converse. I can't imagine that this sort of escape from reality is of any benefit to themselves, or to mankind.

We left Certosa reluctantly, as there was still so much to see, and even dashing about with a guide one barely has time to see even a fraction of it all. I often deliberately did not look at something the guide indicated, as I find it ridiculous for a group of people to stare at something a guide thinks worth looking at. After all, what a person likes is entirely a matter of individual taste; everyone can't like the same things.

Pavia, a little Italian town on the banks of the Po, is not far from Certosa. It is suffused with an air of ancient culture, and its buildings are old and lovely. It is entirely different than a little Hungarian town; from a cultural point of view, far superior; but perhaps our small towns are brighter, gayer.

June 28, 1937

Today I visited the Ambrosiana Gallery, my third museum in Milan. This one is beautiful too—perhaps the most wonderful of the three. I saw two portraits by Leonardo and several of his sketches, a great many etchings by Dürer, paintings by Titian, and canvases by other great masters. I was enormously taken with a huge green vase.

After leaving the Ambrosiana I went to the Duomo again for a spell. No matter how often I were to see it, I think it would impress me differently each time, as there is so much to see that it is hardly possible to see it all in a single lifetime. I don't say everything is of great value. In fact, my impression is that it's the quantity rather than the quality that is remarkable.

July 1, 1937

We visited the famous cemetery of Milan. Somehow I felt it irreverent to tour a cemetery still in use, merely out of curiosity and armed with a camera. But this seems to be the accepted practice here. A group of Hindus visited it when we did, and they were taking one picture after the other.

The entrance to the cemetery is very beautiful too: arcades with crypts leading into them. The entire cemetery is looked after meticulously, and there are many handsome monuments. I recognized the three important ones myself, without the guide having to call my attention to them, which pleased me. The first represents a winding procession of the Calvary; the second consists of three masks: mockery, satire, pain; the third is a huge sculpture symbolizing man's labors and depicts a farmer plowing with two yoked oxen. I was also impressed by a group composed of a nude, and in the background two nuns with bent heads. Opposite were a few atrocious figures in nine-teenth-century dress, artless and ugly. But then they can't all be great works of art.

San Pellegrino, July 5, 1937

I'm writing this while sitting on the grass in San Pellegrino, hills in front of me, hills behind me, a delicious little stream rippling across the valley. It is both a gorgeous picture and a wonderful sensation.

I have a tremendous amount to write about, as I've just spent two of the most fabulous days of my life. I'll try to record everything so I can keep intact the memories these two days have given me.

We started out Saturday morning around nine o'clock. First we stopped in Bresca, but only for a few moments. There we walked about the main square, bought a few odds and ends, then went on. We soon reached Lake Garda, and here the marvelous part of our drive began. Even the beginning of the lake is exquisite, but as one pro-gresses along the lakefront (a heavenly road) the palm gardens, orange and lemon groves, and elegant resorts come into view. Here the color of the lake turns to an indescribable blue, and the hills along the oppo-site shore come closer. In short, the fabulous beauty intensifies.

We stopped and picnicked on the smaller end of the shore, took pictures, and then went on. The road was laced with tunnels, and as we wound in and out of them, again and again the cerulean lake came momentarily into view. We often stopped along the way to stare and to take pictures. Even so, we arrived at the upper reaches of the lake much too soon. I took a brief farewell of it, knowing I would be seeing it again the following day, and we continued our drive toward the hills.

The actual purpose of our excursion was to visit two resorts in order for my hosts to decide where to spend their summer vacation. For a while the road wound around a barren hillside that became a steep, pebble-strewn path, and the car chugged up slowly, reluctantly.

But it was worth the effort, as a little paradise, situated on the summit, greeted us. It is called Cei, and lies in a small pocket of the hills, on the shore of a tiny mountain lake. It has only one hotel, but even that is charming and attractive. I liked it all so very much.

Unfortunately we spent only a half hour in Cei, then started back, for a while following the same road, then on to Lavarone. We made the ascent on a serpentine-like road, and each bend along the hazardous route brought us to another extraordinary panorama until we reached a height of nearly five thousand feet—and Laverone. It, too, is beside a lake, is larger than Cei, and not as friendly. But as we walked about in the soft evening we noted that it, too, was magnificently situated.

Meanwhile it had grown quite late, so we hurriedly made arrangements for hotel rooms, ate supper, and went directly to bed. I awakened early, and as I had a room to myself was able to get up when I liked, and walked about the town. We started out again at eight o'clock, directly after breakfast, drove along the beautiful mountain road, and around ten were back at Lake Garda. This time we drove along the opposite shore, also lovely, but not quite as beautiful as the other side. Along the way we found a cozy little secluded beach, stopped, went swimming, and sunbathed until four o'clock. It was a delicious sensation swimming in that soft, blue water, as if one were in a mound of soft pillows. We all got wonderfully tan, and started back in great spirits. I, at least, wanted to laugh and sing with joy, feeling happy and grateful to everyone for everything. The drive back was cheerful, and we arrived home at nine in the evening, after two perfect, dreamlike days.

Milan, July 7, 1937

As Géza had to return to San Pellegrino yesterday I went with him, and he let me off at Bergamo, which is on the way. The old section of the town is charming, situated high up in the hills, and its most notable building is a very ornate old church whose exterior I much preferred to its interior.

I strolled all over the town, finally sat on a bench to read, and was greatly amused by my "successes." For instance, when I was walking

down one of the streets, two boys wearing dark glasses came opposite, and when they saw me they pushed up their glasses, stared, and
chattered about all sorts of nonsense. I just smiled and went on. This
sort of thing is not at all annoying. But what did bother me was a man
on a bicycle in the busiest section of New Bergamo, who insisted on
pedaling directly beside me and talking incessantly. Of course I
didn't say a word, and didn't even look at him. Finally he went away.

The same thing usually happens if I go to the beach alone.
Generally a group of boys tries to get friendly, and of course I don't
pay any attention. But I am always enormously amused. Here they
think if a girl goes out alone she is just a pickup. Nice Italian girls don't
go to the beach—at least not alone. Girls, poor things, must have a
dull, uninteresting life here. I think they have practically no freedom.

Géza and I had arranged to meet in a café, and I felt very conspicuous sitting there alone. But I simply buried my head in my
book and turned my back to the world.

July 10, 1937

This afternoon we drove all over Milan. We visited the museum that
is part of the Scala, and the most interesting thing in it—I think—is
Rossini's spinet. After that we went into the Opera to see the stage
and auditorium. Both are enormous, but of course during its summer slumber in mothballs and under covers it is not particularly
impressive, apart from its size. It is interesting to note that the stage
slopes, and there is a dome-shaped vault at the back which, when
properly lighted, creates an impression of immensity. We saw all the
percussion instruments used to create sound effects such as thunder,
rain, and wind; also the great bells and the huge organ.

After the Scala we went to visit two churches. The second was
Sant'Ambrogio, which we learned about in school, and I was pleased
to be able to see it. It is plain, simple, Romanesque, with an excellent square courtyard. Built in two different periods, the steeple differs from the church proper.

We also went to Santa Maria del Fiore,[16] where Leonardo da
Vinci's *Last Supper* is hung. It had deteriorated badly, but not as badly

as I had expected from what I have heard and read. The faces are still very distinct, and I enjoyed it very much, the more so since not long ago I read Merezhkovski's book and thus felt closer to the spirit of the painting. The convent itself, the image of the one at Certosa, is inferior.

We saw the Well of St. Francis, a handsome statue so lifelike it seems to move. We merely passed by the War Memorial, the Lido, the City Park, the Municipal Stadium, and the monumental stock exchange building with all its bas-reliefs. But we did stop and visit the great fairground that is in use only two weeks of the year. The rest of the time it is boarded up, its many buildings standing empty. It's a veritable labyrinth, with real, sturdy houses that do not have to be rebuilt every year, the way they are in the fairgrounds of Budapest.

July 12, 1937

I'm in a bad mood today, for the first time since I've been here—and not without reason. I wanted very much to go to Florence for a few days, but Mother won't allow me to. I found the news when we returned from Menaggio last night, and it ruined the wonderful mood I had been in all day. It was such a magnificent day, though very windy, and consequently the lake was really rough. But it's a wonderful sensation to swim in a lake with waves in it. I lay on a sort of wooden platform for a long time, while it was tossed about by the waves. We could clearly see the mountains, even snow-capped Mt. Rosa. All the way home we were in a fabulous mood, singing, laughing, wonderfully happy. And then Mother's letter with the news that Florence is out. What can I do about it? Of course I'll go straight home, but I now plan to stop in Venice and see it for myself. There is no time now to ask Mother's permission, but perhaps it's just as well because she might forbid me to do that too.

On board the train, July 15, 1937

It is seven o'clock, and I have had a great day. When I got off the train at Venice this morning I left my luggage at the station and then, reveling in my independence, took a *vaporetto*. Of course I was already familiar with the Grand Canal from pictures, but even so, it was really interesting to see the steps of the palazzos leading directly into the water. I looked at the various famous buildings, blindingly white, reflected in the water. They are very old, and had they not been restored they would surely have crumbled long ago.

The *vaporetto* stopped near the Frari Monastery.[17] I got off, and after some searching finally found the Franciscan church. Because of my short-sleeved dress, I had to rent some sort of red shawl before I was permitted to enter. There are four world-famed masterpieces there: Titian's *The Assumption*, two Madonnas by Bellini, and the tomb of Canova. I was probably most impressed by the last. Nearly all the frescoes are valuable works, too. I spent approximately three-quarters of an hour there.

I took the *vaporetto* again, and arriving in St. Mark's Square went immediately to a restaurant. I ate, wrote a few postcards, and paid. At about one o'clock I went to the Doges' Palace and across, through the ornate gate, to the courtyard. I looked at the two fountains, took some photos, and walked up the giant staircase. Then I bought a ticket and set out to see the rooms. There are a great many frescoes by Tintoretto, Veronese, Titian, and others. Of course it is impossible to look at everything carefully in such a short time, or even to make mental notes. In the arsenal I saw implements of torture, cannons, and suits of armor. I found Tintoretto's *Paradiso* in the Sala de Gran Consiglio the most beautiful of all the paintings. It is at the end of an enormous room, and as one looks at it from the opposite side one is overwhelmed by the swirling, writhing mass of figures. But taken one by one, and carefully examined, the figures separate and the painting is truly glorious.

I continued through the palace, and on into St. Mark's Cathedral, with time only to glance at the wonders. I even managed to see the Tintoretto exhibition and finished sightseeing at four-thirty. Then I had an orangeade and walked all the way back to the station. I am so glad I stopped in Venice, even if on the run. I saw so many remarkably beautiful things.

Now it is eleven o'clock at night, and since the Yugoslav border

Hannah at sixteen years old.

I've been sharing the compartment with a lady, the two of us alone.
It's extremely pleasant.

Dombóvár, aged sixteen, July 19, 1937

I'm in Dombóvár. Undoubtedly many things are different here, and of
course I am more tied down. There I did almost everything the way
it suited me, whereas here I am once again under Mother's wing. The
meals are entirely different, too. I am no longer used to the filling
Hungarian diet.

At first the beach seemed tiny after the swimming pool at Milan,
but I enjoy not having to sit alone with a book. I have so many girl
friends here with whom I can go bathing. On the other hand, it's
already quite clear that there will be no boys this summer. There are
a great many non-Jewish boys, but the segregation here is so sharply
defined one can't possibly think of mixing, or imagine that a
Christian boy would even go near a Jewish girl. This segregation
often seems comical, but actually it is a very sad and disquieting sign.

July 22, 1937

I'm writing on an empty stomach, as I've supposedly been ill all day.
I write "supposedly" because actually I'm as healthy as a horse. But
they are forever trying to put me on a fattening diet, so I feigned a
little indisposition as a counter-measure. The idea occurred to me
because Évi was actually ill with an upset stomach, and so was Fini
Mama. So I decided upon this little hoax. I had a difficult time convincing myself to do it, as it is, after all, a lie. But then I console
myself that I am hurting no one, and it's really good for the stomach
to fast once in a while.

This morning Mother decided my tongue was coated (!) so I had to
drink some bitter water. Of course I laughed to myself when she
reached this conclusion. My luck is amazing, because Aunt Eliz and
Uncle Steve complained about a stomach upset too. So now they think
we must all have eaten something upsetting. I must admit I'm a surprisingly good liar, but I really don't like to lie—it gives one a most
unpleasant feeling.

Yesterday I finished a very charming and interesting book by Ernst Lothar, *Romance in F Major*. I could hardly put it down. It's the diary of a fifteen-year-old girl, and is very like mine, in both content and style. Now I am reading Nyiro's *In God's Yoke*, which I rather like. But I would never write that way myself, even if I could. Both language and environment are so foreign to me.

Évi and I talk a lot about the future. I have long had an idea for an undertaking that would be called "From Head to Foot," a place where everything in women's wear could be made to order in one day. It would have to be staffed with young, capable people, and I would organize and direct the entire enterprise. I have a hundred other ideas, including hotel keeping and so on. I'm afraid there are too many things I would like to do, and thus won't do anything well. What I would like best of all, of course, would be to become a writer. That's my greatest wish. But I am terrified of the idea of writing to order so as to earn a living. I always end my speculations with the consolation that I still have two years to contemplate the future, which seems such a long time, even though I am only too well aware how time flies.

July 26, 1937

Good lord! I was interviewed! Mr. Szabo, the lawyer, told me yesterday that Mr. A., a journalist connected with the *Tolnamegyei News*, would like to meet me so that he could write an article about the "poetess who is now holidaying in our town." We said there was no point in this, whereupon Mr. A. arrived and proceeded to interview me very thoroughly. He asked a few trite questions, i.e., who is my favorite writer, favorite poet, etc. He then asked for some of my poems, and I read "Dance of the Moments" and gave him "The Tear" to take away. Now I am waiting anxiously to see what he will write about me, because I have a rather poor opinion of journalists and reporters. But perhaps there won't be any trouble.

July 28, 1937

The paper appeared, and in the beginning of the article he wrote about Daddy, then about me. It's quite a good article, and everything would be fine but for one thing: he included the principal of my school in the piece, saying what a high opinion he has of me, or some such. This worries me a great deal, even though it is most unlikely this little paper will ever fall into the hands of the principal. But as this statement is not true, it is embarrassing. Fini Mama is in bed; she has a severe cold, feels very weak, and is suffering a lot.

July 30, 1937

Fini Mama died last night. Sepsis, or some such, the doctor said. But it makes so little difference what it was. The fact is that for two days she suffered tremendously, and now she is gone. The closeness of death last night, when the doctor told us there was no hope, was so horrible that we all sobbed, and were incapable of saying anything. Mama is completely shattered, and I can do absolutely nothing to comfort her. I could only promise to do everything possible for her, to stay near her, as she will be so alone without Fini Mama. Daddy's death is constantly in my mind. I don't believe I have yet been able to grasp Fini Mama's death. Today I can't even cry. I have a continual feeling of strangulation, but otherwise I am quite calm.

Darling Fini Mama. I am happy now for every moment I was good to her, for the times I showed my love, and I think even if I hurt her once in a while, she loved me very much and was never really upset or angry with me.

July 31, 1937

I couldn't continue yesterday, as Évi and I had to run around, helping as much as we could. Mother and Aunt Eliz are incapable of doing anything at all. Mother has been in bed all day, and I'm afraid now of how things will be when we return home. Aunt Manci arrived last night, and I see she has great self-control. I was told, however, that she was up all night, walking, and she, too, has been very much affected by the sudden blow.

I'm so tired. I've been getting up at six every morning, not because it's necessary but because I can't sleep. I feel well enough in spirits, but extremely worried and fearful about Mama. I can understand how difficult life at home will be for her now. I also realize what a silly conceit it was for me to think, even for a moment, that I could replace Fini Mama. But just the same, if Gyuri feels as I do, between us we can make things much easier for Mama. I am going to write to him now in Paris, but Mother doesn't want me to tell him about Fini Mama's death, as he can't return on his own anyway; he must remain with his group.

August 1, 1937

We buried Fini Mama at two o'clock this afternoon. Many relatives came from all over, which meant a great deal of work, of course, so Évi and I were busy all day. The funeral was a little late starting. The entire thing was so awful. The catafalque was in the courtyard, and the rabbi spoke there. Then we accompanied the coffin to the cemetery on foot. It all seems so distant now. S. L., who remained here longer than the others because his train left later, laughed heartily at his own stories, and without wanting to we instinctively laughed with him. Life remains the same regardless. Only Fini Mama has gone. Poor Mama, how will she be once we return home?

There has been considerable discussion as to whether Fini Mama should have been buried in Jánosháza, next to Grandpa, but we finally decided it would be best to bury her here. I was in agreement with this, for after all, the entire ritual is more for the living, so they can occasionally visit the grave. If there is a soul that lives on, it can meet its loved ones anyway; and the body, which quickly disintegrates, doesn't care whether it rests beside the dust of a loved one, or beside that of a stranger. This, however, may be a childish or selfish notion. On the other hand, if it had been the wish of Fini Mama to be buried in Jánosháza, or if we find such a request among her papers, we will exhume her. But I hope this will not happen.

Budapest, August 15, 1937

We've been home since the 12th. Mother hasn't engaged a maid yet, so there is considerable work. I clean the house in the morning and prepare breakfast; we breakfast, and I wash the dishes. In fact, I've even prepared various vegetables to go with some of the food we brought back from the country. I heartily enjoy this sort of work. It's different than anything I've ever done, and I'm happy to be able to do it.

Mother is busy packing, receiving condoling visitors. Our home-coming was certainly very sad for her, poor dear. But I feel she is calmer now. Perhaps this new life won't be as difficult as we had feared. True, when we're back at school it will be terrible for her here alone. She would like some sort of work, not only to fill her time but also because we could use the extra income.

Now I'm going to arrange my pictures and reproductions, which will be a lot of fun.

August 25, 1937

Thanks to my clumsiness I've broken a beautiful hand-engraved glass and two lovely plates. And besides all that, today I put too much salt in the spinach. In connection with this last incident the usual remarks were made, of course.[18]

I can see Mother is convinced I'm in love with Peter, even though I'm now positive I'm not. Pity, because he is a very nice boy, and I am not indifferent to him. But even though I've now known him for six months, we're still so distant, so remote, that it's difficult to imagine we could ever be really good friends. We talk about books and related subjects, but of other matters—not necessarily sentimental ones—such as plans for the future, dreams, hopes, doubts, there is rarely any mention.

September 5, 1937

It's the Jewish New Year, and I wondered whether or not to write on this day. But to my way of thinking this is a prohibition impossible to obey. Religion, in the truest sense, does not consist of such things.

School has started, and everything is much the same except that I've dropped Latin. I already thought about doing that last year, since it takes so much time, and I know I'll never have any use for it because I have no intention of going to the university. Of course I am now hearing a lot of sound advice, i.e., that it would be wiser to continue it—but naturally, this does not have the slightest influence on my decision. There has also been the question that if I don't intend to go to the university, then what profession am I preparing for? This is enormously difficult to answer, because even though I have a lot of ideas, I can't make up my mind what I want to do.

September 16, 1937

A lot of things happened today, among them one that is very unpleasant. At the statutory meeting of the Literary Society I was nominated for office, along with several of my classmates. I was elected. The Literary Society generally accepts officers elected by the class, but in this case they called for a new election, and nominated two other girls to stand with me as candidates. This clearly indicated that they did not want a Jew—me, that is—to become an officer, which hurts me very much. Had I not been elected I would not have said a word, but this way it was a decided insult. Now I don't want to take part in, or have anything to do with the work of the Society, and don't care about it any more.

Fortunately, pleasant things happened as well. I began tutoring Irma today. I am to give her two one-hour lessons a week, for which I will be paid 20 *pengö*. This is really very good. And she invited me to a party at her house next Saturday. There will be some really interesting people there.

Peter telephoned too, and asked whether he could come and see me. We arranged it for Sunday morning.

October 1, 1937

I'm just finishing Daddy's book *The Eleventh Commandment* and am completely captivated by it. Thanks to this book Daddy seems so close, even closer than before. I know a novel has little to do with real life, but just the same, it portrays Daddy's youth—with a bit of exaggeration—and his and Mother's love. It is so dear and charming. I want to read Daddy's other books now. It's really about time!

October 6, 1937

Peter was here this afternoon, and we went for a walk. We talked about all sorts of things that belong in a diary. After a good deal of tactful preamble, he gave me to understand that he loves me. I listened quietly to his declaration—which did not surprise me. Yesterday we went to the cinema, together with Irma and another boy, and Peter kept looking at me in the dark in such a way that what he said today did not catch me unawares. Besides, I thought he probably cared because he wanted to see me today after we had been together just yesterday. He also insisted, at all costs, that we go for a walk.

I was nice to him, too, even though I did not say I loved him, because had I said it, it might well have been untrue. Anyway, I'm happy, as this was the first time I was pleased to hear such a declaration. (I can't say I was ever displeased to hear such a thing, but I certainly had no reciprocal feelings before.) In connection with this we then talked about a lot of things, and thus immediately felt much closer.

I don't know whether I'll tell Mama, though I think I will. It's not very nice of me to have anything to do with any other boys now, considering how Peter feels about me. But the fact is, not long ago Sandor was here again, and we passed the time quite pleasantly. On another day János came. He is a bit shy, but an intelligent fellow. His parents are good friends of Mama, and he came with them.

October 23, 1937

What a long time since I've written! There's not much news, but one can always find little things to note. Since then Peter has been here only once. But we're meeting again this afternoon at the home of a friend.

Life at school is rather dull. I am not really working. At the moment I'm most interested in English. I read Pearl Buck's *East Wind, West Wind* not long ago, and now I'm reading *The Good Earth*. I received a letter from my English pen pal and answered immediately.

January 1, 1938

We spent most of New Year's Eve together, at home, the three of us. As Mother doesn't go anywhere yet, Gyuri and I wanted to stay home too. But then Mama Kiss invited me to a premier at the Comedy Theater. It was really impossible to refuse such a tempting invitation: premier, Comedy Theater, New Year's Eve—so I went.

The play, *Sweet Home*, was relatively weak. I was reminded of those opening nights of Daddy's. I think there must have been more real laughter, more genuine applause on those occasions. And somehow, I was overwhelmed by a strong desire to see one of my own plays performed, and for the audience to roar its approval of it instead of rushing to the wardrobe for their hats and coats immediately after the last act and during the curtain calls, as they did last night. Perhaps it's madness to think of such things, but somehow a writing career no longer seems as impossible as it once did. I think of it more and more; perhaps I could be successful.

Of course I came directly home from the theater, and we listened to the radio. Mama, poor darling, was very sad, and I cried too. We missed Fini Mama so much.

Now I want to summarize the past year. It's wise to do this in order to have a clearer picture of things. I feel I became an adult this year—or at least a young lady. What with my travels and my reading I had a few major experiences. And there was one great sorrow: the death of Fini Mama. In other words, a great many things happened.

As far as my writing is concerned, I believe I made some progress; as a human being I don't think I did. Last year I stated that I expected to improve this year. This has not happened. I don't say I have a great many faults, but I do have some, and I ought to make a great effort to eliminate them. Maybe, maybe this year!

Ah, I just looked out the window and saw something absolutely magnificent. Beyond the white curtain and the white windowsill, the fence is all white—and beyond it the trees. In fact the entire world is white, and it is still snowing. So much whiteness—and all of a different shade. Blue-white, gray-white, sparkling and dull white, all of it indescribably beautiful. But now I must stop. With this entry I have formally and festively begun my diary for 1938.

January 14, 1938

As I leafed through my diary, reading bits and pieces, I noticed that events concerning the Peter affair are not clear. In short, I was already a little bored with him, and he expected a greater response from me. I'm afraid I was not particularly nice to him, and he noticed my indifference. That was that! I wasn't a bit sorry.

At present my school life is quite satisfactory, and I have several interesting assignments. I also have a new pupil. On the whole, I'm very satisfied with things.

January 28, 1938

I've not mentioned Marianne's party before. I should really call it a Big Affair rather than a party; it was truly a large-scale, brilliant evening, the entire atmosphere delightful and gay. Between dancing and good conversation, the hours literally flew. I didn't get home until four in the morning. It's a good thing Pista[19] is here from Dombóvár so we can go out together, and I have no need of an escort.

Mary, my English pen pal, wrote about my proposed trip to England this summer, but I'm afraid it probably won't be possible for me to go until next year, though I would much rather go now, as times are so uncertain.

Saturday afternoon Náday was here again. I really can talk to him; he's such an intelligent, attractive fellow. We ended up discussing differential and integral calculus, but naturally we don't generally talk about such things!

Saturday night we spent in a most delightful manner: we read aloud the letters Daddy wrote Mama. They are such humorous, dear letters that it's a joy to read them. I can imagine how much they meant to Mama. We haven't finished reading all of them. Perhaps we'll continue tonight.

March 7, 1938

I'm really fed up to the teeth with all this bother for the Purim Festival. As president of the Bible Society it's not becoming for me to say such things, but there is so much worry and trouble about the preparation that it's awful. It is to be on the 19th, and among the four scenes we plan to present, only two are ready, and to my way of thinking they're weak too. I am really not in the mood to do anything, and wish the whole thing were over and done with—though I do hope it turns out well.

I am now reading *Chrome Yellow* by Aldous Huxley, a very witty and amusing book. I like his style and concept, though the plot is not too interesting. Before that I read Cronin's *The Citadel*. It's rather good and a bestseller, but I don't think it's a book of any particular value.

March 13, 1938

Today I want to write about two things: political events, and last night. And as in time and importance the political situation is foremost, I'll begin with that.

Not long ago, just before Hitler's annual progress report to the Reichstag (February 20) the Austrian Chancellor, Dr. Kurt von Schuschnigg, went to Germany at the invitation of Hitler. Ostensibly they had a most cordial conference, and we heard little about the question of Anschluss. Arthur Seyss-Inquart, a lawyer and Nazi politician, became a member of the reorganized Austrian cabinet (Minister of Security), but there were no other visible signs of Hitler's influence. Thus, understandably, there was an uproar when Schuschnigg— on Wednesday, if I correctly recall—ordered a plebiscite for Sunday, March 13, for the question of Anschluss: Yes or No. The sudden decision naturally surprised everyone, including those outside Austria, but we all calmly awaited the results, confident the vote would be in favor of independence. This was the situation on Friday.

That evening we happened to turn on the radio, and were appalled to hear the following: "The plebiscite has been postponed. Germany has given an ultimatum demanding the resignation of

Hannah, at sixteen, dressed up for a Purim party in a Hungarian officer's uniform.

Schuschnigg. Compelled to submit to force, Schuschnigg bade farewell to Austria in a radio address, and Seyss-Inquart seized controlling power of Austria. In the interest of establishing peace and order in Austria he urgently requested German troops." Saturday morning (March 12) the occupation of Austria began, troops were on the march, and at this moment Austria is entirely under Nazi control.

These events have caused indescribable tension in Hungary too. In school, on the street, even at parties, it is the main topic of discussion. The lives of many people here are closely affected by these events. But even those not immediately involved are awaiting the mobilization of Czechoslovakia with deep concern and interest, wondering whether she will take steps to insure the safety of the Sudeten Germans. There is also speculation concerning the next moves of England and France (there is a political crisis in the latter), and whom Italy will side with. And not least, what will happen to us in the shadow of an eastward-expanding nation of seventy million?

Hitler is arriving in Vienna today. Setting aside all antipathy, one must admit he accomplished things extremely cleverly and boldly. At the moment everything is at a standstill, and everyone is awaiting developments, apprehensive of the future.

A gayer and lovelier event was the affair last night at Lucy's house, where about forty of us were invited. After the usual leisurely beginning, we danced, had a buffet supper, sang, and the atmosphere became delightful and relaxed. I danced a lot and had a fabulous time.

March 26, 1938

The Purim party took place and went quite well. I don't have much to say about it. I went dancing again last night; there were a lot of rather attractive boys, but not one interesting enough to continue a friendship with.

The tensions caused by the political situation are easing, but now one can feel the far-reaching waves. A great many people here are being affected, and even more are considering the possibility of emigrating. Everyone is afraid and asking, what's going to happen here? It is almost impossible to imagine a conversation that does not branch into this sea of a thousand questions. Everyone is restless and expectant. As far as war is concerned, there doesn't seem to be any danger. Events appear to have been smoothed over amazingly easily and quietly. Evidently, everything happened at the most opportune moment.

April 4, 1938

I'm ashamed not to have written anything about today's depressed, tense, agitated world, and even now I'm writing only to sum up the happenings of Saturday evening. But one talks and hears so much about events in Austria, and one is so nervous about the local situation, that by the time it comes to writing about things, one feels too depressed and discouraged. Of course Gyuri won't go to Austria next year, as planned, but perhaps to France—for good. Thus we'll be torn apart, scattered.

But to get back to Saturday night. We were at Vera's, and I really enjoyed myself. The atmosphere was superb. We danced a lot, and Vera improvised a charming little bar. As usual, the company was wonderful. I spent most of the evening with Gyuri Révész. I don't believe I've mentioned him before, though I've met him several times. When we first met we danced together only occasionally, but lately much more often. He's a wonderful dancer, and a rather nice fellow. He told me, among other things, how much my behavior, manner of speaking, etc., etc., appeal to him. He said he would like his sister to be like me, and "consoled" me with the assurance that, even if I didn't have as many admirers as some of the other "types," I would always have greater success than they with boys who are really worthwhile. It's interesting that Marianne's cousin said exactly the same thing about me not long ago. Of course I danced with a good many other boys besides Révész, and it was daylight by the time the party broke up.

Dombóvár, April 24, 1938

It's been such a long time again since I wrote. Meanwhile really a lot has happened. I've been in Dombóvár a week. Left Budapest Tuesday, and had an exciting adventure on the train. Well, adventure is an exaggeration; let's just call it an encounter. When I got on the train a young man helped me with my bag and sat beside me, and I immediately noticed he wanted to get acquainted. So I got out my book, *The Moon and Sixpence* by Somerset Maugham—a wonderful novel that actually deserves a separate paragraph—and started reading.

"Will it bother you if I smoke?" "Are you going to Dombóvár?" (The conductor had mentioned it when he took my ticket.) "Do you know ... there?" I answered his questions rather laconically. But when I started pulling at the window and he got up and vigorously helped me yank it down, I couldn't do anything but answer his questions. It turned out he is a Presbyterian theologian, and when he tried to convince me that I ought to attend divinity classes, I gave him to understand this would be impossible because...

This did not deter him from asking further questions. On the contrary. He insisted upon knowing my name. However, I did not tell him, whereupon he stated it was evident that we Jews stubbornly withdrew from all possible social contact and integration. We discussed matters in connection with this question, and I assured him that this was certainly not why I wouldn't tell him my name. Whereupon he pretended he was very upset and vowed he would wait for me one day after school. I asked him not to do that, and thus the matter ended

The debate on the Jewish Bill[20] is now in progress. There has been, and continues to be, terrible tension about it, and conjecture as to whether there will be a law concerning this bill. People are talking about it everywhere. Commerce, industry, the theatre, cafés—everything is at a standstill while this matter is under discussion in Parliament. I wonder how all this will end?

Budapest, May 7, 1938

Gyuri's graduation ceremony took place this morning, and this afternoon there was a farewell gathering at the synagogue in honor of the graduates. This has been customary for years, but this year it had a special significance, and was a much sadder occasion than usual. Boys of this year's class will be scattered and can look forward only to an uncertain future. Ivan spoke, and attempted to make his message strong and hopeful, but even so it was such a hopeless and resigned speech. True, one can hardly feel otherwise these days. At any rate, it was a sad affair, and particularly so for me because of Gyuri. It was only then that I actually realized what it means to have him leaving home immediately after graduation, without knowing what will become of him, or when he will be able to return. How awful it must be for Mother.

Among Gyuri's classmates there are a few Arrow-Crossers,[21] and he asked them to look after Mother and me if there should be any trouble. It's horrible how everyone takes it so much for granted that there will be trouble, and very naïve to think these boys would do anything for us if the need arose. At any rate, it was dear of Gyuri to speak to them.

May 30, 1938

I'm writing this after another "night of revelry." I try to convince myself that my diary is not concerned only with such events, but at any rate I've only remembered to make an entry about it now.

We were at Mari's house. I went with Péter and wore my new dress—the muslin de soie over blue taffeta, with a pink flower in the belt. It's really adorable. I did my own hair and was a bit nervous it wouldn't turn out right. But it looked quite good.

I ought to mention, as a preliminary, that I was somewhat dubious about going to Mari's party, as her family has only recently converted to Christianity, and I very much condemn this. But my desire for a night of fun conquered my reluctance. We got there at ten-fifteen, the last to arrive. They had just begun serving supper. I sat at a small table with a very pleasant group. After supper we danced, and it was a most enjoyable affair.

I have some big news: the Virágs have invited me to spend the summer at Lelle, where I will help a bit in their guest house. I'm delighted, as this sort of work interests me greatly. My trip to England is out of the question anyway, so this will be very nice.

I've written a new poem. It's called "Blue." I like it very much.

June 15, 1938

Today was the last day of school. I got A's in everything and won second prize in the photography competition. This year it was the only activity in which I competed. I haven't participated in the Literary Society since the incident last autumn. On the whole, I was rather lax the entire term. Next term I'll work harder.

I think a worthy manner in which to close today is to note that I just finished reading *Crime and Punishment*. I was enormously impressed by the characterization and somehow—subconsciously— felt there was considerable similarity in family traits and characteristics between the family portrayed in the book and ours. Of course only in certain particulars.

This diary has also come to an end. I think it will belong among my most cherished mementos.

June 23, 1938

I'm starting a new diary once again. This will be my third, and I'm beginning it with considerable emotion. I'm reminded of the words of Mr. Tót, the schoolmaster at Dombóvár who encouraged me to start my first diary four years ago. He told me it would be such a delightful memento that if ever a fire broke out in my house the diary would be the first thing I would think of saving! Perhaps he was right.

I can only write a few lines now. I'm in the midst of feverish packing and general commotion, as I'm leaving for Lelle this afternoon. It will be very difficult to say good-bye to Gyuri.

Lelle, June 25, 1938

This is my second day here. There is practically no work, and we spend the days walking, bathing in Lake Balaton, playing ping-pong, etc. The whole thing is really delightful. Erzsi and I get along very well. We're good friends, have a lot to talk about, and so on. Otherwise I have nothing much to write about. I doubt this summer my diary will be as full of entries as it was after last summer's vacation.

June 28, 1938

I'm going home. I am terribly ashamed at not being able to adapt myself to the principles of Erzsi's mother. The only real pastime here is bathing in the Balaton, but near the shore the water is so shallow it's only possible to wade and splash about. I was given to understand that Erzsi's mother would not permit us to swim beyond the point where we could touch the bottom, so I swam out to about shoulder depth. This, however, is relatively far out, so it's difficult to see a white bathing cap in the distance. Today, when Erzsi's mother came to the beach and saw how "terribly far" I had swum, she had palpitations and became extremely upset. When I begged her pardon, she declared she was not disposed to be upset by me, etc., etc. I gathered she thought it would be best if I went home. I remained relatively calm and spoke politely, but felt near to breaking point and began crying, so ran to my room. I locked the door, and cried for a long time. Meanwhile I began writing in my diary.

I was infinitely hurt by the entire thing, and am ashamed to think I'm going home under these circumstances … I was sitting like this, crying, when Erzsi and her mother came to the door. Erzsi's mother was very kind then and asked me to believe she was only concerned about my safety and welfare, and that she realized she had been hasty. In other words, she had cooled down. She asked me not to let the same thing happen again, kissed me, and entreated me to stop crying. Of course this is easier said than done. Now I must stop writing, as I have to go down to lunch. I hope my eyes aren't too red.

It's now afternoon. The storm is over; everything has calmed down and seems to be all right. But it has left a deep impression on me. If I stay on, even if I try to convince myself it was all due only to tension, worry, and basic good will followed by kind words, I think I'll still have difficulty forgetting this morning's scene. I could still cry if I weren't making a considerable effort to contain myself. I don't think I'll stay beyond the middle of July, unless there is more work, things to see and learn that would fill my days. In other words, I'll see how things go.

July 2, 1938

I've already forgotten the incident of the other day. Since then everything has been going very nicely. These last two days we've spent a lot of time boating, and I've even learned to row, which I've enjoyed tremendously. What we do, Erzsi and I, is take the rowing boat out, sit in it, sunbathe, read, and watch the D-22, a beautiful big sailing boat which circles around us a good deal ... of course not empty, but with its three masters. This is the only interesting boy situation, as the young chap at the guest house really doesn't count. If he comes down in the afternoon and stretches out in a hammock near us, I immediately start reading *The Village Notary*[22] and laugh when he wonders how I can read this "required" reading matter during my holidays.

Matters concerning Gyuri's emigration, i.e., foreign currency, documents, etc., have been settled, thank God, and he'll soon be leaving. I am so glad everything is finally in order for his departure, regardless of how my heart aches at his going. If his train passes through Lelle we're going to the station to see him. Poor Mother; I'm so sorry for her. I know she's crushed, but I'm sure this is best for Gyuri—as far as anyone can tell these days.

July 4, 1938

I think I'll shorten my stay here after all. Not because of the people—they're all really very nice and kind—but because this aimless, completely idle, and unproductive existence is not for me. As far as I'm concerned, there are only two kinds of vacation: complete rest or work. But the possibility of working, or even being of any use here, is nil. Thus I have no opportunity of learning anything either. On the other hand, although I enjoy being with Erzsi, and one of the reasons I came was to spend time with her, she is busy to a certain extent so that I'm always waiting for her to finish something she's doing. This is really not for me, as I'm just wasting my time, accomplishing nothing at all.

I haven't written any of this to Mother, as she would probably worry that I'm unhappy. I'm also still hoping there will be more guests, thus more work, and that the situation will improve.

Bela was here over the weekend. He is the most observant member of this family. He saw things weren't entirely in order and asked me if anything was the matter. But I didn't want to discuss it. Besides, he wouldn't really understand the situation, so I said I feel very well but that one can't always smile and be gay. Of course this was not a very satisfactory answer, but he didn't pursue the matter further. In any event, he was very sweet, and I could almost have fallen in love with him—probably because I feel very lonely here and could still start crying at a moment's notice.

July 10, 1938

I've now settled into the situation and can adapt myself much better. But I've written Mother that I don't want to stay after the 15th. It was difficult to write her, and it will be still more difficult to announce my departure here when they've all been so kind, and have done everything to make me comfortable. It would be extremely ungrateful of me to offend them.

I see I've neglected to report that we boarded Gyuri's train according to plan, and managed to exchange a few words with him. I don't know when I'll see the "old man" again. The farewell itself wasn't really emotional, since we confined our conversation to all sorts of banalities, such as a new tennis racket, my Italian lessons, my suntan, mutual friends, and so on. The train had already begun moving when I told him the length of the swimming pool in Milan. But behind it all was the fact that he is starting out in life on his own. It must be very difficult for poor Mother, home alone. She writes that fortunately she has a lot to do. I would like her to have a holiday too this year, without fail. She's the one who has the greatest need of a bit of rest and peace.

Today the weather is ugly, stormy. But Lake Balaton is perhaps most beautiful at such times, though the colors and vistas are so wonderful most mornings and evenings that it's impossible to say when it's loveliest.

I wrote this poem, "Farewell," for Gyuri's departure:

Farewell[23]

You left. We waved a long while.
Porters clattered behind.
We watched and you disappeared.

Life took you. You were happy.
Maybe your heart had songs within.
Our tears were well hidden.

Wordless, we went home
Watching the sky, pale and blue,
And our soul, unseen and secretly
Is waving still to you.

July 13, 1938

I've been in bed for two days. Perhaps I'll get up today, as I no
longer have any temperature. Actually the whole thing lasted only a
day. When I got up the other morning I felt there was something
wrong: I was dizzy, and even went back to bed for a few moments.
But in the end I foolishly got dressed, with some difficulty, because
I didn't want to say there was anything the matter with me. In the
morning I helped in the kitchen but felt awfully ill. When I finally
came up to my room and took my temperature, I found it to be
nearly 102. We were careful about telling Erzsi's mother and did so
only gradually. I slept most of the afternoon, took some medication
in the evening, and yesterday the fever was already gone.

I read all day and finished *The Village Notary*. Toward the end it
positively interested me. I wasn't bored by it at all, as there is so
much truth in it even today—sorry to say. For instance, Hungary
leads all other countries in parliamentary sessions because we're
working in the interests of others as well as our own, for the welfare of Hungarians in the ceded territories, and such matters. Of

course this is not entirely without self-interest. Naturally, the characters in the book are entirely imaginary. It's a good book, but
because of its obsolete and diffused style difficult to read. And now
I have nothing left to read and don't know what I'll do all day. As
long as I had books I wasn't bored and had no need of people. But
even if I had, it would have made no difference, as everyone is busy
now. I'm very upset that I'm ill just at the time there is so much to
do. It's a most uncomfortable feeling, but I can do nothing about
it. I have a suspicion that the reason for my illness lies in the fact
I've been eating an enormous amount of meat. In these last three
years, since I've eaten meat only sparingly, I've not had any kind of
illness with a temperature. Of course I'm not saying one develops
a sore throat directly from eating meat, but it's possible that if one
eats a lot of it, one's system is more susceptible to infections.
Naturally I keep all such thoughts to myself, as Erzsi's family would
think me a half-wit were I to voice such theories.

In the end I'll probably write as much this summer as I did last,
though the subjects are dissimilar. This time last summer! Perhaps I
was in Certosa, or around Lake Garda. I don't remember the exact
dates any more, but I think there was hardly a day I did not see
something beautiful. Of course, my vacation thus far this year is
entirely different, but I'm not at all sorry. I saw one or two interesting things this year too, had a few pleasant days, met a variety of
people, and if I was a bit disappointed that was because I expected
too much.

It looks as if this diary will be the opposite of last year's, which
was full of "boy matters." Here there is little mention of them,
unless I mention Hevai, who wrote yesterday that he is coming to
Lelle on the 23rd. But I'll send word that I won't be here by then.
Sometimes it would be good to have someone to talk to about
everything, tranquilly. No matter. I'm really not one who can't be
alone. If worse comes to worse, I can always write in my diary, and
that makes everything all right.

July 14, 1938

I stayed in bed yesterday too and spent the entire day writing. Outside my diary I wrote letters, post cards, and a poem which I think is quite good, not yet titled, but which I'll probably call "Storm" or some such.

Mother wrote to say that she showed some of my poems to Alkalay, a journalist and translator, and that he was surprised and favorably impressed by them. I'll hear all the particulars when I get home. He mentioned someone to whom I could take the poems, and I shall do so. I now need honest and serious criticism, not just the praise of family and close friends.

I feel that writing isn't difficult for me, and if something turns out well it gives one such a great feeling. The other day, in a weak moment, I recited for Erzsi the farewell poem I wrote for Gyuri. I think it's good because of its simplicity and informality. Whereupon she remarked how nice it is when a person can write a poem when he wants to, and that she wrote her last poem when she was twelve, but since then hasn't felt like writing poems. I could have used greater discrimination in my choice of audience, but sometimes the overwhelming need to share and confide gets the best of one.

A while ago I had a great adventure: for 60 *fillér* I found out about my future. A gypsy read my left palm. I need not say what a disappointment such a thing can be. When I'm eighteen I am going to be a bride, my husband is going to own a car…. Later she said that he won't be rich but that we're going to have a very happy and satisfying life together. I am going to have only one son. She couldn't tell me much about the rest of this year, but for 1939 she predicted a lot of happiness.

As for the present and immediate future, according to her I've been in love twice—which I can just barely accept—though as far as I'm concerned in neither case was it really love. She said I have had one suitor, and that someone living abroad is thinking of me (of course such a person doesn't exist). She said I'd receive a letter that will please me soon. I've recorded all this so I can "control" what she said at some future time. The gypsy girl had beautiful eyes, but otherwise, as someone noted, she didn't read from cards or palms, but from left field.

Budapest, aged seventeen, July 21, 1938

I finally arrived home on Tuesday night. The last days at Lelle were quite pleasant. G. came on Saturday. It was good to be able to talk to him. Saturday evening a rather large group of us went out and celebrated my birthday—my seventeenth. At midnight we drank to my health, danced a bit, and at about two in the morning went home. Sunday morning a lot of people congratulated me; G. sent flowers. In the morning we went swimming and rowing, and played ping-pong. The lake was a bit rough, which I enjoyed tremendously.

That afternoon I said good-bye to everyone and left. Arrived back at nine in the evening and am wonderfully happy to be home again. Mother and I were so delighted to see each other, but we're already discussing the possibility of my going away, somewhere in the mountains.

July 25, 1938

It's been settled. I'm going to Biela Voda, near Tátralomnic. They say it's a very beautiful and pleasant place. I'm very happy now about the idea, though at first I really didn't have much desire to go. I'm leaving on the 30th and staying until August 20, just three weeks. It will cost 220 *pengö* plus the fare, which is expensive. But somehow everyone has now lost the value of money, wondering whether what has happened in Vienna will happen here. If it does, it will make really very little difference how much one has left for them to confiscate. Perhaps one should not take this attitude, but we're so thoroughly prepared for the worst and feel it's really only a matter of time.

July 28, 1938

Yesterday I went to see Piroska Reichard, one of the journalists on *The Nyugat*.[24] I have long wanted the opinion of a professional, and believe I got exactly that from her. She received me by saying the poems surprised her, and she thinks I'm talented. She said they are definitely better than average, and thinks I will become a writer, though not necessarily a poet. Judging by the poems, she doesn't consider me entirely lyrical. She then told me what the faults are: they are apt to be long, and she feels I compromise the form for the sake of content. She also feels that sometimes my manner of expression is still rather immature. But on the whole, she finds me talented. I was terribly pleased. Somehow, one has more confidence after professional criticism.

Day after tomorrow I leave for Biela Voda. It's near Teplic, and I believe it will be very nice. Évi and I are going together; she's arriving today from Dombóvár, and I'm meeting her at the station. I have an awful lot to do: packing, shopping for a few things, and so on.

I still have to mention the Dini affair. Not long ago I received a letter from him in which, among other things, he wrote that he has been in love with me for years. He claims he made such an enormous effort to do well at school only to please me, and feels he could eventually go quite far—for my sake. He asks me to answer yes or no.

I was tremendously surprised by this letter. I didn't consider Dini an idealist, one who silently struggles and suffers (he claims he suffered too!). At any rate, the entire affair was quite uncomfortable, but I answered at once because if what he writes is true, then he actually does take the whole thing most seriously, and I don't want to keep him waiting for my answer. I was very kind but firm in my refusal. I am not saying he's not a very decent fellow, but he has certain characteristics which preclude my taking his proposal seriously even for a moment.

Biela Voda, July 31, 1938

We arrived in Biela Voda yesterday. The road up was lovely, particularly the second half, after we reached the mountains and pine forests. We got off at Poprad, where Aunt Magda and a few girls were waiting for us. We came up by car along a magnificent road. Biela Voda itself is fabulous. The house is very attractive, the mountains glorious. There is a forest, and paths for walking right in the heart of it. It's truly wonderful. I don't have much time to write now.

August 4, 1938

It's early in the morning; everyone is asleep. I'm sitting in a sunny meadow attempting to reconstruct the most outstanding events of the last few days. For instance: we went to the beach at Lomnic. Magnificent. I had a sort of feeling of release, joyousness, and weight-lessness all combined as I stood beside a lake embedded in the hills. I don't know whether I've described the sensation correctly, but that it's wonderful is for sure. Besides, we were gay, joked and teased constantly, and it was all quite fantastic.

Tuesday we went to Ratzenberg, leaving at seven in the morning. Rest periods included, we reached six thousand feet, our goal, around noon. That stretch of the road was rather tiring. At the top we sunbathed, rested, ate. (This always belongs to the most important part of the schedule.) Then we made our way across a steep, pebbly, craggy path to Steinbach Sea. This is a tiny, clear, delightful mountain lake, and one can feel its icy coldness just by looking at it. There is a hospice nearby, where we rested, ate, and drank, then made the three-hour hike to Lomnic. From Lomnic we came back by car, and I won't deny we were quite tired.

August 12, 1938

I feel wonderful here. Since I last wrote we made an excursion to Moses Springs, from where the view is breathtaking, even frighten-ing. Then we went back to Steinbach Sea and descended along a rather long road to Gemse, where there is a perfectly situated hostel. On the most beautiful section of this road there is a magnificent foaming-white waterfall that springs from an extremely precipitous cliff. It's really an extravagant sight. From there we hiked down to Lomnic, and that evening arrived home dead tired.

Now ping-pong is in full force, and I won the championship. Such simple pleasures still exist in this world.

August 22, 1938

We went to Tátrafüred, all of us jammed into a bus, singing, laughing, carefree, and from there, on some sort of cogwheel railways up to Gemse. We quickly reached Great Waterfall and continued from there—in the wrong direction! But we were not sorry, as we went up a fantastic side road faced on both sides by cloud-shrouded rock walls. We were sad we could not continue along this road, but as it did not lead to Five Seas we had to turn back.

We quickly reached the waterfall again, admired it once more, and continued on the road to the Magistrale. The view was breathtaking all the way. The stream, which is the source of the waterfall, appears like a silver streak in the green forest, and there are cliff walls and pine trees everywhere. In one spot we drove through snow, and it was a remarkable sensation to do so in August. Fortunately, when we reached the top there was brilliant sunshine. But before reaching the top, and on our way down, we certainly swallowed a lot of fog, and it even rained.

At the peak we went to the hospice and fell into chairs. We were tired and hungry, and along with the plate of soup each of us ordered, we ate our picnic lunch. Then, after wrapping ourselves in the warm things we had brought along (as it was extremely cold), we went to look around. We found all five lakes and took pictures, but unfortunately it is not possible to capture on film all the beauty one sees. We started back to Magistrale and to the pebble-strewn stream, where we rested again, and then on home!

Meanwhile we had a terrific argument with a German boy about a philosophic subject: whether or not there is a God. Needless to say, we reached no agreement or decision. However, we miscalculated the time and had to stumble through the forest in the dark, which was a somewhat eerie sensation, but beautiful. It was eight-thirty by the time we burst into the house, yet after dinner went again for a walk, just to prove we weren't the least bit tired! Next day came the packing and other such sad things. It was difficult to say good-bye. We reached home late at night, exhausted.

In short, they were three glorious, memorable weeks. I hope I shall not forget them. I don't want to say "never," because according to Oscar Wilde this is a big, meaningless word that women are fond of using. So instead I'll write, "I won't forget them for a long time." It's not the vistas that I would like to carry within me, but the moods, the stillness of the mountains, the feeling of peace, of height. Perhaps I'll succeed.

Budapest, August 30, 1938

This summer, like all the others, has gone by so quickly. School starts on the 3rd. In times past I was always glad to return to classes, but this year I await the opening with mixed emotions. I am partially prepared for serious work; on the other hand I feel some concern about the Literary Society and the likelihood of similar unpleasantnesses cropping up—and they probably will. And then the knowledge that this is my last year of school is so strange. At home we're already beginning to discuss the choice of a career. I never imagined it would be as difficult for me to choose as it is for most others.

At the moment we're considering hotel management, but in the background there is always the possibility of writing professionally—and whatever I do, the biggest question is where? Here, or somewhere abroad? It's not easy to find a job anywhere. It can't be said we were born into an easy world, my generation.

Now everyone is again talking about war, but this doesn't even interest me any more because for the past six months the situation has been vacillating from dangerous to less dangerous. I'm trying not to be too concerned with things because I know I'll have great need of good, steady nerves in the near future, and it would be a pity to ruin them now.

September 17, 1938

We're living through indescribably tense days. The question is, Will there be war? The mobilization going on in various countries doesn't fill one with a great deal of confidence. No recent news concerning the discussions of Hitler and Chamberlain. The entire world is united in fearful suspense. I, for one, feel a numbing indifference because of all this waiting. The situation changes from minute to minute. Even the idea there may be war is abominable enough.

From my point of view, I'm glad Gyuri is in France, though Mother is extremely worried about him. Of course this is understandable. The devil take the Sudeten Germans and all the other Germans, along with their führer. One feels better saying these things. Why is it necessary to ruin the world, turn it topsy-turvy, when everything could be so pleasant? Or is that impossible? Is it contrary to the nature of man? G. sees the war entirely differently. Materialistically. To him the annihilation of mankind is unimportant. And he is able to defend his point of view so ingeniously that one can hardly stand up to him with a counter-argument.

September 27, 1938

Ten days have passed since my last entry, and the situation remains unchanged. Negotiations, Mussolini's and Hitler's speeches, Chamberlain's flights back and forth, news bulletins concerning mobilization, denials. There have been practice air-raid alerts, and the situation remains unchanged. One wonders, will there be war, or won't there? Though the atmosphere is explosive, I still believe there will be peace, perhaps only because I just can't possibly imagine war.

Under these circumstances, one can't look forward to the Jewish New Year holidays as a time of renewed hope and peace. For us Jews the situation is doubly serious, and it's difficult to imagine how all this will be solved. I am going to the synagogue now, though not with any great enthusiasm. There will be some sort of youth service, though the situation doesn't arouse much feeling of devotion in one. But I'm going just the same.

September 29, 1938

I think one can safely state that the excitement and tension have reached a peak. Hitler's ultimatum[25] runs out tomorrow, and peace is only possible if Czechoslovakia hands over the territories Hitler demands—free of Czech nationals. This is impossible. Today, at the last moment, Chamberlain, Hitler, Daladier, and Mussolini are making a final attempt to save the peace. Though until now I believed in the possibility of maintaining the peace, I am now beginning to have doubts. Mobilization has started everywhere. Perhaps Gyuri has already left France. I feel so sorry that the poor boy has to make such difficult decisions alone. Perhaps he'll return home; perhaps he'll be lucky and manage to get to Switzerland. Mother's tension is understandable, but everyone has something or someone to worry about.

Now an entirely different subject: I recently had a letter from Bela. It went even further than Dini's. I don't know how to answer him. It's a difficult business. And my usual luck—I don't like him the tiniest bit.

October 1, 1938

It is the Saturday before the Day of Atonement. I should have gone to synagogue, but instead I wrote a poem, and now I would rather attempt some self-analysis in my diary.

I don't quite know where to begin. That I made many errors this past year (though I don't feel I actually sinned), I know. Errors against God, righteousness, people, and above all against Mother, and even against myself. I know I have many mistakes to answer for, and see them all clearly in my mind's eye. But I find myself incapable of enumerating them, of writing them all down. Perhaps deep down I'm afraid that someday someone might read what I have written. And I am really incapable of "confessing."

I would like to be as good as possible to Mother, to wear my Jewishness with pride, to be well thought of in my class at school, and I would very much like always to be able to believe and trust in God. There are times I cannot, and at such times I attempt to force myself to believe completely, firmly, with total certainty. I wonder, though, if anyone exists who has never doubted? Yet, I don't think it is possible to have complete faith until after one has known some doubt and considerable deep meditation.

October 27, 1938

I don't know whether I've already mentioned that I've become a
Zionist. This word stands for a tremendous number of things. To me
it means, in short, that I now consciously and strongly feel I am a
Jew, and am proud of it. My primary aim is to go to Palestine, to
work for it. Of course this did not develop from one day to the next;
it was a somewhat gradual development. There was first talk of it
about three years ago, and at that time I vehemently attacked the
Zionist Movement. Since then people, events, times have all brought
me closer to the idea, and I am immeasurably happy that I've found
this ideal, that I now feel firm ground under my feet and can see a
definite goal toward which it is really worth striving. I am going to
start learning Hebrew, and I'll attend one of the youth groups. In
short, I'm really going to knuckle down properly. I've become a different person, and it's a very good feeling.

One needs something to believe in, something for which one can
have whole-hearted enthusiasm. One needs to feel that one's life has
meaning, that one is needed in this world. Zionism fulfills all this for
me. One hears a good many arguments against the Movement, but
this doesn't matter. I believe in it, and that's the important thing. I'm
convinced Zionism is Jewry's solution to its problems and that the
outstanding work being done in Palestine is not in vain.

November 12, 1938

I have so much to write about I don't even know where to begin. We
have got back the upper part of Northern Hungary.[26] From the 2nd
of November until the 10th, the joyous and enthusiastic entry of
Hungarian troops took place from Komárom to Kassa. We had no
school, and thanks to the radio we too felt involved in the entry. And
this morning the four senior classes, in groups of ten, attended a special holiday sitting of Parliament, which was very interesting. But I
must honestly state that to me the road I am now following in the
Zionist Movement means far more, both emotionally and spiritually.

I am learning Hebrew, reading about Palestine, and am also reading

Szechenyi's *Peoples of the East*, a brilliant book that gives fundamental facts concerning the lives of all the people of the world. On the whole, I'm reading considerably more, and about far more serious subjects than hitherto.

I am determinedly and purposefully preparing for life in Palestine. And although I confess that in many respects it's painful to tear myself from my Hungarian sentiments, I must do so in my own interest, and the interests of Jewry. Our two-thousand-year history justifies us; the present compels us; the future gives us confidence. Whoever is aware of his Jewishness cannot continue with his eyes shut. As yet, our aims are not entirely definite, nor am I sure what profession I'll choose. But I don't want to work only for myself and in my own interests, but for the mutual good of Jewish aims. Perhaps these are but the vague and confused thoughts and fantasies of youth, but I think I will have the fortitude, strength, and ability to realize these dreams.

Mother is having difficulty accepting the idea that I will eventually emigrate, but because she is completely unselfish she won't place obstacles in my way. Naturally I would be so happy if she came too. The three of us must not be torn apart, must not go three different ways.

Gyuri is well, and we are always eagerly awaiting news from him. Recently he won a ping-pong tournament in Lyon; his picture was even in the papers there. We were so pleased for him.

I must close for the time being. Certainly it will be a long time before I'll write again, but I'll try not to let it be too long. And next time I'll write in the style of Szechenyi: instead of writing about events, I'll note my thoughts.

November 20, 1938

The thought that now occupies my every waking moment is Palestine. Everything in connection with it interests me; everything else is entirely secondary. Even school has lost some of its meaning, and the only thing I am studying hard is Hebrew. I already know a little … a few words. Éva Beregi is teaching me. She is remarkably kind and won't accept any money from me, so I'm racking my brains to find some possible way of reciprocating. I have also joined a correspondence course. They send lessons, and it's quite good.

I'm almost positive I'll choose some sort of profession connected with agriculture. I'll probably study dairy farming and cheese production. A woman who was in Palestine, and enchanted by it, gave me the idea. She also told me all sorts of wonderful things about the Land. Listening to her was a joy. Everything that is beautiful, cheerful, and of some consolation to the Jews stems from Palestine.

Here the situation is constantly deteriorating. A new Jewish Law[27] is soon to be proclaimed. It will be the "most urgent" thus far. They are going to "solve" land reform by distributing the land at present in Jewish hands—and only that. The truly great estates won't be touched. But of course this was to be expected.

December 11, 1938

It's nine o'clock in the morning, but I'm the only one up—surrounded by paper streamers and an untidy mess. Yesterday I finally had my "evening"—or whatever one can call it, as it was six-thirty in the morning by the time I got to bed. Whether it was a successful party I can't say. I would be pleased to state that it was, but to me the entire thing was somehow a disappointment. Perhaps one of the contributing factors was that I personally didn't enjoy myself very much. By this I mean there was no one with whom I spent any great length of time, or who really interested me. But there is something else: the times. And above all, my ideological point of view has so vastly changed since last year that I could not help but consider the affair frivolous, empty, and in a certain measure quite unnecessary at a time such as we're now going through.

There were nearly thirty people here, and only a few among them seriously interested me. I kept thinking how nice it would have been to have put all the money the party cost into the collection box of the Keren Kayemet.[28] Oh, dear, I would like best of all to go to Palestine now. I would be glad to forfeit my graduation, everything. I don't know what has happened to me, but I just can't live here any longer, can't stand my old group of friends, studying, or any of the things with which I've been familiar up till now.

December 21, 1938

This is the first day of vacation, so I again have time to write. This morning I studied Hebrew and spent some time reading *Bambi,* at one time one of my favorite books. It was delightful to read it again. Though I really can't allow myself to spend time reading this sort of thing, as I have so many new books I ought to read, and am now constantly reading all sorts of travel books about Palestine.

Yesterday afternoon I was at the home of Judit Kiss, and it was evidently her determined intention to dissuade me from going to Palestine. Naturally she didn't succeed. On the contrary, she finally said perhaps I am right. She was infinitely kind, and I promised I would write her about myself from Palestine, and we would see which of us was right.

I've completely stopped writing now, and am sorry about it. I would like to be advanced enough in Hebrew to write in it, but of course that is still far in the future, as I am merely at the beginning of the beginning.

February 6, 1939

I've been ill for several days, and I'm not going to school today either. I would like to write a few words about the book I finished yesterday: Ludwig Lewisohn's *The Island Within.* I liked it enormously. Perhaps now that I am so immersed in Jewishness I understood and enjoyed this book doubly. More so, certainly, than if I had read it perhaps a year ago. He chronicles the lives of four generations of Jews, from the ghetto to New York, from belief and unity to complete spiritual and emotional insecurity and family disunity. He relates the struggles of the rootless fourth generation and its recognition of the essence of Jewishness. In other words, he presents all these deep and burning problems incisively and with clarity. I would like to give everyone who wonders why he is a Jew (and there are a tremendous number of such people) this book to read. It's a must!

Meanwhile I've leafed back through my diary and see I mentioned Bela. I must finish that story. While he was in town he was here a couple of times, then when he returned to Kolozsvár (Cluj) he wrote me very warm letters—which I answered, though with considerably less warmth.

When the first Jewish Bill[29] was introduced I received a letter from him in which he wrote that now he understood why I was so reserved: I must have thought that he, a Gentile, would be disturbed by the fact I am Jewish, whereas, etc., etc. When I read this I instantly sat down and replied that evidently he could not believe a Jewish girl still had pride and self-respect. I told him that if he felt I was an "exception to the rule" (that Jews are inferior), I did not want to be considered as such (exceptional) and to please remember that he can safely include Jews among those about whom he can safely say something good.

This is a paper I read at a meeting of the Bible Society:

ROOTS OF ZIONISM OR
THE FUNDAMENTALS OF ZIONISM

When anyone in Hungary spoke of Zionism five or even two years ago, Jewish public opinion condemned him as a traitor to Hungary, laughed at him, considered him a mad visionary, and under no circumstances heard him out.

Today, due perhaps in large measure to the recent blows suffered, Hungarian Jews are beginning to concern themselves with Zionism. At least so it seems when they ask, "How big is Palestine? How many people can it accommodate?" and "Is there room for me in the expanding country?" Often the answers to these questions decide whether or not the questioner will become a Zionist.

But the question least frequently voiced is, "What is the purpose of Zionism, its basic aim?"

I would like to deal exactly with this seldom-voiced question, because I believe it to be the most important of all. When

one understands and feels this and applies it to oneself, one
will become a Zionist, regardless of how many can emigrate
to Palestine today or tomorrow, whether conditions here will
improve or deteriorate, whether or not there are possibilities
of emigrating to other countries.

Thus, without relating it to the times and circumstances
under which we are now living—in fact apart from all per-
tinent circumstances and situations—I would like to summarize absolute Zionism.

If we had to define Zionism briefly, perhaps we could
best do so in the words of Nachum Sokolov[30]: "Zionism is
the movement of the Jewish people for its revival."

Perhaps many are at this very moment mentally vetoing
this with the thought that Jews do not constitute a people.
But how is a nation created out of a community? From a
common origin; a common past, present, and future; common laws; a common language; and a native land.

In ancient Palestine these motives were united and
formed a complete background. Then the native land ceased
to exist, and gradually the language link to the ancient land
weakened. But the consciousness of the people was saved by
the Torah, that invisible but all-powerful mobile State.

It is, however, inconceivable that in the stateless world of
the Middle Ages, when religion was the focal point of life,
the self-assurance of the ghetto-bound Jew could have
become so strengthened that he could have expressed his
longing for a nation, or the restoration of his own way of life,
or that he would have thought of rebuilding his own country. Yet, the yearning expressed in the holiday greeting "Next
Year in Jerusalem" is absolute proof that the hope of regain-
ing the Homeland never died within the Jew.

Then came the human rights laws of the nineteenth century and with them new ideas and concepts of national values.
From the peoples of the greatest countries to those in the
smallest Balkan enclaves, all attempted to find themselves and
their rights. It was the time of decision. Did a Jewish people

still exist, and, if so, would it be influenced by the strength of the spirit of the new movement?

The greater part of Jewry asked only for human rights, happily accepting the good will of the people among whom it lived, and in exchange casting off individuality and ancient characteristics. But a few hundred inspired zealots, young men from Russia, started off toward Zion, and shortly thereafter Herzl[31] wrote *The Jewish State*. Thousands upon thousands endorsed the concept and ideals of Zionism, and suddenly there was a Jewish nation. He who feels there is not, let him speak for himself, but let him not forget those to whom Jewishness means more than the vital statistics on a birth certificate.

One of the fundamentals of Zionism is the realization that anti-Semitism is an illness that can neither be fought against with words, nor cured with superficial treatment. On the contrary, it must be treated and healed at its very roots.

Jewry is living under unnatural conditions, unable to realize its noble characteristics, to utilize its natural talents and capabilities. Thus, it cannot cultivate its natural and immortal attributes or fulfill its destiny.

It is not true that during the Diaspora we have become teachers of the people, leaders. On the contrary, we have turned into imitators, servants, become the whipping boys for the sins and errors of those among whom we live. We have lost our individuality and renounced the most fundamental conditions of life.

How many great Jewish ideas and ideals died behind the walls of ghettoes during the Middle Ages even before seeing the light of day, or behind the invisible ghetto walls of modern Jewry?

If we compare the accomplishments of the five-hundred thousand Jews now living in Palestine with the same number of Jews living in Hungary today, perhaps we will no longer voice the opinion that we can reach our aims only in the Diaspora. Thus, dispersion cannot be our aim, and certainly the sufferings of the Jews must be alleviated.

We don't want charity. We want only our lawful property and rights, and our freedom, for which we have struggled with our own labors. It is our human and national duty to demand these rights. We want to create a homeland for the Jewish spirit and the Jewish people. The solution seems so very clear: we need a Jewish state.

"The Jewish State has become a universal necessity; thus it will become a reality," stated Herzl. Those Jews who want it will create it, and they will have earned it and deserved it. If we renounce Zionism, we renounce tradition, honor, truth, the right of man to live.

We cannot renounce a single one of our rights, not even if the ridiculous accusation were true—that Zionism breeds anti-Semitism. Anti-Semitism is not the result of Zionism, but of dispersion.

But even if this were not so, woe to the individual who attempts to ingratiate himself with the enemy instead of following his own route. We can't renounce Zionism even if it does strengthen anti-Semitism. But amazingly enough, Zionism is the least attacked in this area. On the contrary, the only hope of lessening or ending anti-Semitism is to realize the ideals of Zionism. Then Jewry can live its own life peacefully, alongside other nations. For only Zionism and the establishment of a Jewish state could ever bring about the possibility of the Jews in the Diaspora being able to make manifest their love for their homeland. Because then they could choose to be part of their homeland—not from necessity, but by free will and free choice.

When the possibility of a new homeland came up for discussion, the general Zionist opinion unanimously opted for Palestine. By so doing it gave assurance that its aim was not only to create a homeland, or haven for persecuted Jews in any spot on earth, but that it definitely wanted a homeland, and that it wanted to create that homeland on the very ground to which its history and religious heritage binds it.

I don't want to talk about the work that has been going on in Palestine for several decades, because that has nothing to do with the ideals of Zionism. That is, instead, a part of the realization of the homeland. But one thing must be said at this time: that reality—that which is happening in Palestine—has justified and verified many times over the concepts and ideals of Zionism. The Jew has proved his will to live, his love of work, his ability to establish a state; and he has shown that the name of Palestine is so powerful that it is capable of gathering in Jews from any and all parts of the world.

This tiny piece of land on the shores of the Mediterranean which, after two thousand years, the Jew can again feel to be his own, is big enough to enable the new Jewish life and modern Jewish culture to be attached to its ancient, fundamental ways, and flourish.

Even today, in its mutilated form, Palestine is big enough to be an island in the sea of seemingly hopeless Jewish destiny, an island upon which we can peacefully build a lighthouse to beam its light into the darkness, a light of everlasting human values, the light of the one God.

March 10, 1939

The only thing I'm committed to, in which I believe, is Zionism. Everything connected with it, no matter how remotely, interests me. I can barely think of anything else. I am not afraid of being one-sided. Until now I have had to cast my sights in many directions. Now I have the right to look only in one direction—the direction of Jewry, Palestine, and our future.

The Round Table Conference,[32] predictably, will end without achieving any particular results. I think that the Yishuv[33] is ready for anything, even battle, if they don't find a reasonable solution to the question.

I am sending off my application to the Nahalal Girls' Farm. If only they'll accept me!

Graduation is fairly close, but it leaves me completely cold, and I'm not studying. What possible use will Hungarian history, geography, or history of art be to me? And as far as German is concerned, it only brings horrible things to mind. I'll have no use for French in Palestine, which leaves algebra and physics, and, of course, Hebrew. Unfortunately, this last is not taught in my school. Instead, we are discussing the Jewish Question in connection with the nineteenth century, and the subject is presented in the most malicious way possible.

A copy of the letter I sent to the Girls' Agricultural School at Nahalal, Palestine. I wrote it in Hebrew:

> To the Management:
>
> Attached to my application is my curriculum vitae.
>
> My name: Hannah Senesh. Mother's name: Catherine, maiden name, Salzberger, widow of Bela Senesh, writer. I was born July 17, 1921, in Budapest. I am a Hungarian citizen. I completed my elementary schooling in a state school. Since 1931 I have been a student at a high school for girls. I will graduate at the end of this term. So far I have completed all my studies with honors.
>
> Apart from French and German—the languages I learned in school—I also speak English.
>
> Even before the tragic turn of events concerning our people in my native land, I longed to live in Palestine, and for the way of life there.
>
> I decided to learn this profession so that I could take an active part in the creation of the state and the cultivation of the land.
>
> Following this decision, I have learned a fair amount of Hebrew and am continuing to improve my knowledge of it, in the hope that I will have no language difficulties when I am there.
>
> May I request a favorable decision? An acceptance to the school would give me great joy and happiness. It would be the first step toward the realization of my life's ambition.
>
> With cordial Zionist greetings,
>
> Hannah Senesh

April 22, 1939

We were in Lyon for ten days to see Gyuri. We have already been back a week—and so far I've not written a single word about it. Yet, it was all so delightful, so nice. The trip itself was wonderful, even though I had already seen it all—except for the stretch after Milan. The most beautiful part is the landscape before and after the Franco-Italian border, the snow-capped rocky mountains, the valley, the precipices, waterfalls, streams, little houses crammed one next to the other, carefully guarded and cared-for strips of land, enormous power stations, sparkling white winding roads, viaducts, tunnels. On the way back we passed through the same area at dawn, and I watched the contour of the mountains as it emerged from the shadows of the night. Then suddenly, as daylight increased, all the peaks wore red caps, and scarlet colored the entire mountain range, tinting the sky. Sunrise was glorious.

But the outstanding beauty and wonder of the countryside were dwarfed by the joy and importance of seeing Gyuri again. He doesn't want to remain in France but wants to go to Palestine, too. He has also become an ardent Zionist, and it was wonderful to talk to him about these things and to discover how alike our thinking is about such matters. He showed us his school. It's a handsome, modern, richly appointed institute, and I think he likes his profession.

Oh, dear, I could write so much more about Gyuri and how perfect it was to see him again.

June 18, 1939

I don't want to do any more studying before tomorrow's final examinations, and I'm in the mood to write in my diary. Perhaps I'm just a tiny bit nervous, even though the question of *praeclara*[34] is entirely a matter of vanity and means absolutely nothing otherwise.

Of late I've been going regularly to the Zionist Organization. I like being there and feel comfortable with the members. We have a great many problems in common, and there are always a lot of intelligent people there to talk to. It's so comforting to feel that despite their many faults these are our people. Judging by the sort of faults they have, I dare say that, for the most, they are the results of years of exile, of living in Diaspora. It's possible, however, that their many qualities are due to the exile as well. But perhaps in Palestine we'll succeed, at least in part, in throwing off the faults and retaining the advantages. Immediately after graduation I want to busy myself with Hebrew and Zionism.[35]

I want to read the Bible in Hebrew. I know it will be very difficult, but it is the true language and the most beautiful; in it is the spirit of our people. I am now writing this without a dictionary, alone, and—certainly—with many mistakes, but this makes me happy, for I see that I'll be able to learn Hebrew quickly. I want to write some more: about Gyuri, my brother. He's also learning Hebrew and, at the end of one of his letters, he wrote: "It's good to die for our land." Recently that sentence has taken on real meaning, for these are difficult times in Palestine. The British have concocted a White Paper of awful content, and, understandably, the entire Jewish community decries this betrayal.

Dombóvár, July 16, 1939

I couldn't write; I was too busy packing and unpacking. But now we're all settled, and I'm very happy to be here again. Yesterday was the first day since my tonsillectomy that I was allowed to swim, to play tennis, to be out in the sun—in short, to do everything that is pleasant and healthy. I enjoyed it all so very much, because I've missed being active.

There's nothing new concerning *aliyah*.[36] I go to sleep every night and wake up every morning with the thought: perhaps I'll succeed; perhaps I'll get the immigration certificate. It's possible, but there is still some doubt. At the moment there's nothing I can do but hope. If I can't immigrate, I'll go on *hachshara* (pioneer training), but I'm still hoping, always hoping. And why not? Do other girls also want to immigrate so badly? Of course I mean those who, like me, are waiting for certificates.

Well, we'll see.

Yesterday we saw an excellent movie: *L'abîme*; it's a French film, and true art. I don't know enough Hebrew to write what I felt and what my impressions were afterward, but I must say that it was a great experience.

Aged eighteen, July 17, 1939

Today is my birthday. I am eighteen. It is so hard for me to see myself as such an "old lady." But I know these are the most beautiful years of my life, and I enjoy my young ideas, my youth. I am happy with my life, with everything that surrounds me. I believe in the future. My ideal fills my entire being, and I hope I'll be able to realize it without disappointment. The reaction of friends and many relatives is that I will be disappointed in Eretz.[37] But I think I have a good grasp of the situation; I know the people living there make mistakes too. What I love about it is the opportunity to create an outstanding and beautiful Jewish state, and the future depends on this. I want to do everything within my power to bring this dream closer to reality— or the reverse, to bring reality close to the dream. I am writing in Hebrew all the time now, and though I write less than if I were writing in Hungarian, I do better thinking in a bit of Hebrew than in a lot of Hungarian. Perhaps in a few more months I'll write less awkwardly, with less difficulty.

July 21, 1939

I've got it; I've got it—the certificate! I'm filled with joy and happiness! I don't know what to write; I can't believe it. I read and reread the letter bearing the good news; now I can't find words to express what I feel. I have no feeling other than overwhelming happiness. But I can understand that Mother can't see the matter as I do; she is filled with conflicting emotions, and is really very brave. I won't ever forget her sacrifice. Not many mothers would behave as she is behaving.

I have to be in Palestine by the end of September. I still don't know when I'll leave. I won't write any more now, but there is one more thing I would like to say to everyone, to all those who helped me, to God, to my mother: Thank you!

Yesterday we went to Pécs. It was a beautiful day, very pleasant. But I can't write about the trip because it is nothing compared to what happened today.

July 22, 1939

I spent all day reading an interesting book, *The Singing Valley* by Sholem Asch. Everything takes place in the Emek Valley[38] at the time of the difficult beginning in Palestine. I was very happy to find this book and finished it in a day and a half. I read another book and went to copy a selection from it into my diary so that I won't forget it. The book is a translation of Lion Feuchtwanger's *The Jew of Rome.* I'll try to translate the thought into Hebrew. "Jewish history is the history of this war, in which the spirit must battle the antispiritual tendencies, and what is common to Jewish history is common to the spirit, too." This sentence appeals to me; I feel it is true.

That I'm happy is self-evident.

Budapest, August 14, 1939

I don't know how to begin. It's so dreadful. I'm afraid I'm not well. I still haven't been to see a doctor; I still haven't told my mother; and I don't want to believe it yet. I pray it's not true, that it will pass. The fact is I feel a small pain in my heart, day after day, even now as I write. I'm close to tears because if my heart is not well at this early age it is the worst possible thing that could happen to me. But my father had a sick heart from the age of eighteen, and lived with the knowledge. If fate so wills it, I shall also be able to bear the knowledge. But that's not the worst of it. For me the important thing is *aliyah*. I'll be going to an agricultural school; that means I'll have to undergo considerable physical labor. I'm going where I most longed to go, where so many girls long to go. But if I'm really ill and now give my place to someone else, I'll never again have the opportunity of emigration to Palestine, and that will be the end of my great good fortune, of my life's goal. But if I go to Palestine as I am, ill, and wait for them to discover I'm not fit for work, in the eyes of the Zionists I'll be an irresponsible, supremely reckless girl.

What shall I do? I can't discuss this with Mother. I must decide alone. At the most difficult moments in life everyone is alone. I want to see a doctor. My God, my God, let this be just a bad dream.

August 21, 1939

I went to the doctor with Mother. First I telephoned and told him what it was all about. But I told Mother I merely wanted him to check to see if there was any postoperative problem concerning my tonsils. The doctor examined me thoroughly, checked me through the fluoroscope, and the result is—I can work. There is nothing wrong with my heart, or anything else, beyond a nervous tension that is causing the pain.

August 22, 1939

I happened to open my diary at the place where I wrote nearly a year ago about the excitement concerning the possibility of war. If I want to, I could discuss this now, as the danger of war is again imminent. In times of such crises we humans are like animals about to go to the slaughter. Just today I read in the newspaper about a sudden and dreadful thing: the Germans have concluded an agreement with Russia. In terms of German politics this is an extremely inconsistent step, since only a few months ago the Anti-Comintern Pact was formed solely as a protection against Russia—and the one who spoke the loudest at that time was, of course, Germany. And certainly what was then said on Russian radio about "the brown dog" was not exactly friendly.

September 8, 1939

Much has happened, but I have had neither the time nor the desire to write about it. The war we feared has begun. It broke out over the matter of Danzig and the Polish Corridor. Danzig itself is a small

place, and while its population is actually German, all of Poland—
and finally all Europe—is in danger. If they had really wanted to they
could have preserved the peace. But they didn't want to—so there is
now war between Germany and Poland. The Germans have already
captured a large part of Poland, and France and England, Poland's
allies, have entered the war. There is nothing they can do as yet to be
of any real help, but they're standing by, arms at the ready. Italy is still
neutral, as are Hungary and many other countries. They are all aware
that war nowadays will cause more destruction than ever before, and
they are doing everything to prevent it. That is politics.

As for our private lives, Gyuri is in France, and Mother doesn't
know whether he should return to Hungary or stay there. We are still
at peace, and France is at war. But who knows whether Hungary will
participate or not; to be a Hungarian soldier now is not a particularly pleasant thing. And who knows what will happen to foreigners
in France? Our situation is difficult, and we can't decide.

And now for myself. I received the certificate, and yesterday I also
received the visa. I long to leave already, even though a sea journey
now is not particularly safe.

*The following two letters to her mother are included with her Diary, rather
than her Letters, since they form a transitional link between Hungary and
Palestine.*

Mezötúr, September 13, 1939

Dearest Mother,

So both of us can enjoy the advantage of this fabulous little typewriter as quickly as possible, I am starting a letter to you here, on the
train, at 4:45 p.m., which I can perhaps send even before reaching the
border. After that I shall get used to using postcards and telegrams.

Truly, Mother dear, that moment when the train started and I
could not control myself was extremely difficult. Regardless of the
fact I was so overjoyed about the journey, I forgot all my dreams,
plans, and hopes, and at that moment felt only the pain of parting
with you for a very long time.

The other farewells weren't difficult. Yes, when we left our little house—that was painful too. After all, it is more or less the symbol of my life so far. But even so, it was the easiest part of the farewell. How I felt about leaving you—what purpose does it serve to write about it in detail? You surely must know.

Certainly we won't be spending the Jewish holidays in the happiest of circumstances, and I'm afraid, Mother dear, these will be very sad days for you too. No matter how preoccupied I am with my plans and the journey itself, my thoughts are constantly with you, and I shall spend this New Year holiday with you in spirit.

Don't be upset, Mother, that this letter is so empty. When one has a great deal to say one can't find words—beyond these two: dearest Mother.

On board the *Bessarabia,* September 17, 1939

Dearest Mother,

Our ship is anchored in Constantinople, and I am on deck, my typewriter on my knees. I hope you received my telegram from Constanta and have not been at all worried about me. There really has been no cause for any concern. Everything went perfectly. I saw very little of Constanta, as the train went straight to the docks. From on board ship I was able to glance around a bit, but by then it was already evening, so only the illuminated casino was visible.

I can see a trifle more of Constantinople, since we will be tied up in the harbor for about three hours; but of course we are not permitted to leave the ship. Nevertheless, I can see mosques, towers, narrow streets, watermelon carts, stevedores, a coffee bazaar, and on the hillside quite modern and attractive buildings. On the other hand, there are horribly run-down shacks, too, so there must be great contrasts here.

Life aboard ship is extremely pleasant, and the cabin is quite comfortable. I asked for an upper berth, and it's right next to the porthole, so it's nice and airy. I slept wonderfully well; perhaps being tired had a lot to do with it! My cabinmates are congenial people—women, that is—Polish and Palestinian, so we speak a lot of Hebrew, and my French has been useful as well.

This morning I got up at six because I couldn't stand staying in bed when I saw how beautiful the sunrise was. I walked about the ship, all over the decks, and though I'm already quite familiar with it, there are times when I still can't find my cabin in the maze.

The majority of the Jewish passengers are from Palestine, returning from visits to relatives. But there are a great many Poles and Czechs as well, and a lot of children from Palestine, who are adorable and speak only Hebrew. There are opportunities to practice my Hebrew with them, and as there are a great many people who speak Hebrew as a general rule, I grab every opportunity to accustom myself to speaking the language.

There are differing opinions about life in Palestine. There are many on board who already live in kibbutzim, and others who are headed for kibbutzim. And of course there are city people who are returning, and already feel Palestine is their home, accept the hardships, and are content. One thing is certain: everyone can barely wait to get there. But this does not mean the voyage is not extremely pleasant. I'm enjoying it enormously. For instance now, at a quarter of seven in the morning, I'm sitting on deck and while writing look up now and then to gaze at the beautiful seascape. Yesterday afternoon and last night we lay in our deck chairs too. I read a lot, as my book is extremely interesting. My wardrobe is first-rate. I'm wearing my gray slacks now and my checked blouse, and I'm making every attempt not to be too disheveled, entirely out of regard for you.

Don't be angry, but I can't write more now. The view is so beautiful that it's a pity to miss a single moment of it. I think we'll soon be in Athens.

Nahalal Agricultural School, Palestine, September 23, 1939

Today I must write in Hungarian, as there are such an endless number of things to write about, so many impressions to record, that I can't possibly cope with them all in Hebrew as yet.

I would like to be able to clearly express today, on Yom Kippur,

Hannah on her first day in Palestine
(Haifa, September 19, 1939).

the Day of Atonement, all that I want to say. I would like to be able to record what these first days in Palestine mean to me. Because I have been here four days.

A little sabra[39] is climbing up the olive tree directly behind me; in front of me are cypress trees, cacti, the Emek Valley.

I am in Nahalal, in Eretz. I am home.

The being "home" does not refer to school. After all, I have been here only two days and haven't become a part of the regular life yet. But the entire country's atmosphere, the people—all of them so friendly—one feels as if one had always lived here. And in a way this is true, since, after all, I've always lived among Jews. But not among such free, industrious, calm, and, I think, contented Jews. I know I still see things idealistically, and I know there will be difficult days.

Yesterday, on Erev Yom Kippur, I was very low. I mean spiritually. I made an accounting of what I had left behind and what I had found here, and I didn't know whether the move would prove worthwhile. For a moment I lost sight of the goal. I deliberately let myself go because once in a while one must completely relax from all one's tensions and from being constantly on guard. It felt good to let go, to cry for once. But even behind the tears I felt I had done the right thing. This is where my life's ambition—I might even say my vocation—binds me; because I would like to feel that by being here I am fulfilling a mission, not just vegetating. Here almost every life is the fulfillment of a mission.

To write a stage-by-stage account of the two-day, exciting train journey, the five-day voyage on the *Bessarabia* (a Romanian ship), of the inexplicably pleasant experience of disembarking in Tel Aviv and Haifa and of being among Jewish porters and officials, and what this means to a person … to write about Haifa, Beth Olim, the Krausz family, where I went on the recommendation of Art Thieben,[40] and where I found a most warm welcome … to write of the drive by bus to the Emek and of the arrival at the school … somehow or other I can not write any of this now. But everything is beautiful, everything is good, and I am happy that I'm able to be here. I would like Gyuri to come as soon as possible. And then Mother.

November 2, 1939

I haven't written for a long while. It's true I'm working hard, but there are other reasons. My new surroundings interest me so much that I cannot focus on personal matters.

There is much I could write about my life here. I do simple work in the laundry, and frankly I must admit it has little educational value. I've learned to launder and iron a bit … I'm learning somewhat more in the courses, both in content and in terms of language. This month they devote more time to working than to studying farming or a craft; this is the program for all first-year students. I don't mind. Just that I sometimes think I could use this year for more important studies.

I'd like to continue in Hungarian because I feel I'm not writing exactly what I would like to express. At the same time, however, I want to overcome this difficulty and will continue in Hebrew. I must get accustomed to it.

Shabbat here is very nice. I've already got to know some people, and sometimes I even have visitors. I read, play ping-pong, or visit the kibbutzim and other neighboring places. Thus, there is some variation. Mother writes regularly, but I didn't get a letter from her last week. A postcard came today, however. She writes that all is well with her, and that Gyuri is able to continue his studies in Lyon.

The girls occasionally ask whether I'm homesick; I always answer, No, and it's the truth. The atmosphere of home, and the general environment, I really don't miss. But I do miss Mother and Gyuri very much. If I could at least see Gyuri. I haven't seen him for so long. Mother I saw only a month ago. But we're so far from each other. That's the only hard part. The only one? I think so. All the rest is nothing compared to it.

I love the Land. Rather, I want to love it, but don't know it well enough yet to say how it impresses me. Of course, the great difference between the Diaspora and the Land is something I feel every day in the school and everywhere else. The liberty, the humaneness … oh, it's so difficult as yet for me to say all I want to….

November 22, 1939

I write so rarely now that this will become a very incomplete diary. Pity, because a great many things are happening, not so much around me as within me. I don't know much about events on the outside: war, politics—all of Europe seems so far away. Mother and Gyuri encompass all that binds me to it.

And what binds me here? My plans, my goal, all that I have built within me this last year. Sometimes I feel it's a very shaky building, and at times I feel that what I've done was badly blundered. If in these moments of self-doubt I were to sit down to write, perhaps the ink would be somewhat washed away by tears. But fortunately in those moments I can't very well write, as I'm probably just in the midst of washing dishes, or sweeping, or simply too depressed to write. Those are, however, only moments, sometimes a day. But the weeks, the two months I've already been here, prove that in the long run I made the right decision. (Though even this may be autosuggestion.)

Not that I learn so much in school. On the contrary: the school has many faults. But I feel those very faults may, at some future time, be of considerable use to me. Frankly speaking, I can't imagine that I could ever be a worker in the true sense of the word. When I think of the future, I can only imagine myself doing something in connection with teaching. Nevertheless, I feel very well here. I want to concentrate on learning Hebrew now. I've already made considerable progress.

December 16, 1939

I'm now working in the dairy. I was very happy to be assigned to dairy work, because I once wanted to choose it. For the first three weeks I'll be cleaning up, but that's all right.

What has been happening to me during this long interval? Well, there was the Hanukah holiday—my first in the Land—and I visited the Krausz family in Haifa, where I spent two pleasant days. I also went to some parties, danced and sang a lot. I saw city life and was again convinced it won't be difficult to do without it. I am very content in the country, in Nahalal, even at school.

Since I'm keeping a diary, and it is proper to confide to a diary about boys, I'll give the news on that front briefly. Miki and Ben wrote to me from Hungary, and each proposed. It's funny. They both write as if it were a very serious matter. I answered them. I didn't have to think for a moment what the answer should be. That was really simple, because they don't interest me. I've got to know some boys here, too. They come to Nahalal for an evening … to stroll, to converse a bit. At first I was happy to spend some time with them, but then I realized it wasn't really worthwhile. We'll see.…

During my holiday I didn't just dance and sing, I also saw something of life in the Land. I saw hardship and mistakes, but I also saw those interesting people, the first *chalutzim* (pioneers), who have been living here many years. But I still lack the vocabulary to write about all this. I lack fluency in the language, and besides that, I don't have time. In a few minutes we'll be going to the *Oneg Shabbat*,[41] so I must stop.

January 1, 1940

I'll write again now, if only to enter the new date in my diary: 1940. It's incredible and frightening how time flies. Though this day is not considered a holiday here, it will do no harm to make a little accounting, as I used to at home. After all, the past year, 1939, brought so many changes in my way of life—and within me. It was a year filled with constant tension, excitement, and fear, and last autumn World War II began. The year also contained the anxiety of the Jewish Laws, the crisis in the internal politics of Hungary, and what were of even greater concern to me (even though still so distant): the riots here in the Land, and the excitement of the conferences. Because of these outer pressures, plus my personal leanings and abilities, I became a Zionist, and a real Jew.

I need not comment to what extent emigration has changed me. And now when I look back upon the past year I see how very eventful and difficult it was, what an emotional struggle. It was a year that ended one of my life's chapters, and began another. A year filled with tension and excitement, yes. But, withal, it was a very rewarding year in which I became aware of, and sensitive to, many things.

What do I expect of 1940? For myself, work, study, progress in Hebrew, and—if I succeed—to draw closer to, and become familiar with, the life and the people here. And if God intends this year to be a very beautiful one for me, then perhaps I'll see Gyuri here too, and even Mother. And for Eretz perhaps this year will bring a bit of prosperity, which it could use so very, very much. I think in the "outside world" this year will be no calmer, no more peaceful than the last was.

January 16, 1940

What shall I write about? I feel very well, love my work (dairy production), my quiet simple life, and my friends, and I'm extremely interested in my studies and surroundings. But to write ... what shall I write about? I write home about my work and daily routine. About my thoughts? I don't have many. I feel this period of my life is serving as a time to gather impressions, to see, to hear, to feel—and perhaps afterwards will come a time when I'll talk about it all, perhaps even write about everything. Presently I even lack a language. Hungarian? No ... no more. Hebrew? No, not yet. I'll read now. This is not the time for a diary.

February 17, 1940

Several days ago my interest was caught by two things: a postcard from Budapest in which Évi describes a friend's party, and then how, after reading it, my gaze, unintentionally, wandered to my work-scarred hands. Suddenly I asked myself, wasn't it foolhardy romanticism, against my instincts, to leave the easy life, to choose a life of hard work, virtually that of a laborer? But I was immediately reassured, since I'm absolutely convinced I couldn't possibly live in the Diaspora again. My place is here in the Land.

The only question is, did I choose the best way? But I believe I did. I don't think I'll remain an ordinary laborer. I have the drive and strength of will to develop, to improve, and hope eventually I shall also have the necessary know-how. Yesterday a minor occurrence again proved to me I have organizational ability. We dedicated the reading room here. I organized everything, and it was so gratifying to see how the girls suddenly began showing interest in the project, pitched in and worked, and how extremely enthusiastic they were. I think it exceedingly important, particularly here in Eretz, to strengthen the intellectual interest of the people, to influence their spiritual and emotional moods and states, as nearly everyone has problems and faces hardships.

It is so very difficult to write about all this in Hebrew. And difficult, in general, to write clearly about matters that are not yet entirely clear to me.

March 6, 1940

What can I write when there are such a tremendous number of things that I can't clarify even to myself? Recently the stringent laws decreed by the British White Paper have been strengthened. There is great bitterness and opposition in the entire Land. There have been demonstrations in the cities, victims, curfew, and a seemingly hopeless situation.

War against the British rule—it seems that is the desperate, bitter public opinion, and the country's leaders incline in the same direction. I don't know what it is within me—love for the Land and the people, or horror of all wars, or perhaps a point of view that belongs in another world—but I still condemn any step that leads to hopeless, unnecessary bloodshed.

As far as I'm concerned, I think they ought to build with greatly renewed energy within the designated areas, and then, when the existing lands are irrevocably in our hands, and if the British political situation does not change meanwhile—then if we still must fight, we can do so with guns. But bloody encounters—or, more exactly, fighting in the cities just so we can show "the world" that we protest—would be a meaningless waste of blood and life. This is what my common sense tells me. But the majority judge and see things differently, and it is possible they are right.

National manifestations—force, guns—are undoubtedly the implements of today. But not in our hands—at least not yet. Perhaps despair will supplant what we lack in number. It would be so good and so simple if with a prayer such as "My Lord, help Your people … our people" one could trust and believe, and not pry into, or dwell upon, the possibilities of the future.

Or if one had the sagacity to find the reason for the incomprehensible, and to understand the possibilities of the future. In me neither is strong enough. I think my faith is the strongest. I am not speaking of religious faith, rather faith in the people, in the mission, in the future of Eretz. Or are these just words that get lost in the rat-a-tat-tat of gunfire? Who can answer these questions? I feel very much alone. Sometimes I feel as if I am thinking of important things in a dream, making decisions about my life, and not understanding what it is all about.

March 25, 1940

I've been working in the kitchen for nearly two months, and for the past two weeks I've been cooking. Of the outer aspects of the work I don't have time to write in detail, nor is that so important now, at four-thirty in the morning. As far as I'm concerned, it is more interesting to observe myself a bit in this work. I am astonishingly clumsy and slow. I'm a bit surprised, as I don't think I'm so lacking in ability in other things, and above all, I don't consider myself stupid. But during these last two weeks I really wonder at myself at times, at the lack of intelligence with which I work, not to mention my clumsiness.

And in connection with this, a good many things have come to mind: I wonder wasn't it perhaps a mistake to ignore my intellectual capabilities entirely, and to choose a field I can probably have little success in, or, to be exact, in which I am not worth much? I don't know whether it's just in kitchen work that I am like this, but as a matter of fact, I wasn't much different in the dairy, or in other, more responsible assignments.

Mother warned me before I came, but I thought just because I was so incompetent in this field it would be good for me to do this kind of work. Perhaps I'll finally learn to be orderly and spotless. To be quite frank, I only realize now I had very little idea about either when I came. The work itself is often quite hard and tiring, and it consists of a lot of scrubbing up and scrubbing down. I often think if all this energy ... but I suppose everyone goes through this phase who, either by necessity or voluntarily, changes from an intellectual field to one that is mechanical and physically hard. Perhaps this is even more difficult when a person has assumed the work of his own free will.

Yet, despite everything, I think I am starting life in Eretz from the right point, and in the right way.

I have not yet written about something extremely beautiful: about two weeks ago we were in Yagur at a Hubermann concert. It was during an excursion into the hills, where we hitchhiked, then to the Kibbutz Yagur. There was excitement about getting tickets for the concert, and finally getting in free, and then about the magnificent concert itself: Mendelssohn's Violin Concerto, Bach, Chopin. Then back home in the car of Kibbutz Sarid. I didn't finish last time, but now only this: it was wonderful. There is great detail about all this, and also about last Sunday's excursion to Tiberias in a letter to mother.

April 10, 1940

My thoughts are generally motivated by existing conditions and return to "idealism." For example, while sorting grapefruit in the storeroom, selecting the beautiful, good ones, and putting them at the bottom, the battered, weak ones on top, the comparison ran through my mind that this is the way God arranged our people. He piled the strong at the bottom so they could bear the pressure that represented the weight of a developing country, while the battered remain for the top. And within me a request was born: My Lord, may our people be like wholesome, faultless, stainless fruit so Your hand won't have to search among those which will bear the weight and those which are weak. Or, if possible, let there not be a lower and an upper level, but rather a great, wide shelf upon which everyone is placed side by side. But I can't really believe in this.

Lately we have been learning primarily about root cells, which are the first to penetrate into the earth and prepare the way for the entire root. Meanwhile, they die. My teacher used the comparison: these cells are the pioneers of the plants.

I think the words flew over the heads of the other pupils; but here, in Nahalal, if one examines the lined faces of the farmers—who are young in years—one can't help but be struck by the strong imprint left by their battle with the soil, and this is not difficult to understand. They were the cells that perished so they could penetrate the soil and help to create roots for every plant. Shall our generation become such root cells, too? Is this the fate of the farmers of all nations? These questions are of far greater interest to me than the study of botany.

Hebrew has become part of me. I write it easily now (though incorrectly), but lines that came to mind this morning during my walk in the meadow came in Hungarian.[42] I don't think I shall ever be able to write poetry in Hebrew. Here are the four lines, translated; I don't feel like adding more:

> Our people are working the black soil,
> Their arms reap the gold-bound sheaves,
> And now when the last ear its stalk leaves
> Our faces glitter as with golden oil.

Our people. How dear those words are to me. But do we actually have a people? And if we do, where? For those who are here are not yet a people, a nation. Or perhaps they really are a people but not consciously. I am going to bed now. I'm very tired.

April 20, 1940

I would now like to write about the boy question, though it's really not worth going into detail; in fact it's best to generalize. Since I've been here, five or six boys have tried to approach me. Now and then I go walking with them of an evening, but generally break off quite abruptly. I can clarify the reason to myself: I would love to have someone who loved me, and I would like to really love someone. That's why when I meet someone the thought immediately arises:

perhaps this will be the real one. But when I see I have been wrong, I prefer breaking off completely because I can no longer go on with these little courtships. I feel that it must be a serious friendship—or let's just be forthright and say, I need a real love affair—or nothing. It's fine to talk a bit, to take walks, but the boys, for the most, are not satisfied with just this; and I, too, begrudge the time wasted on this sort of thing.

Day after tomorrow I am going to Jerusalem. I have a lot of friends there, particularly Alex, who is waiting for me, and who proves he often thinks of me by doing delightful, thoughtful little things to please me. And several people have told me that he finds me attractive. I don't know him very well yet, so I don't want to pass judgment. But deep in my heart I already feel it's no. And I am sorry because I would so like it to be yes, at last.

Yesterday we went to a kibbutz for the Passover program and concert. I watched the faces meanwhile and thought perhaps the one I have been looking for might be there, and that we would pass one another without realizing it. Or perhaps he is so far away that we will never meet. But I'm too much of an optimist to really believe this.

May 14, 1940

I was sitting, studying a notebook on general agriculture, when suddenly I was struck by the realization of how cut off I am from the world. How can I have the patience to study and prepare for an exam while the greatest war in history is raging in Europe? We are witnessing, in general, times that will determine the fate of man. The European war is engulfing vast areas, and fear that it will spread to our land is understandable. The entire world is gripped by tension. Germany grows mightier daily. And with the entire world on the edge of an abyss, it is difficult to deal with minor problems, even more difficult to believe that personal problems are of any importance.

It is impossible for me to continue writing now. My roommates are chattering about all manner of things, and besides, I am tired. There is no time even to think a bit, and it's almost impossible to express one's self. Especially in Hebrew. Though the language doesn't

Egy virág is van a levélben, ezt nem csak azért küldöm, hogy lásd, milyen tavasz van nálunk, hanem a helyett a virág helyett, amit apuka sirjára vinnék ki most, ha otthon lennék. 19.-án még többet fogok Rád gondolni anyukám, mint máskor, ha ugyan az lehet.

Ami Gyurka vizsgáit illeti, nem is csodálnám, ha a gyerek a mostani körülmények között nem tanult volna olyan rendesen, de remélem, hogy mégsem olyan veszélyes a helzet, mint gondolod. Ezerszer csókolom őt is, remélem megkapta a levelemet, amit nemrég irtam.

Számtalanszor csókollak

Part of a letter Hannah Senesh wrote from the Nahalal Agricultural School, adorned with sketches and light-hearted comments about falling into a manure heap and having to be helped out (left) and about her work with the cows (right).

cause me much difficulty now, simple words and simple phrases can still only express simple thoughts.

I felt very good in Jerusalem. I had a pleasant vacation but discovered many new aspects of life in the city that have given me considerable food for thought. After the long recess I again debated a bit, but faced facts optimistically (and they're putting out the lights....).

May 18, 1940

There are so many things I don't understand, least of all myself. I would like to know who and what I really am, but I can only ask the questions, not answer them. Either I have changed a lot, or the world around me has changed. Or have the eyes with which I see myself changed?

I feel uncertain, undecided, positive and negative at one and the same time. I'm attracted and repelled, I feel selfish and cooperative, and above all, I feel so superficial that I'm ashamed to admit it even to myself. Perhaps I feel this way only compared to Miryam because she knows her direction and her judgment is more positive than mine; she can penetrate more deeply to the heart of things. Or is it because she is two years older than I? I'm already making excuses for myself, afraid to face facts. I say it's being optimistic to see the good side of everything. This is an easy attitude, but it doesn't lead very far.

My behavior toward others is so unnatural, so distant. Boys? I am really searching for someone, but I don't want second best. I'm kind, perhaps from habit—until I'm bored with being kind. I'm capricious, fickle, supercilious; perhaps I'm rough. Is this my nature? I want to believe it is not. But then why ... ?

Today I listened to music. Sound after sound melts into harmony, each in itself but a delicate touch, empty, colorless, pointless, but all together—music. One tone soft, one loud, staccato or long, resonant, melodious, vibrant. What am I? How do the many tones within me sound all together? Are they harmonious?

We are studying water plants, whose job it is to serve as nourishment for superior animals. I wonder whether our mission is other than to serve as some sort of high substance for one of nature's higher orders? But if we're serving a law, then we ought to at least realize that it is not only to serve our own ends. Perhaps only in this is man superior to animal.

May 26, 1940

A few words about electrolysis (or the problems of education). There is a certain chemical solution that contains charged atomic particles that circulate without purpose. Immediately upon the introduction of an electric current, the atoms are disrupted and drawn toward the two poles, where they deposit their charges, and as free atoms, discharged of electricity, leave them.

I began thinking of our people, and about education here. Our youth was once composed of many different elements, yet bound by a common denominator: Jewishness. Then currents more powerful than electricity were introduced, which drew the atoms to many opposing poles and separated the poles from each other. Then there no longer existed "Jewish Youth" or "Hebrew Youth" (for the atoms deposited their energy, their inner tensions, at the poles—the political parties), and in their stead there remained only poles with atoms clustered around them. Who knows whether the atoms will or will not deposit their inner tensions at these poles, and whether the time will come when at the very moment they will have to start functioning, to become charged, they won't lose their energy, that their tension won't abate?

Are we so great and powerful a people that we can afford to distinguish between brothers (between Jew and Jew) and predetermine paths leading to diametrically opposed poles? Isn't it too great a responsibility to drag people along in the current before they can see for themselves where the paths are, and where they lead?

Electrolysis … I've closed my chemistry notebook.

I must now record that I am reading some wonderful books. The poems of Rachel, and a book in German by Martin Buber entitled *Talks on Judaism*. In Rachel I feel many things. In Buber I understand many things about Judaism and about myself that I didn't know before. In the sense Buber interprets Judaism, I am a true Jewess. Reading this makes me happy.

I wonder, isn't it our duty to create a unified, concentrated solution that will be capable of taking action when the time comes— Hebrew Youth? I had sensed Jewishness within me before, too, but to have an explanation of such intimate matters is much more than I expected to find in a book. I'm continuing to read it.

I took my exams in general agriculture and in dairy production. I hope I passed. Yesterday I visited Kfar Avoda, an educational institution for problem children. I found it very interesting. But it is difficult to study the most interesting aspects of the school in such a superficial manner. I hope I'll have another opportunity of studying the institution and the children more closely.

June 4, 1940

Budapest—Lyon—Nahalal.

Between these three points my thoughts flash with lightning speed. Meanwhile the cities are becoming more constricted and confining, and the thought of Mother, Gyuri, and myself is all that remains to me of the cities and countries. Through this I feel all the tensions of these nerve-racking days. All tensions? I know this is a lie. I can't feel a thousandth part of what Mother must now be living through. She is suffering for our plans, dreams, which perhaps in this world holocaust will turn to ashes. If at least Gyuri were already here. But I'm so afraid that it's already too late. And if it is, it's due to my recklessness. It's all my fault.

And the Land? The future, the ordeals we're headed for? I trust in the future of the Land, through all fires and storms. I am not afraid for myself. This has nothing to do with unselfishness. It's only another manifestation of selfishness. One wants to protect one's self from those indescribable agonies that can touch one through the loss of those one loves most, and the things one most values.

The sky is a brilliant blue; peace and fertility encompass the Land. I would like to shout into the radio, "It isn't true! It's a lie! It's a fraud that there are a million dead and countless injured, bombings, cities destroyed!" Who could have wanted this? Who can understand the historic mission of this butchery? To lay Europe waste and then, upon its ruins, build a new world? But who will build it, for whom and why? Only so there will be a new Europe to destroy? "Struggle Man, and trustingly trust."[43] But why struggle? I won't write the second question. I want to believe.

June 17, 1940

The Germans are on the threshold of Paris. Perhaps today the city will fall. Paris and France, and the entire world. What is going to become of us? All I ask is, how long? Because that Hitler must fall, I don't doubt. But how long has he been given? Fifteen years, like Napoleon? How history repeats itself. Napoleon's career, life, battles; but a twentieth-century German version turns everything into inexpressible horror.

Italy has also "stepped into the war"—one hears a thousand times over. Because of this, the immediate danger has increased here also. We are preparing as much as possible. If we are still alive ten to fifteen years from now, perhaps we will know why this is happening. Or perhaps it will take a hundred years before this life becomes history.

June 29, 1940

France, Gyuri, my mother ... ? It's difficult to say what hurts most as the days pass. France has negotiated a shameful peace. It has actually ceased to exist.

Communications with Gyuri have been cut off completely. His certificate arrived too late. I've no idea where he is now. But I'm still hopeful; perhaps he'll still come; perhaps he'll still be able to leave. I study the face of every young man, secretly hopeful.... Oh, how awful it is to feel that I'm to blame, that I'm responsible for matters, insofar as they concern Gyuri. On the other hand, I know that in times like these, during a war, no one is to blame. It is impossible to judge, to decide whether it is best to be here or elsewhere.

And Mother.... I can imagine her spending sleepless nights, getting up in the morning worried, searching the newspapers, waiting for the post, locking all her worries and sadness in her heart because she is much too noble to burden others with her worries. And I, thousands of miles away, cannot sit beside her, smooth her creased brow, calm her, share the worries.

I'm working in the field, gathering hay, reaching—or imagining I'm reaching—my goals. And my goals are, I think, worthy—even beautiful. But does one have the right to long for what is distant, and give up what is close at hand? The only possible way I can answer this question is by saying that I would not have been able to continue living the life I led in Hungary. I would have been miserable. Each of us must find his own way, his own place and calling, even though the entire world is on fire, even though everything is in turmoil. No, I can't look for explanations, reasons. The "aye" and the "nay" storm within me, the one contradicting the other.

Here everything is quiet. But where in this world do internal peace and tranquility exist? The wheel of history rattles on, crushing one's soul; nothing remains untrammeled.

Kfar Gil'adi, July 3, 1940

I'm at Kfar Gil'adi. Miryam and I set out this morning, and we're headed for Metulla, in the extreme north. We took a wonderful route: the Kinneret,[44] then the hills, cliffs, isolated settlements. And now— Kfar Gil'adi. Winds, hills, quiet. Perhaps in Hungarian I could write about the distant blue hills, about the sky, the trees, the people. This is the first day of our excursion. I hope it will all be as nice as this.

In the Land, aged nineteen, July 5–26, 1940

How shall I begin? I have seen and felt so much during these past days. At the moment we're in a eucalyptus grove near Kfar Gil'adi. Miryam is carving her name on a tree, and I'm trying to record everything before a car comes along to take us further.

Early Saturday morning I climbed the hills facing Kfar Gil'adi. Wonderful scenery. And in the brilliance of the beautiful morning I understood why Moses received the Torah on a mountaintop. Only on the mountains is it possible to receive orders from above, when one sees how small is man yet feels secure in the nearness of God.

From there one's horizons broaden in every respect, and the order of things becomes more understandable. In the mountains one can believe—and must believe. In the mountains one involuntarily hears the query, "Whom shall I send?" And the answer, "Send me to serve the beautiful and the good!" Will I succeed? Will I be able to fulfill God's command?

In the morning we went on an excursion with several members of the kibbutz. We rode up to Metulla in a kibbutz truck, and from there, along beautiful paths, to Tannur. We returned around noon, and immediately got a ride as far as Dan.

What else can I say about Kfar Gil'adi? It's a large, pleasant, orderly, well-developed kibbutz. Among its members I particularly want to remember Gershon, a kind, charming man. We got to know him on the road, and he took particular care of us. A real pioneer, a man of good will; I was delighted to meet him.

Another spot we visited was Dan. It's a little settlement, an island in the heart of a luxuriant region. Its members, mostly Transylvanian immigrants, received us warmly. One of them took particularly devoted care of us. He guided us to Tel-El-Kadi, the source of the River Dan. It's an enchanting spring, next to it a primitive Arab mill. I must note how well, in general, the inhabitants of Dan get on with their Arab neighbors, and even with the Syrians who live across the border. Of course they can't depend entirely upon their good will, but the friendly relationship adds to their feeling of security.

We spent a night at Dan and set out the next morning to tour the countryside. Sasa, Dafna, Sh'ar Yashuv—new settlements whose situations are still difficult. The soil is good; water is abundant; but the land must be cleared of stones, and from a political point of view carefully guarded. However, should their development remain unhampered by events, they can look forward to a happy future. They have all the requirements to develop into fertile agricultural settlements.

We also visited some of the girls who have graduated from the school at Nahalal. All of them are getting along well, and judging by this we concluded that the school has really prepared them properly and given them a sound foundation.

The following day we waited at the roadside until evening and nearly gave up. Toward nightfall we lost patience and agreed to wait only another fifteen minutes, though we certainly did not feel like returning to Kfar Gil'adi. Even Tel-Hai, which lay ahead, is more a symbol than a good place to spend the night. But finally a car came along. If Mother had seen me standing in the middle of the road, hitchhiking! In fact, if she could have seen me at any time throughout the trip, I wonder what she would have said! But then here everything happens in an atmosphere so completely different from that to which one is accustomed. And that's exactly what's so nice about it.

We reached Hulata that very evening. It's a young collective with a charming group in a wonderful setting. Excellent opportunities to swim and row. It's superfluous to add that I enjoyed myself enormously.

We rowed on to the mouth of the Jordan, the place where it flows into Lake Huleh. The region is tropical, with papyrus reeds, water lilies, and flamingoes, and the placid green waters reflect the surrounding beauty. Later we went rowing with two of the fishermen (twenty men from the collective are fishermen). One of them, Moshe, was "mine"; the other, Miryam's. I saw he liked me, and I liked him a little too. He is really an attractive young man, strong, handsome, simple, likable.

That evening we went out with the entire fishing fleet to watch them at work. It was a moonlit night. The lake was absolutely calm, and the night still. We could hear only the soft and monotonous splashing of the oars. The muscular bodies of the fishermen swayed left and right in the course of their work. They are familiar with the marshes, with the places where the fish teem, thus cast their nets with assurance. We returned to the collective at ten-thirty; the nets were left in the marshes until early morning.

When we reached home, Moshe visited us for a while. He said he loved me, wanted to kiss me, but I wouldn't let him. He suggested we keep in touch, but I said that although I had enjoyed the day we spent together, I saw no point in corresponding, since we had so little in common, and in all honesty I was not that interested in him. I wanted to part with a handshake, but he kissed my hand.

I thought about him after he left and realized I had actually been rather foolish, and even apprehensive. What harm would there have been in a kiss? Yet I could not.... I suppose it's ridiculous that I'm still "waiting for the right one...."

We went on early next morning and reached Safed, the ancient city high in the hills. The scenery is beautiful; the types of people fascinating. We wandered about the town for hours, just looking. Then we turned back to Rosh Pina, and from there continued on to Kibbutz Ginosar, where we spent the night. It's a settlement of young people who are struggling against great odds and are having considerable difficulty with the soil. We didn't have time to see much of the kibbutz because we left early in the morning so as to reach Kibbutz Afikim before noon.

If only I could describe it all: Lake Kinneret, the Yarmuk River, the Jordan, the old and new kibbutzim, the delightful people we met everywhere, the beautiful excursions we arranged to places around Kibbutz Afikim, Ya'akov who "sort of" fell in love with me, the beautiful vineyards, the ride to Yarmuk on horseback, the soft nights sitting on the grass, talking, discussing life. It was all beautiful, and I could fill an entire notebook describing everything, particularly the way a kibbutz is run and managed. In short, it was all wonderful, absolutely wonderful.

We spent about five days there, then finally left the Jordan Valley by train for the Emek. We saw Kibbutz Bet-Alfa, Tel Amal, Ein-Harod in the distance, and before we knew it our journey ended. I spent the last day of my holiday with the Farkas family at *moshav*[45] Merhavya. They were very friendly and hospitable, and the warm family atmosphere was most welcome after so many days of communal life in the various kibbutzim, and I was happy to have the opportunity of comparing the two different ways of life.

Beyond a doubt the kibbutz, economically speaking, is far more rational, and from the point of view of working conditions, simpler; and life, lived on a communal basis, is easier on the kibbutz. But from a spiritual point of view, village life has its positive advantages. Certainly it's very obvious that not everyone is suited to life on a kibbutz. I suppose in a matter of years a middle-of-the-road way will be found, which may successfully combine the advantages of both.

Personally, I prefer the kibbutz. I'm not yet so devoted to agricultural work that I can feel sufficient strength to work at it unceasingly. And whenever I visit an educational institution on a kibbutz, the old desire to study, to learn, returns. But what and how? At any rate, this year I want to devote myself to my chosen field (poultry farming) and to learning the language. What happens after ... well, we'll see.

The entire vacation was glorious. I was so strongly aware of the beauty of youth in everything I did and saw: in song, in laughter, in boundless energy, in my overwhelming desire to see and absorb everything, to enjoy all the wonders of the Land, to glory in it. And certainly there was endless opportunity to sample every phase of life in the Land, to see all its wonders. This holiday strengthened my faith in the country, in myself, and in our common future. For two weeks I forgot that there is a war raging, that it is so close to us. Haifa has been bombed twice, and on the second occasion there were a good many victims. Here, in Nahalal, life continues as before. At night, blackout; and when Haifa is bombed we hurry to our shelter.

My work consists of field work and housework. Four hours indoors, four hours outdoors.

The books I'm reading: Rachel's poems, which are beautiful, and Kautsky on socialism. This last is a fundamental explanation of Marx's *Das Kapital*. I wasn't acquainted with these works, but now I must familiarize myself with them as well.

Nahalal, September 6, 1940

About boys: Today A. called upon me, and then B. I would be pleased to trade both for one—one I really like. And I'd give even that "certain one" for my own brother. I'm longing to see him.

Life continues in its usual way, relatively monotonously. It's only at night that I'm sometimes overwhelmed by the feeling that things can't go on this way! It's been two years since I last saw my brother, except for the few days spent in Lyon, and I'm so afraid that by the time we meet again we'll be like strangers. The title of a book keeps ringing in my ears: *The Burnt-out Soul* by Lajos Zilahy. It's about two people who are separated for a long time, grow apart, and when they finally meet have nothing to talk about, no mutual interests, and stare at each other like strangers. Two years ... and how many more? I'm still hopeful. I want to continue being hopeful.

Impressions of my work, of the harvest:

The crop covers the fields, and as the harvester mows it, it falls to the ground and there is no one to gather it. One would like to protect it from the sun's torrid heat, from the drying winds, so it won't all be scattered. Bundles are stacked, and that which escapes the bundles is picked up by the wind. This is the way of our people too ... they scatter after the harvest.

There is a broken broom in the barn with which we clean the stalls. It's an annoying implement, and whenever I use it I have a strong desire to repair it. Recently I decided to do just that, so one day after work I got hold of some wire, a small piece of wood, and set to. When I realized I couldn't manage it, I went to the workshop and one of the carpenters took pity on me and repaired it so expertly it was a joy to watch his fingers fly. I was enormously pleased. I had invested only a bit of time and everyone would benefit. It takes only one person to start a project, and someone will always follow suit.

To me the broom symbolized improvement, growth, achievement. The first thing I said to my fellow workers in the barn next morning was, "Well, what do you think of our old broom?"

"Great! Wonderful!" they exclaimed.

I was immeasurably pleased.

That very afternoon one of the girls informed me that the broom was rather shaky. It seems they were too hard on the poor old thing. The following morning the broom was broken again. Is it possible that what is damaged cannot be repaired, what is old renovated? Is there no solution but that everything must be new?

When I wash the walls of the barn, or take out the manure and scrub the floors, I wonder whether I'm not stealing time from things that are far more important to me. But what things would actually be more important? I'm too enthused about the work and life here to pose the question to myself, and to expect an objective answer. I want to follow the path I've chosen.

I would like so much to talk with Mother a bit.

October 11, 1940, Yom Kippur eve

I want to make a confession, to give an accounting to myself, and to God. In other words, to measure my life and actions against the lofty ideals I've set for myself. To compare that which should have been with that which was.

I'll begin my confession in the name of mankind. There is no sin that has not been committed seven times over this year. There is nothing left with which to punish us because our every step and deed are self-punishment. We are all being punished for sins that we think we did not commit, or which we felt we were compelled to commit. I would not say that only "certain ones," primarily the dictators, brought about this horrible war, this spiritual destruction, this great darkness, and that only they are responsible for everything.

Who, then, is to blame? Everyone individually? Perhaps not. But all of us—the entire establishment, the entire order, the existing morality. In short, all of humanity. Yet those who are most to blame are the ones who feel the least guilt, and only Jewry confesses, "We have sinned."

And I … I've sinned against my mother by not considering her situation more thoroughly before making my decision to emigrate. I've sinned against my brother by not treating the question of his *aliyah* more seriously. I sinned against this Land when I judged it superficially, without sufficiently interesting myself in its problems. I've sinned against certain people by being indifferent to them, by being insincerely friendly. And I've sinned against myself by squandering my strength and talents, by my negligence, my lack of spiritual development.

Even so, I'm not afraid of being judged. I sinned for a good purpose and with good will. If I failed, if I didn't find the way, if I wasn't strong enough, I'm not ashamed, but sorry.

My plan for the new year is to study and immerse myself in my

Hannah relaxing in the fields near Nahalal.

work, in the language, to search for the right road—and to become a real human being. I'm afraid circumstances here make this last resolution difficult to achieve. But I'll try my best, as this is the only road that's worth the effort. But how? I'll know by the time the year is over; I'll know—if I succeed.

I want to record a poem I've attempted in Hebrew.[46]

In the fires of war, in the flame, in the flare,
In the eye-blinding, searing glare
My little lantern I carry high
To search, to search for true Man.

In the glare, the light of my lantern burns dim,
In the fire-glow my eye cannot see;
How to look, to see, to discover, to know
When he stands there facing me?

Set a sign, O Lord, set a sign on his brow
That in heat, fire and burning I may
Know the pure, the eternal spark
Of what I seek: true Man.

November 2, 1940

I dream and plan as if there were nothing happening in the world; as if there were no war, no destruction; as if thousands upon thousands were not being killed daily; as if Germany, England, Italy, and Greece were not destroying each other. Only in our little country—which is also in danger and may yet find itself in the center of hostilities—is there an illusion of peace and quiet. And I'm sitting here, thinking of the future. And what do I think about my personal future?

One of my most beautiful plans is to be a poultry farming instructor, to travel from one farm to another, to visit settlements, to advise and to assist, to organize, to introduce record-keeping, to develop this branch of the economy. In the evenings I would conduct brief seminars for kibbutz members, teach them the important facets of the trade. And at the same time I would get to know the people, their way of life, and would be able to travel about the country.

My other plan is to instruct (seems I only want to teach) children in some sort of school. Perhaps in the institute at Shfeya, or in a regional agricultural school. The old dream is to combine agricultural work with child guidance and teaching.

My third plan—a plan I consider only rarely—has nothing to do with agriculture or children, but with writing. (As I write this the *Unfinished Symphony* is being played on the radio downstairs.) I want to write books, or plays, or I don't know what. Sometimes I think I have talent and that it's sinful to waste or neglect it. Sometimes I think that if I really do have talent I'll eventually write without worrying about it—that if I feel the need of self-expression, the urge to write, I'll write. The important thing is to have a command of the language. I've made considerable progress during this first year in the Land, but I must do better.

And I've yet another plan. I'd like to live on a kibbutz. This can, however, be in conjunction with the other plans. I'm quite sure I would fit in, if only the possibility of working at something that really interested me existed.

When I visited Merhavya during my vacation, I was able to imagine myself finding purpose and satisfaction in a *moshav*, but this way of life seems to me to be the least satisfactory. Generally speaking, it's difficult to discover what suits me best, since I take easily to all conditions, environments, kinds of work.

I don't think I've written anything about my daily life. I haven't even mentioned my work in the chicken house, which I really like very much. Nor have I said anything about the Bible Society, nor about the end-of-term celebration. Yesterday was both Pnina's and Miryam's birthday, which I didn't mention either. Nor about my relationship with them, nor my feelings about the school, nor about my visit to the Vadash family in Kfar Baruch. They're really very nice people.

I haven't mentioned my horseback riding, one of my greatest pleasures and one in which, unfortunately, I can indulge only rarely.

But that's all right … I don't mind leaving all these things out of my diary, but it's impossible for me not to write about a book I recently read. It's called *Jeremiah* and was written by Kastein.[47] This book made a tremendous impression on me. Considering the present situation of world Jewry, it is extremely timely. He penetrates and analyzes the basic questions of the Jewish religion through his characterization of the Prophet Jeremiah. It is impossible not to be impressed. It was doubly interesting to me, since it gave expression to my own interpretation of religion.

Before I was familiar with the point of view of the prophets, and what, in general, the Jewish religion was about, I instinctively objected to empty religious forms and searched for its true content and morality as expressed in deeds. Needless to say, I only searched but did not always find. Yet, at least I tried. I was never able to pray in the usual manner, by rote, and even now neither can nor want to. But the dialogue man holds with his Creator, and about which the prophet preaches, is what I, too, have found. I see the sincere, inner link, even if it comes through struggle within myself and through some doubt. But I cannot fit into a conventional mold that is, in part, dead, and which, in part, crystallizes thoughts that are so foreign to me. The book touched my heart because of its sharp expression of all this. In many respects I had the same feeling about Buber's book.

In any event, a book that involves me directly, and offers me fulfillment, touches me. And this book affords a historical view of the fate of the Jewish people in its relationship to the Covenant, and to God, as the pure way of life. It is written with such consistency and logic, with such simplicity, that even a child could understand it and live according to its moral teachings.

November 27, 1940

A ship filled with illegal immigrants reached the coast. The British would not allow them to disembark for "strategic reasons" and for fear there might be spies among them. The ship sank. Some of the passengers drowned; some were saved and taken to Atlit. I brood over this and ask, What is right? From a humane point of view there is no question, no doubt. One must cry out, Let them land! Haven't they endured enough, suffered enough? Do you want to send them far away until the end of the war? They came home; they want to rest; who has the right to prevent them from doing so? But from the point of view of the country … really, who knows? They come from German-occupied countries. Perhaps there are elements among them likely to endanger the peace of the Land, particularly at a time when the front is drawing closer.

We argued about these matters among ourselves today. I tried to take the side of the British but didn't believe in my own argument. Perhaps this is born of our fear of objectively seeing our insoluble dilemma—a tiny country between two formidable adversaries: one the representative of anti-Semitism, the other the author of the White Paper. Needless to say, we have but one road: to side with Britain against Germany. The British are taking advantage of our situation. We stand here powerless, awaiting events. We can do nothing else; we're forbidden to take action, though there is certainly a difference between passivity and inactivity.

They're putting out the lights. I don't have time to explain now. That's the way life goes on here. I don't have time to clarify these burning problems even to myself, to get any deep knowledge of the issues involved and to reach a conclusion. I feel superficial and wanting, lacking in the years normally devoted to contemplation and dedication. I'm afraid those years will never come, not because of my age but because of circumstances.

December 14, 1940

A ship of refugees sailed for New Zealand. The demonstrations and protests didn't help. The entire Jewish community unanimously demanded that they be allowed to remain in the Land. But the ship sailed during the night, stealthily leaving the coast and Haifa. What is there to add? What can we feel as human beings, as a people? And the question arises, How much longer?

Today is the Sabbath. An empty Sabbath, which offers only a part of the day's significance: a day of rest, but not a holiday, not a day of festivity. I read a bit of *The Mother* by Sholem Asch, and an article in a trade journal. There is an emptiness about me; I've no interest in reading any more. I would like to go riding or to meet people. Perhaps this is a strange parallel, but it stems from the same source: I'd like to break out of my physical bounds, to fly across the fields and feel the wind in my face as I once did during a storm on my way back from the village. Running in the wind, I want to cast off everyday shackles, to use words I don't use every day, to meet people I don't meet day after day. As I have no choice, I am content with my surroundings, in which I have thus far not been disappointed.

There are all sorts of things I want to tell myself, and it's good and enjoyable to do so in writing. I feel I could not possibly live without writing, even if only for myself, in my diary. Or perhaps other things. A thought that is not put on paper is as if it had never been born. I can only truly grasp a thought when I've expressed it in writing.

What shall I write? There is so much. I would like to erect a statue to my mother, who allowed us, my brother and me, to go off into the world, to find our own way, and renounced her right to prevent us from leaving. But this is not a portrait of just my mother, but of all Jewish mothers of this generation, or of many of them. But it appears to me that there are few mothers who have been as heroic, as modest, as quietly patient as my mother—the very qualities that have made her, in my estimation, so great. If I were truly talented I could express all this in a quatrain. But if I lack that ability, even a thousand pages would not suffice to portray her.

January 2, 1941

Another New Year. If I want to give an accounting of the past year I must differentiate between two worlds: the external and the internal. The external world was bellicose and stormy, filled with bloodshed and destruction, purposeless. The inner world was at peace. My "inner construction" continues. There is a definite beginning of clarification, of better perspective, more penetrating perception. I note only a beginning, but hope for progress in this field.

What can one hope for from "that" (external) world? I think one can dare hope for British victory, but one has no idea what bearing this will have on our situation. I'm fearful of passing judgment on our own land, as I was far away from the happenings, and because of this I may be wrongly condemning it for its lack of action. But I have no doubt whatever that ceaseless negligence and countless errors are spoiling our lives.

I was ill for a few days. I had jaundice. I'm not yet completely recovered. But what worries me most is that I again have those stabbing pains in my heart. I'm terrified by the thought that there may be something wrong. I'm afraid not only of dying young (I really do love life) but also that this may prevent me from following my chosen path and from choosing the work I like best. I haven't spoken to the doctor yet; I postpone doing so from day to day. I want to reassure myself that it amounts to nothing at all. This is what is known as "ostrich diplomacy."

February 25, 1941

It's time I wrote about Alex. Even though it's more "his" affair than something we share. Several things happened last month that I didn't write about, not only because I was busy working at the incubator but also because I find it difficult to write about matters that aren't entirely clear to me, or about which I am undecided.

I've known Alex for about a year, but only recently have our meetings become more frequent. There is no question at all but that he is extremely fond of me and that he is serious about me. But what I'm not sure about are my feelings toward him. He is honest, decent, good, and loves me. But I'm convinced we aren't suited. Our educational background, our interests and perspectives are too different. I could probably live a pleasant, simple life with him, but one that would not satisfy or fulfill me.

He recently told me he loves me, and asked me to marry him. I told him that although I respect and like him, I don't feel as he does. Nonetheless, I couldn't say this with absolute certainty, and the matter was left unresolved. He comes to see me as usual, but I asked him to wait a while before demanding a definite answer.

Why this hesitation? If I feel so certain the relationship ought to be discontinued, why continue it? Perhaps because I feel a certain responsibility toward him, and toward myself as well. I want to be as sure as possible before making a decision one way or the other.

But what about myself? This question raises many problems concerning my future—problems not too clear to me and therefore difficult to solve. In theory, I've opted for a life of farm work. I want to be involved with the working people of the Land. I need them, and they need me. This is what determines my decision for the future and will, in the end, decide where I'll settle. And this is not mere theory, as the way I've chosen already influences my daily life and even determines my attitude toward people and events.

But all this is not quite clear to me yet, as I have conflicting emotions. Thus, my decisions are certainly not concrete. And until I am sure of myself, there is no possibility of deciding my future course. Sometimes I feel one way, sometimes another. In any event, I must try kibbutz life in order to see if it suits me. But even if it does not, I know I want to stay in agriculture, though not on a *moshav* because the field of activity there is much too restricted.

I think living on a kibbutz is likely to be an interesting experience for a year or two. But I can't see myself living out my entire life on a kibbutz. On the one hand, I feel bound to some form of public service; yet, everyone must have personal freedom, quiet, an opportunity for individual initiative and development.

My problem is a tendency to confusion. Sometimes I feel one way, sometimes another. And if not this way, and not that way, then what ... ?

My point of view, my attitude toward society, toward socialism, are beginning to develop. I don't feel any sudden "internal revolution," only a slow development based upon knowledge, comprehension, and perhaps even more on intuition. My education, family background, my nature bind me, in many respects, to that "other life." The advantages of that life have nothing to do with the coffee houses, fine clothes, beautiful home, and luxury. But it does offer opportunity and free time to study, read, think. The last is what I miss most. Lack of time for reading has an adverse effect upon my development, but I don't suffer as much from it. But there are times when I feel the days are running away, and I must content myself with the thoughts to which my work limits me. And while they interest and occupy me, I'm pained when I stop and think how many areas of life and thought I've not had the opportunity of knowing well, or knowing at all, and that are now completely lost to me. I regret this because I think it is more than a personal loss.

Of course I am fully aware of the advantages of a working life, and of the opportunities it offers. I constantly have new ideas concerning my work, "invent" things that are reasonably good and make the work easier. I'm now working on a plan connected with the automatic brooder, which is really keeping me busy. I have an idea (though I still don't know whether it's feasible) that entails introducing colored chalk or some other coloring agent into the chicken, which would then mark every egg. Each hen would have its special marking. This sounds a bit strange and comical, but I don't think the idea is impossible, and want to pursue it further.

However, I think poultry farming, and agriculture in general, are relatively well organized here, or at least eventually will be without any help from me! The agrarian economy is based on a firm foundation and is in good hands. The general problem here is organizational. Political, educational, and social conditions are very disorganized, though these are exactly the areas in which our future and our fate are determined. I wonder whether I wasn't really meant to lend a helping hand in government? I've noticed at times that I have the ability to influence people, to comfort and reassure them, or to inspire them. Have I the right to waste this facility, hide it, ignore it, and to think about the automatic brooder instead? I don't know whether it's a blessing or a curse that everything I become involved with stimulates my interest so that I instantly begin thinking of ways of repairing, renovating, improving, developing whatever I come in contact with, be it the filling of sacks with potatoes, or the problems of mankind.

But I lose myself in the thick of things, my entity. What, I wonder, will happen when I will no longer have the flexibility to adapt myself, or the enthusiasm to create? There are times I feel I'm being dishonest with myself, that I'm cheating myself, that I'm playing games, and that I'm actually pleased the khaki slacks and blue work shirt are becoming to me, happy I can do the work anyone else can do, and willingly renounce doing things only those endowed with specific talents can accomplish.

I'm not afraid of overestimating myself, and I'm not bragging about my positive qualities. It's not to my credit that I have been given these attributes; I didn't do anything to merit them. They're talents I was born with, probably inherited. The joy is in the knowledge I was granted them, and I think it's my duty to utilize them. I wonder, will I be able to take advantage of them? I wonder, is this way I've chosen the right one? Whatever my future, I won't regret these two years for an instant. Wherever I am, these two years will make it possible for me to understand everything, everyone better: the working man, and all kinds of crafts and trades. These two years will bind me to the Hebrew village, both in deed and spirit.

I started to write about Alex and seem to have gone far afield. But perhaps therein lies the answer. The problem I now face is whether to marry a man "just like that"—to disrupt my plans, give up my independence. Naturally, it's difficult not to be impressed and flattered by the love of a man of character, a man you respect and esteem. But this is still not love, and thus there is really no reason to continue.

I've written a great deal and chaotically. But that's the way my thoughts and emotions live within me at this time. One contradicts the other, one fights with the other. And there is no one around who notices this, or with whom I have any desire to discuss any of this. Miryam is a good friend, but I can't discuss these questions with her. She, too, is at war with herself. In these matters no one can help. Only by facing the realities of life can I come to terms with the question. I hope I'll be courageous enough to search my own soul, my own heart, and, if necessary, to make a wise decision.

April 12, 1941

Really, this is absurd. I think of myself as an empty jug, or more specifically, a jug with a hole in the bottom through which everything that has been poured in drains out. Nothing I do makes sense. I need people. Not just hunks of flesh, but people who are akin to me in thought and spirit. It's not even "people" I need, but just one person.

I'm afraid there is a hidden thermostat within me that neither lets me warm up nor cool off beyond the required degree. Although this uniform temperature is conducive to developing the embryo in the egg and helps it to hatch, it kills the spirit of the young human.

Why am I so lonely? Not long ago I strolled through the *moshav* one evening. It was a fabulous, starry night. Small lights glittered in the lanes and in the middle of the wide road. Sounds of music, songs, conversation, and laughter came from all around; and far, far in the distance I heard the barking of dogs. The houses seemed so distant; only the stars were near.

Suddenly I was gripped by fear. Where is life leading me? Will I always go on alone in the night, looking at the sparkling stars, thinking they are close? Will I be unable to hear the songs … the songs and the laughter around me? Will I fail to turn off the lonely road in order to enter the little houses? What must I choose? The weak lights, filtering through the chinks in the houses, or the distant light of the stars? Worst of all, when I'm among the stars I long for the small lights, and when I find my way into one of the little houses my soul yearns for the heavenly bodies. I'm filled with discontent, hesitancy, insecurity, anxiety, lack of confidence.

Sometimes I feel I am an emissary who has been entrusted with a mission. What this mission is—is not clear to me. (After all, everyone has a mission in life.) I feel I have a duty toward others, as if I were obligated to them. At times this appears to be all sheer nonsense, and I wonder why all this individual effort … and why particularly me?

There is no longer a postal connection with home. The war is constantly spreading. And I'm almost indifferent to it. I'm actually afraid of myself. I'd like to feel something, to laugh, to cry—but heartily, sincerely.

April 23, 1941

Yugoslavia has fallen. In Greece the British and Greeks are retreating. The fighting in Libya is heavy and the results still uncertain. And Palestine is deadlocked in weakness, misunderstanding, and lack of purpose. Everyone is discussing politics; everyone is positive the front is getting closer. But no one dares ask, what will happen if the Germans come here? The words are meaningless—on paper. But if we close our eyes and listen only to our hearts, we hear the pounding of fear. I'm not afraid for my life. It's dear to me, but there are things I hold dearer. Whether I want to or not, I must imagine what the fate of the Land will be if it has to confront Germany. I'm afraid to look into the depth of the abyss, but I'm convinced that despite our lack of weapons and preparedness, we won't surrender without resisting strongly. Half a million people can face up to a force, no matter how greatly it is armed. And I'm sure Britain will help us— or, to be more exact, will do all it can on its own behalf. And I continue to believe in a British victory.

But will there still be an Eretz? Will it be able to survive? It's dreadful to contemplate the possibility of its end at close hand. And though everyone wants to be hopeful, to reassure himself, deep within is submerged the thought ... perhaps.... And no man has come along yet with the ability to unite the people and to stop, even for a moment, the interparty conflicts. There is no one to say, "Enough!" No one to whom they will listen. I feel a deep sense of responsibility: perhaps I ought to say the word! But this is not my job. I don't have the opportunity to do so, or the knowledge. But even if I had the courage to rise up and speak, they wouldn't listen to me. Who and what am I to assume such a task? I can't do this, of course. But to do nothing, merely to look on from afar—that I can't do either. As if in a nightmare, I would like to scream, but no voice comes from my throat; I'd like to run, but my legs lack the strength. I can't come to terms with the thought that everything must be lost, destroyed, without us having the slightest say or influence on the course of things.

I want to believe that the catastrophe won't come to pass. But if it does, I hope we'll face it with honor. And if we can't hold out, that we will fall honorably.

The words of Shneur[48] ring in my ears: "It's glorious to die the death of the saints, and to leave the world to the inglorious." What is a heroic death? To consecrate God's name? Is it possible to consecrate God's name in a manner divorced from life itself? Is there anything more holy than life itself?

It's three o'clock. I must go to work.

May 17, 1941

There is a certain feeling of transition in our lives now. We plan something and add, "If meanwhile …" and don't finish the sentence. Everyone understands. I don't think about dying, in any sense, though objectively speaking the possibility is very close. But I feel I still have a lot to do in this life and that I cannot die before doing it all. Obviously everyone feels this way, particularly the young people who have already met death, and those who will yet meet it during this dreadful war. Our entire young country, filled with love and the will to live, feels this way.

June 14, 1941

Greece has fallen, and so has Crete. The war is now raging in Egypt and Syria. The British army marched into Syria three days ago, so the war is now virtually on our doorstep. Haifa was bombed for two nights. We went outside and listened to the bombs exploding, and the firing. Today we heard that Tel Aviv was bombed last night, too, leaving many dead and wounded. The city is defenseless, an easy prey. It looks now as if the war is starting here.

At times one wants to view things from a longer range, from an historical rather than a fatalistic point of view, to seek explanations for things that can't be explained.

Look, let me draw a picture of a fruit orchard: an orchard of people. Saplings and full-grown trees, good trees and bad trees. They have blossomed, yielded fruit; winter has come, and their leaves have fallen. The gardener comes and sees their dry, stunted branches. He thinks of the spring and mercilessly trims and prunes, thereby strengthening them.

An ancient tree stands in the middle of the orchard, its trunk thick, its roots and branches spreading over and under the orchard. Its branches have dried up; the earth's life-giving moisture is unable to reach it. The gardener's eye notes that its roots are still vigorous, its trunk healthy. It's a noble tree, still able to yield fruit. But it must be more carefully pruned and tended than the other trees. He unhesitatingly cuts off the thick branches, and the pruning hook leaves fresh, golden wounds.

Will the tree survive? Look! In place of the amputated branches new ones are budding. A small twig appears near the roots, with fresh, full buds containing the hope of renewed life. Does the pruning hook snip it off too? Is it possible the gardener will fail to recognize the new life under the gray bark? And should the unseeing hand trim it off … will the Tree of Israel ever blossom again?

July 9, 1941

They haven't started pruning yet. At least not for the time being. The pruning hook has turned toward Russia, where the fiercest battles since the beginning of the war are now raging. Germany attacked Russia about two weeks ago and swiftly captured Russian Poland, as well as a good part of Finland, and has begun advancing toward the interior of Russia. According to newspaper and radio reports, the Nazis are now encountering strong Russian opposition. Everyone knows that the results of this struggle will be decisive to the future of the world; thus, the suspense is enormous. The bombings have become frequent here, too, and it's a miracle there have been so few casualties.

Yesterday I received a telegram from Mother that came via Turkey, and I gather she is frightened and worried about me. It's awful to think that while I'm living a normal, comfortable, peaceful life Mother is worried sick, envisioning me in all sorts of frightful situations, allowing herself no peace. I'm conscious-stricken that I have it so good and easy here while others are suffering, and feel I ought to do something—something exerting, demanding—to justify my existence.

I've had enough of schoolwork and am impatiently waiting for the end of exams. I know my life will be, in many respects, more difficult after I leave school. But "difficult" is a relative term. It is "difficult" to lift a heavy stone, for instance, but it's far more difficult to stop breathing—although this requires no physical effort.

Aged twenty, July 30, 1941

We handed in our vocational theses today and talked with Levine, one of our teachers. My grades were all 9s and 10s—the highest. Only one other girl did as well. Naturally I was enormously pleased and happy. The results of the other exams don't particularly interest me, and I'm impatiently awaiting the end of school.

And what comes next? First, excursions, making the rounds of the kibbutzim. It's difficult to imagine myself tied to one place. I feel as if all the Land were mine, as if I belonged to the entire Land. But to settle in one place, to give all my energies to it, to live there all my life … ? I have a fear of permanent ties. I can't, as yet, think of any definite ties, such as marriage (besides, the man is lacking), and even the thought is foreign to me.

We're about to begin a one-week seminar at Kibbutz Gesher in order to familiarize ourselves with one of the new projects of Working Youth. I'm eagerly looking forward to this. Though I'm not a member of Working Youth, I'm interested in its projects. Zionist Youth, Working Youth, Youth, and even the Shomer Hatzair[49] are fighting over me now. They know I haven't committed myself as yet, and each wants me to join it. Strangest of all was the invitation of the Hungarian founders of Kibbutz Dan. They made a special journey just to speak to me, though I don't know the reason for all this sudden attention. Perhaps I'll visit them, but I have no intention of joining them, since I have no reason for doing so.

How can I explain my dissatisfaction with myself? Sometimes I almost hate myself. I say something and immediately regret it. I do something and feel dissatisfied. I want to be alone, yet feel the lack of "someone," someone whose company I would enjoy, who would be important to me. It's dreadful to think that in all the Land there is no one who truly loves me, who cares what happens to me. I have friends; I have acquaintances. But what do they all mean to me? I feel I've lost much of my flexibility in this place, my spiritual strength, but hope I'm wrong: that they are merely dormant, that future activities and a normal, stimulating life away from here will reawaken them. There is one thing, though, with which my stay here can be credited: it taught me to see things and people differently, less idealistically. I don't know whom to blame for this, but I don't think I'm far wrong in saying that the cold, arid life here is partially responsible.

Enough now! I have two more exams and must prepare for them.

August 3, 1941

I'm completing this diary[50] the day before the school's annual excursion, and think my stay at Nahalal will end at the same time. It seems to me that a period of my life has ended—a twenty-year period of preparation—and that now I must repay society what it has invested in me. I think my first step toward life will be the week to be spent at Gesher. Though it's hard to define that specific "life." After all, didn't I breathe, eat, think, meet people, laugh and cry, have ideas thus far? Wasn't all that "life"? But all those actions lacked a certain sense of responsibility, probably because of a feeling of transition and insecurity connected with the way of life. In this respect I probably won't feel any immediate change in the kibbutz, as the struggle for existence there is not pronounced or noticeable. But I intend to write about everything that lies ahead.

August 25, 1941

If I wanted to yield to symbolism, I'd put off starting my new diary until my departure from school, which is fast drawing to a close. But after three weeks of holiday, I have a lot to write about and won't postpone doing so for the sake of symbolism. I won't have enough time now for everything, since the work bell will soon ring, but I'll take advantage of this bit of free time before work to write a few paragraphs. I'll start with Gesher.

For the eight of us interested in joining the United Kibbutz—or, to be more exact, a project of Working Youth—a seminar was arranged to introduce us simultaneously to both the kibbutz system and the new project. Behind this general plan lay the special purpose of the seminar's organizer, Razi, to convince us to join Kibbutz Gesher, which is greatly in need of additional personnel.

We left for Gesher in the morning. We were really looking forward to the days ahead, our first in a kibbutz, and were convinced beforehand we would enjoy ourselves.

A minor incident on our trip (we hitchhiked, as usual) is worth mentioning. Three South African officers, two of them Jews, gave us a lift. They had come up from Egypt on leave and were touring the Jordan Valley, as well as the rest of the country. They were very decent chaps, especially one of them, named Roy, and were sincerely interested in everything that is happening here and in the life in general. The kibbutz concept struck them as a bit odd. They asked a thousand questions, were very impressed by our answers, and liked everything we told them. They were not too eager to return to Egypt. I hate writing about this meeting so colorlessly and meaninglessly, because at the time I was very taken by their behavior and by the interest they showed in all the questions of vital interest to me. We all went swimming in the Kinneret and traveled up to Kibbutz Daganya, and then they drove us over to Gesher. It was really a pity we had to say good-bye.

But to return to present matters. We reached Gesher, and the seminar started the following day. I'll sum it up: lectures, discussions, readings concerning the course of the Workers' Movements in the Land, the United Kibbutz Movement, Working Youth, economic problems, the organization of a kibbutz. We worked a few days too, and sat in on kibbutz meetings.

Considering the short time we spent there, I managed to learn a lot and familiarize myself with things, and was favorably impressed with the place. There are a number of outstanding people there with whom it would really be interesting to work, and the entire group made a good impression.

But there are two factors against my joining: first of all, the kibbutz is perhaps too young for me, though this is not a serious reason. The real crux of the matter is that the spot is two hundred meters below sea level, and the heat is awful; the place to be eventually chosen for the permanent settlement will most likely be in the same area. This, in itself, should not be decisive. But I'm hesitant because the doctor used to insist that I go to the mountains every summer because of my heart. Though concern for my health may be a justifiable excuse, I'm not being entirely honest. Actually, my convictions are not strong enough to renounce half my life. This probably sounds exaggerated, but it's true. During the summer, in such climate, doing hard work, one can't become involved or interested in anything else but the kibbutz. And I feel I would be giving up more than I want to.

Naturally, this isn't a decent excuse. After all, hundreds settle in the Negev Desert, in the Bet Shean Valley, and even down by the Dead Sea. I would too if I were linked with a group. But to choose such a spot of my own free will, knowing what it means, is too difficult a step for me. Nevertheless, the kibbutz's atmosphere tempts me, and I haven't completely decided against it.

From there I went on to visit the young group at Kinneret, composed of the Transylvanians who were in Kibbutz Afikim last year. They understood that my visit was not merely for fun, and made it possible for me, despite the brief three-day visit, to get to know something of the place and the people. My impression in brief: they are serious, well-educated intellectuals who enjoy human comforts (they're home-loving, which is in their favor), and are still partially tied to the Diaspora, particularly in language and culture.

On the basis of all this, it would seem they are really closest to my taste. But opposites attract, and thus I'm drawn to the settlements where the atmosphere is different. They, on the other hand, are considering the possibility of amalgamating with a Palestinian group, which would really be a good solution for them. But that's still in the future. At any rate, I'm not sure there is anything to be gained by my joining a specifically Transylvanian group, since our common origin would be of little advantage and would only hamper my progress in Hebrew and Hebrew culture. That's why I left Kinneret feeling that although pleasant, it was not the answer for me. But at the same time … maybe—perhaps. It seems the more one sees, the more difficult it is to decide.

While at Gesher, I heard there would be a week's course given in Jerusalem on poultry ailments and decided to attend. I returned to Nahalal, went on to Herzliya (where I spent a heavenly day on the beach), then to Petach Tikva, and finally on up to Jerusalem. Professor Fekete welcomed me cordially, as usual, and arranged for me to attend the course at the university.

The week was really interesting and pleasant. I went to the university daily, attended the lectures, participated in the laboratory work, i.e., microscopic investigations, and so on. In the evenings I met friends, went to the theatre and the cinema, had long talks, visited the Hadassah and university buildings and the local branch of Working Youth. And in my spare time I read an excellent book, *Gone with the Wind*.

During this week I realized I'm not the same liberal, sociable girl I was two (or three) years ago, able to acknowledge and accept all strata of society, all modes of living. I can no longer pass the time, or chat "just for fun," aimlessly. I can't help seeing shallowness, even though at times I know I carry my criticism and faultfinding too far. Involuntarily I find myself judging the far too many faults of society to such a degree that it spoils my fun. But I would be less than truthful were I to say I didn't enjoy the week in Jerusalem, despite the fact that my critical voice and scrutinizing glance were constantly active.

I'm back in Nahalal now, preparing for my final departure. Everyone asks what my plans are, and they're amazed I haven't made a decision yet. As far as I'm concerned, I'm in no hurry to make up my mind, and not in the least bit worried. I have a fatalistic attitude based on the conviction that I'll find the right answer when the time comes.

My ideological point of view is clear to me now. I want to join a Working Youth project that will become part of the United Kibbutz

Hannah and friends on a boat in the
Sea of Galilee.

Movement. Many people argue against this from a social standpoint, and they are against the United Kibbutz. But personally I respect it despite—or perhaps because of—the great difficulties with which it must contend. The ideologies of the Kibbutz Groups Association, the Hashomer Hatzair, and the Pioneering Zionist Youth don't appeal to me. Others are of the opinion that in practice things differ from theory, and that my thinking will change after a direct confrontation with the kibbutz. I think they're wrong, just as those were in the Diaspora who prophesied all manner of things I would find when I got here.

Now back to work in the garden. That's always a pleasant chore.

September 2, 1941

Yesterday was commencement: the festive, ceremonial end to two years. It was a very successful party. I addressed the school in the name of the class, and afterwards could barely shake hands with all those who wanted to congratulate me because they thought my farewell address was very beautiful. There were some who actually wept when they heard it, and that certainly was not my purpose.

In short, the day is over and we are free. I'm starting to pack and hope to finish soon. I'm leaving for a kibbutz, filled with energy and excitement. My only doubt is—where to go, which one to choose. I hope I'll soon be able to make a decision, and find a permanent place—though absolute permanency is something I find difficult to imagine.

A few days ago Nahalal celebrated its twentieth anniversary. Those twenty years are etched into the village and into the faces of its members. One has blossomed during this period; the other has withered. It's as if the sap of life were drained from tiller to soil, and there turned into flora and fauna. Or, in short, become "property and chattels" whose development and growth are charted on that graph now on display at the village exhibit. By the way, the display at the village school was a flop. The natural display, the village itself, speaks more eloquently for itself than any chart or speech ever could.

September 6, 1941

The last week, the last Sabbath, the last afternoon at Nahalal. The room is a mess. Miryam and I have been packing. I just finished and will be leaving tomorrow morning. While packing I again realized how much unnecessary stuff I have. To be more exact, how many of the things I brought along will be superfluous to the kind of life I've chosen. At any rate, it's important that I have what I need; the surplus can't hurt.

I'm taking advantage of this last opportunity to talk to Miryam, to clarify matters, since we certainly won't have a great deal of time together in the future (apart from a brief excursion we've already planned). I think Miryam was my best friend. Whether I've got to know her well is difficult to say. There were times when I felt she was distant, that beneath the outer layer of self-control, which she acquired through self-discipline, she is entirely different, and that the "two Miryams" are contradictory.

I don't think our friendship was as candid and genuine as it might have been, because our aims and dispositions are too much alike, which has always tended to create competition between us. We had many heated arguments besides our long ideological discussions and differences. There were times when our wrangling ended abruptly and in anger, as one or the other would say, "I don't want to discuss this with you any further," or would suddenly end the argument in mid-sentence with "That's enough! I want to sleep!" These heated discussions generally took place at night, after ten o'clock, and more than once were so stormy that our neighbors yelled, "Stop it!"

There were times I felt she was depressing and sullen, and longed for gayer, more stimulating friends. But despite all this, I think she is still my best friend and probably always will be.

What did our friendship stem from? At first, shared experiences. We arrived at Nahalal at the same time; we were both newcomers; both of us knew little Hebrew but were zealously determined and eager to learn it. We shared similar backgrounds and similar cultures, aspired toward similar goals, and had similar ideas, though there were vast differences in our outlook, in our ideological education and expression. We both wanted to give our surroundings everything we had to offer, and to receive from them whatever they had to give. We were both too tense, too avid for everything in the Land. We both had the same attitude to our work—a hazy, idealistic attitude. We both desperately wanted a new way of life.

Those were the traits we had in common that drew us close. Our differences, on the other hand, served as opposite forces to attract us and to strengthen our friendship, much as the depressions and bumps on the little discs that fit one into the other to form snap-fasteners.

These, briefly, are our opposite traits: she is more thoughtful, tends to exaggerate more. She is apt to worry herself to death about trifles. I'm more superficial, more easygoing, ready to see the good and beautiful in life. She often remarked that she found my judgments and decisions too easygoing. I pointed out the happier side of life to her. She is more impulsive, quick-tempered; I'm more restrained, better balanced. Her perception is more theoretical; mine, on the other hand, more realistic.

What is most important is that I was able to turn to her with all my problems, tell her everything. I knew she understood me and was able to give me advice. I always valued her opinions. And she felt the same way about me, and sought my opinion and advice. This was of considerable help to both of us in overcoming both minor and major problems. But it wasn't only this. We also glanced at the world together, laughed together at its expense, poking fun at ourselves all the while, and at the people around us. We criticized the entire world, but in a constructive way. In short, it took but a glance, a single word, or even just a hint, and we understood each other.

We both laughed at boys, but both of us would have been happy to have found "the" one—not just anyone. And because we didn't find that right one, we kept making fun of those who were interested in us, who came to court us.

Petach Tikva, September 8, 1941

As I expected, parting was not too difficult except from Miryam and Pnina. When the rounded outline of the village disappeared beyond the horizon, I felt myself bound to it as well as to the entire surrounding valley, and I knew a chapter of my life entitled "Studies and Preparations" had come to an end. This sort of spoiled the pleasure of that happiness I had so long looked forward to—that moment of going out into the world and facing life on my own.

But perhaps that's an empty phrase at the moment, as I'm just visiting friends and acquaintances. But the freedom of making my own decisions day in and day out, of being responsible for all my own actions from now on—all this, as far as I'm concerned, constitutes the meaning of that well-worn phrase "going out into life."

Today, on my way from Haifa to Petach Tikva, I traveled with a Revisionist[51] who tried to explain his and his friends' political views. I'm sad when I hear and see how great the political split is growing, and all in the name of "unity," "nationalism," and "Greater Eretz Yisra'el." (And this is not only against the Revisionists.) He naturally emphasized his political attitude toward England, and there was considerable truth in what he said. But he didn't mention the "social-Socialist" aspect. However, the conversation was interesting, and I must admit my knowledge of party matters and perspectives is very limited. My views are merely instinctive, and subconscious rather than conscious....

September 14, 1941

I'm writing a play.[52] I don't have proper working conditions because I can only write when it's quiet. Everyone keeps asking what I'm writing.... People generally think I'm bored when I'm alone.

Ness Tziyona, September 21, 1941

It's the eve of Rosh Hashanah. Two years have already passed since I left home. Two years away from my mother, my home; from my brother I've been away three years; and I've lived two years in the Land. If I could, I would write a few words to my mother. I have so much to tell her. It's hard to know what I'd talk to her about were we to meet now. I would tell her about these years, about my dreams, my plans, my anxieties. I would tell her how I felt yesterday: I was so desperately depressed that I cried. I felt I was faced with two possibilities: to seek personal happiness and shut my eyes to all the faults in my surroundings, or else to invest my efforts in the difficult and devastating war for the things I deem good and proper.

But I don't think the decision is up to me. I feel that hidden traits within me will determine my course, even though all the hardship and suffering it will entail are clear to me. But I wonder whether I have the strength and the ability to achieve what I want. I also wonder if what I want will be the right thing?

Dear God, if You've kindled a fire in my heart, allow me to burn that which should be burned in my house—the House of Israel. And as You've given me an all-seeing eye, and an all-hearing ear, give me, as well, the strength to scourge, to caress, to uplift. And grant that these words be not empty phrases but a credo for my life. Toward what am I aiming? Toward all that which is best in the world, and of which there is a spark within me.

I wouldn't talk about all this with Mother. But perhaps even if I said nothing, she would understand. Here I'm among strangers. They don't know me, don't understand me. Nor do I know them. I sometimes think I'm lacking in sensitivity and feeling. I don't love anyone. As a matter of fact, I like everyone and look for the good in people, and if I find it, I like and respect them to a certain extent. But this doesn't count. I've really only loved Mother, my brother, Grandmother, and the memory of my father.

Here I love only the Land. But it's far too big, too vast to return my love—and besides, this is not a living love.

Perhaps subconsciously I love myself—but not the way others love themselves. For other things take precedence on my scale of values—which is why people call me an idealist. I find this ridiculous. Even if I wanted to, I could not be different than I am. I couldn't possibly live without looking for that which seems right to me, without attempting to make the things that are right attainable. And this is certainly not to my credit. It's all a part of my nature.

So much for myself. Now what can I say about the world around me—the world that is virtually destroying itself? Or about the tens of thousands of people perishing daily? How shall I grieve for them on the eve of Rosh Hashanah? About the suffering, the pain, the injustice … what can I say, and to whom? He knows—thus there is nothing for me to say on this solemn evening.

Do I believe in God? I don't know. For me He is more a symbol and expression of the moral forces in which I believe. Despite everything, I believe the world was created for good and that there is nothing on earth so evil that a ray of light can't seep through, or a pinch of good can't be seen.

These are just words. But life will speak for itself; it will justify itself. I know my words are those of one who knows very little about the suffering and evil in the world. My road still lies ahead....

I'm entirely alone, independent, responsible only to myself. Presently that's what's good about my life.

September 22, 1941

Yesterday I wrote only a few words, impressions, inner feelings. Today, however, I would like to take stock of my impressions of the Land itself. This is difficult for me, as my impressions are still very scanty, and I can only make fragmentary reports.

There are striking problems in the Land: a destructive political partisanship—and at the same time a shocking lack of organization. Along with these there is great bitterness and a feeling of hopelessness. Everyone blames the other, everyone considers himself innocent and hates the other. Everyone thinks that outside factors influence deteriorating conditions. Nonsense! Internal rot is the primary problem, and if our internal condition were more sound and stable, our external situation would be different too.

We're a very sick people. We need a great doctor to heal us, and perhaps the sun and air of Eretz will help. But it's a mistake to think the two alone will serve as a cure-all for our ills. In any event, the character of the new generation is better, more honest than that of the previous one. They—the youth—are fit and willing to carry on. But the impetus needed to get them started, to lay a foundation, is lacking. Nor can they have it, really. Only people from the Diaspora can begin, and the sabras can complete the building of the country.

I know there is too much empty philosophizing in all this, and as long as this mood has gotten the best of me, I had better not write.

But one more question interests me: what will my future be? Will I write or be active in the land? Or both? Or neither?

Kiryat Hayim, September 28, 1941

On my last day in Ness Tziyona we went on a pleasant outing that included Givat Brenner, Kibbutz Schiller, and the experimental station in Rehovot. The experimental station, where everything was completely and interestingly explained to us, particularly impressed us. We saw Givat Brenner only superficially.

On my way back from Ness Tziyona I stopped at the home of Avigdor Hameiri, the author, in Ramat Gan. The first thing he said was, "You look exactly like your father." He couldn't get over how much I resembled him. It seems he knew Father well as a young writer, and he reminisced about their common past. Then he discussed the trend of the theatre in Palestine and in general, and its future possibilities. He said Father's plays, deliciously humorous and entirely devoid of political or social tendencies or implications, would be completely unacceptable to the theater here.

I then told him a "friend of mine" had asked me to show him some of her poems and to ask for his opinion. I said my friend, a twenty-year-old girl from a well-to-do family, had arrived in the Land two years ago and had learned Hebrew here. I read him "Moment" and "To the Galil." He listened attentively, and said they were "interesting examples; showed technique, facility of expression, and simplicity." In short, he considered my "friend" talented and said he would like to send "To the Galil" to his newspaper for publication. I said I was not authorized to submit the poem (because this isn't really important to me, but I was happy to have the objective opinion of an expert). He asked me to send him the poem, but I don't know whether I will. I don't think this is the right time.

Now I'm in Kiryat Hayim, helping Ilonka[53] a bit in the garden, in the poultry yard, and in the house. I've come to the conclusion that working a small farm doesn't suit me. I now recall that even as a child I always imagined that whatever I would do in my life would be on a large scale. I guess this is one of the traits that impels me toward the kibbutz.

Yesterday I attended an interesting lecture on the Labor Party in England. In the afternoon I visited Sdot Yam. Day before yesterday I spent an evening with Working Youth.

No news from home, or from my brother.

Erev Yom Kippur, September 30, 1941

This evening too—Erev Yom Kippur—my thoughts are with them. What's happening to them? Had I definitely known things would turn out like this, would I have left them? I think yes. After all, I knew even then that this possibility existed, and perhaps only wanted to quiet my fears with the futile hope that my brother would join me in a year, my mother in two years. That was probably the argument I gave myself in order to ease my conscience about the irrevocable decision I had made to come to this Land.

I must now ask myself, by what right did I consider my *aliyah* justified at a time when so many tens of thousands of young Jews continued to live in the Diaspora? My only answer—and an absolutely selfish one—is that only here can I find any meaning to my life. This is absolutely clear to me.

Difficult as it is, I must confess I have no one here, and am completely alone by my own choice. This is the only way, the only possibility for me to decide, freely and independently, about my future. But as with everything, one must pay the price. In this case, however, I think it is Mother who is paying instead of me. And I'll never be able to repay my debt to her.

I'm not fasting because I don't feel the need. In my opinion, the only value of fasting is for the Jews in the Diaspora to express their solidarity. I feel I have other ways of expressing my ties with Judaism, and I'll forgo this one, which is completely alien to me. However, I'll observe the essence of the day by soul-searching and confessing.

I sinned by being apathetic, by failing to act—that is, not backing

MAGYAR VÖRÖS-KERESZT
UNGARISCHES ROTES KREUZ
CROIX-ROUGE HONGROISE
BUDAPEST, VIII, BAROSS-UTCA 15. HONGRIE

Demandeur — Érdeklődő — Anfragesteller
Nom — Családi név — Name: Szenes
Prénom — Keresztnév — Vorname: Béláné
Rue — utca — Strasse: II. Bimbó-ut 28.
Localité — Város, község — Wohnort: Budapest
Département — Megye — Komitat:
Pays — Orszag — Land: Hungary

Message à transmettre — Üzenet — Nachricht
(25 mots au maximum, nouvelles de caractère strictement personnel et familial —
legfeljebb 25 szó, kizárólag személlyi természetű)
Höchstens 25 Worte rein persönlichen Inhaltes.

George and I perfectly well. He got your
letter of May. Write him again. Should
knew your further plans. What about Lici?
Fondest love
Mother

Date — Kelt: 26.VIII.1941.

Destinataire — Cimzett — Empfänger: Szenes
Nom — Családi név — Name: Szenes
Prénom — Keresztnév — Vorname: Anna
Rue — utca — Strasse: Agricultural School for Girls
Localité — Város, község — Wohnort: Nahalal
Province — Megye — Komitat:
Pays — Orszag — Land: Palestine

Prière d'écrire très lisiblement — Gépírást kérünk!
Réponse au verso — Válasz a túloldalon.
Bitte deutlich zu schreiben! — Antwort auf der Rückseite!

20 OCT 1944

Magyar Vörös-Kereszt Egylet
(Croix-Rouge Hongroise)
Budapest (Hongrie),
VIII., Baross-u. 15.
Modele A.

Agence centrale de renseignements sur les prisonniers de guerre.
COMITÉ INTERNATIONAL DE LA CROIX-ROUGE
Palais du Conseil Général—Genève—Suisse

La formulaire rempli devra être mis sous enveloppe et envoyé
par la poste à l'adresse ci-dessus.

DEMANDEUR
(Feleir) Az érdeklődő:

Nom (Nazwisko) neve: Szenes
Prénom (Immanie) utóneve: Béláné
Rue (Ulica) utca: Bimbó-ut 28
Localité (Miejscowosc) város (község): Budapest
Pays (Kraj) ország: Hungary

Message à transmettre ou destinataire.
Známde maximum 25 słów.
Zniadomośti personnelles.

Ziecenie do przyjmcia do Lensat.
(Maximum 25 séd.)
Szigodna czek személlyi közös label.

Was glad with telegram through Turky - Just returned
summerholiday Damóvár - Perfectly well - George will
work August-Octobre in Beorgsin - What plans have you
after graduation?

Date (Dote) Kelt: Budapest, 26.VII.1941.

DESTINATAIRE
(Odbiorca) A cimzett:

Nom (Nazwisko) neve: Szenes
Prénom (Imanie) utóneve: Anna
Rue (Ulica) utca: Agricultural School
Localité (Miejscowosc) város (község): Nahalal
Pays (Kraj) ország: Palestine

Écrire très lisiblement
La réponse sera écrite au dos du formulaire.

Passé bardzo wyraznie.
Odpowiedz powinnabc nas
pisana z drugiejstrony
kwestjonarjusza.

Otważkora kerelő!
A válasz pap-túloldalon
kéllőbb legyük írni.

Two telegrams that were sent by Catherine Senesh in Budapest to Hannah in Palestine (delivered by the Red Cross during World War II).

up my statements with actions; by wasting time and energy; by being inconsiderate and rash; by being irresponsible. But I constantly sought the right way. Many consider me an idealist and say I'll change when I finally face life on my own. But I don't think I will, nor will I stop looking for the whys and wherefores in life.

I recall seeing a wonderful painting at the museum in Tel Aviv called *Yom Kippur Prayer*. I was enormously impressed by its power, the force of expression in the faces, the hands, and the bodies of the men at prayer. And I saw something else that was beautiful: an Abel Pann[54] exhibition in Tel Aviv. Burning Jewish eyes, and depth and simplicity of expression such as I've never seen before in paintings. I'm certain that both as an artist and as a Jew, Pann belongs among the great. The mayor's speech at the opening, in which he lauded himself far more than he did the artist, annoyed me. It was obvious he had no idea of the magnitude of the works. I could barely look at him.

The Hungarian radio is blaring in my ears. These days I speak a lot of Hungarian; I'm in a Hungarian atmosphere. It's time to go "home" to the kibbutz, to my atmosphere. It's time for the first step—renewal at either Sdot Yam or Kibbutz Ginosar.

October 7, 1941

I've been at Ilonka's for two weeks now, and tomorrow I'm going to Sdot Yam, the kibbutz. I find it difficult to explain even to myself exactly why I chose Sdot Yam. Naturally, I'm just going for a trial period now, but why did I choose this particular kibbutz in the first place?

I was looking for a group composed of young people my own age, attached to the Working Youth Movement, socially and politically alert and spirited. Besides, I'm very much attracted by their plans of settling in Caesarea.[55] The only difficulty lies in joining a group entirely new to me, not only as far as the individual members are concerned, but in its general structure. At least that's how I feel about it now; however, I don't want to make any decisions in advance. I'll see soon enough.

But I want to give myself a simple word of warning even before starting out, and which I want to repeat in the difficult moments that may be ahead—a warning I don't want to forget: I don't feel as if I'm going into the kibbutz for the rest of my life. I can justify kibbutz life, and insofar as I've come to know it, I like it. It's the way of life I've chosen. Nevertheless, I feel it is merely the first stage on a long route. At the moment I'm all excited about the next few weeks, of course, and want to tell myself something "for the road": something to remember at difficult moments, to remember I said it and thought it before I joined.

It's important to know whether the ideological basis of the kibbutz—a constructive socialist society in the Land—is correct. If it is, everything must be done to implement it, despite all the hardships. Its ideals look beautiful on paper and in books, but it is not easy to put them into practice and live by them. There is no need to follow the written word with one's eyes closed and meanwhile forget that the ideal must serve people, the individual. The basic function of the kibbutz is to afford satisfaction to all its members. No one is able to live long as a blind instrument used only to further a social aim. He will only be content if he himself moves toward his goal.

Even if a socialist slogan is placed on a mountain peak as a constant spur and incentive, we must not forget that if the members do not feel fresh air all around them when they reach the peak, if they do not sense a broader horizon, if they do not feel free—if they are considered only as working robots who blindly come and go—then all the efforts will have been wasted. For what is the use of a man reaching the mountain peak if he can't appreciate all the beauty around him because he is broken in body and spirit?

And another thing: I'll never say I'm disappointed with the kibbutz. I have nothing to be disappointed with, except myself. If I can't take that kind of life, the fault lies within me, in my character. I'm afraid only of one thing: I may miss my solitude. Were I certain I'd find a quiet corner for myself now and then, I'd have no qualms whatever. But I'll see. Why conjecture? Why prophesy?

Sdot Yam, October 12, 1941

I've already been here a few days. It's difficult to form impressions after only three or four days, but I feel kibbutz life suits me, and I'm enjoying it. The only question is whether this is the right kibbutz for me. The group is not particularly well developed, or perhaps I haven't got to know them well enough yet. I'm mostly concerned about the girls, since the development of the character of the kibbutz is, to a considerable extent, in their hands.

As to the work: at the moment I'm working in the kitchen. There is no chance to do anything but indoor work, since there is no agricultural development as yet. I may have to spend several years in "service," which is a pity, and really a waste of my time and ability. I no longer have the patience to "take turns" the way I did in Nahalal, where it was important to become familiar with every phase of farming as well as with inside work. Now I feel the need of some sort of work to which I can give maximum effort. I would also like to be active in the Movement. Obviously there will be an opportunity for this while I'm here, but getting started is difficult. What attracts me to this place is that there is a great deal to do, and they have a beautiful plan for the settlement. The conditions are difficult, but not without hope and possibilities. The fundamental problem is the people. I must get to know them better.

Kibbutz Ginosar, November 13, 1941

I left Sdot Yam with favorable impressions and many invitations to return. I really don't know if it's right to leave a group you enjoy in order to get to know a second and a third group. Every place has its good and bad aspects, and in the end it makes it that much harder to decide.

I spent two days in Tel Aviv, met Miryam there, and was glad to exchange impressions of everything that had happened to us both in the month since we parted. I saw two plays, *Alleys of Jerusalem* and *The Eternal Jew*. I wasn't particularly impressed by either, nor did I think the acting very good.

After Tel Aviv I made the rounds: Petach Tikva, Nahalal, Merhavya (a beautiful place, where I enjoyed the heartiness and simplicity of everyone), Balfouriya, Yagur. In Yagur I heard an interesting discussion at a general meeting on the subject of quarriers. And finally I returned to Ilonka in Kiryat Hayim.

I came to Kibbutz Ginosar with mixed feelings. On the one hand, I was curious and honestly eager to become acquainted with it, and on the other I knew in advance I wouldn't stay. Sdot Yam still attracts me. I have some kind of aversion to joining a settlement that has got past its initial hardships and has begun to enjoy the fruits of its difficult years. I don't want anything "ready-made"—though in the few days I've spent here I've come to realize that things aren't so "ready" here either, that everything is still pretty much in a state of formation. Even so, my original reaction hasn't changed. The group's age suits me, as a matter of fact, and its composition also seems right for me. True, I don't know the people well enough to judge them, but meanwhile I'm simply staying on, working, and for the time being have no inclination to come to a final decision.

Besides, there's another thing: it's possible we'll form a unit of Nahalal girls and look for a place to settle. I appreciate the value of such a group, but I am not prepared to give up the idea of going to a settlement I like for the sake of it. I'll see how things stand when the time comes that I must decide.

By chance I happened to chat with some members who are not too contented, and not in agreement with the kibbutz. It's interesting to note the apparently insignificant factors that determine a member's feelings, and the complaints against the kibbutz. The conclusion I drew from talking with them is that they feel a decided lack of personal contact with members, a need for a more communal approach. There may even be a lack of equality in certain areas, particularly insofar as money for each person is concerned. This is the decisive factor in the majority of cases. The complaints, for the most, are focused on problems of supplies—i.e., clothing and such, and upon housing and travel expenses. In other words, the elementary needs of each member.

It would seem the pioneering spirit has already vanished. There is no longer a willingness to do without things. People demand full lives, and the kibbutz, if it wishes to survive the test, must be able to satisfy them and their basic needs. The older kibbutzim have achieved this, to some degree, but a young kibbutz cannot do without some measure of personal sacrifice. Perhaps this is what is now missing in the kibbutz spirit.

November 18, 1941

I've been in Kibbutz Ginosar for over a week now. Naturally, it's still difficult to decide. I can speak only according to first impressions. I've found a number of very intelligent people in the group here. I'm sure I'd find them interesting and become good friends with them. But the group, in its entirety, is not sufficiently alert. Nonetheless, they have made a good impression on me. To be more specific, it's a group composed of many fine individuals, but it lacks the means of expressing itself in such a way as to form a common bond. This lack of expression is noticeable in every field of mutual endeavor, beginning with the reading room, all the way to the general assembly. I feel my sentence is murky and not totally justified.

Many of the members lack kibbutz ideology. Their ties consist of a love for the place, personal friendships, or simply the fact that they like it here—all factors that are, at times, more apt to bind one to a settlement than any ideology. But they neither sufficiently further and develop the life of the group, nor move it in the desired direction. "Desired" is a difficult word. It's very relative. Perhaps the most desirable thing is to let life develop along a simple, natural course, without any particular ideological direction.

Of course, as far as I'm concerned, I can't agree with this, nor can the kibbutz. The right course can be attained only by comparison, by examining—and fulfilling—the natural daily requirements of the individuals and directing them according to an understandable ideological point of view.

Regarding the work, I have no physical difficulties. I work wherever I'm assigned—in the garden, the laundry, the warehouse. But I feel as if there were a "fire within me." I don't feel I'm using all my abilities, but rather that I'm wasting myself. Throughout the Movement they complain of a lack of youth leaders, and a two-month leadership course is being started in the very near future. I may be wrong, but think (in fact I'm convinced) I could do very well in this kind of work. The only doubt I have is whether, with my limited knowledge, I can fulfill such an assignment. I'm quite confused about the issue—a thousand arguments, pro and con, race through my mind. Though the decision is out of my hands, and actually I don't even have the possibility of attending such a seminar, as no one knows me here, so there is no one who can send or recommend me for training. I must wait, not be so impatient. At the moment the most important thing is to attach myself to a settlement.

At times I wonder whether my choice of agriculture as a vocation was wise. I answer yes on every occasion, as acquiring a basic knowledge of agriculture, of work in general, was absolutely essential. Had I been able to obtain this as part of kibbutz training it might have meant a good deal—in the accepted sense. But I would have lost my freedom of decision, the opportunity of developing at my own pace, and a personal choice concerning a kibbutz.

Histadrut[56] elections will be held soon. Battles preceding the convention are already stormy. It's a good thing there's a spirit of sharp criticism, but here's hoping it won't undermine the Histadrut's prestige more than necessary, and weaken it instead of strengthening it.

Sdot Yam, December 25, 1941

I'm back at Sdot Yam, this time not as a guest but as a candidate. Five girls from my class decided to come here. I was also in favor, but the group, as a whole, accepted the decision—or, to be more exact, the suggestion—of Ruth Hakati, a member of the United Kibbutz Secretariat. I was attracted by Caesarea's future, the challenge it offers, the fact that it is at the starting point, and the group in general. I still don't know the members well but think it's a very good gang. My only worry is that they're too young, particularly the boys. In this sense, Kibbutz Ginosar may have been more suitable, but this point of view may be a carryover from my home environment—

though it certainly has some basis in fact. I'm firmly convinced that my ultimate decision is wise, and that this will be my permanent home.

But I'm still intrigued by that unconscious, hesitant voice that says, "Perhaps you shouldn't...." And it finds expression in the minor—though major—fact that I didn't bring all my things with me. I explain this to myself by thinking I'll wait until I've been accepted as a permanent member. But it's weighing on my conscience, and I already regret not bringing everything along. On the other hand, it's a pity there are so many things I like that I won't ever be using again. I now sense in myself the elemental battle with egoistic inclinations that every person—regardless of ideology—must wage upon parting from something he likes and is accustomed to. And on a lower level—from something he simply knows is his.

January 2, 1942

I'll try to write a bit, though my hands are nearly frozen. Outside— a fearful storm. Five tents were blown down during the night. Ours didn't collapse, but the wind is howling around it on all sides, sand has covered everything, and my bed is rocking ceaselessly with a monotonous beat.

Today is my Sabbath, my day off. I've wrapped one rag on top of another around myself and am now in one of the rooms, since it's impossible to remain in the tent. I want to write about the past year. Without noticing, we stepped into 1942.

It is a gray, rainy day that depresses one's very soul, and though the rain doesn't penetrate the room, it robs me of the incentive to do anything.

It's difficult to believe this gray, dismal rain will ever stop—and the same applies to the war. It doesn't touch us, yet locks us in our rooms and denies us our peace of mind—though we do not suffer from it the way the peoples of Europe are suffering. It's hard to imagine that spring and sunshine will come again, and difficult even in this little house to do anything, to clean it, pretty it up a bit. One just doesn't have the desire to do anything. It's possible that the rain will come in, that there may be leaks. But who wants to go out in the pouring rain to build, to mend, to do?

In any event, I'll concentrate on personal matters. This past year I decided on my direction for the future. I chose to affiliate myself with a Working Youth Kibbutz—with Sdot Yam. At the moment I want to examine the "little things" that determine the character of the kibbutz. To achieve concreteness in life I want to see minor matters realistically in order to achieve the great ideal.

I am tormented by grave doubts concerning my work. I stand on my feet nine hours daily, washing clothes. And I ask myself, is this my purpose in life? I'm willing to do this kind of work but feel my potential is wasted, and this is extremely depressing. While this may be purely a period of transition, still, it's been nearly three years since I arrived in the Land—the most fruitful years of development, of study, important years in the school of life, decisive years. Did I achieve everything I could and should have? This is not just my personal worry. It is also that of tens of thousands of young Jews. But each must fight his own battle.

Certainly by choosing Sdot Yam I picked one of the most difficult kibbutzim, both socially and economically. At the same time, I feel it's a worthwhile project, and I have every intention of devoting my best possible efforts and abilities to this settlement. I hope I succeed.

About Mother and my brother I have nothing to say. It's hard to write even a single word about them. The great distance that separates us worries me, and there are times I can't believe we'll ever meet again. Common sense tells me we will, but at the moment this isn't enough.

January 7, 1942

It's difficult for me to write. My hands are nearly frozen after a day of washing. I work in the laundry regularly, and even in this work one can find some interest and satisfaction. But the days are much too short. After a day's work I have neither the time nor the strength to read, study, or pursue social contacts. There's time for a little of everything, but not enough to do anything thoroughly.

Yesterday a closed session was held on cultural matters. I was invited too, and they wanted to elect me to be on the Committee for Cultural Activities. I thought that at the beginning I would not participate in any specific project or serve on committees. I consider it a sign of weakness that they have no one for the job other than a member who has been in the group only a very short while. But at the same time I see there are not many who are both willing and qualified to serve in this field, so perhaps I had better accept the assignment.

As far as my social integration is concerned—it's too soon to tell. I'm still almost a complete stranger here, meeting members only at work or at meals. Of course a good deal depends upon me, but I want to use my free time to read and study.

I'm reading an excellent book by Maxim Gorky, *The Mother*, and I've begun Kant's *On Absolute Peace*. I've also got hold of a copy of *The Communist Manifesto* but haven't finished it yet. No time.

Miryam visited me. We were delighted to see each other. It was good to talk to someone freely and in detail. She's the only person in the Land with whom I can discuss everything that concerns me, and who understands. Sometimes I look about me and realize how very alone I am among my colleagues and acquaintances. I wonder if everyone feels this way, or am I unique? I read my poem "Kibbutz Ginosar" to Miryam.

January 15, 1942

I don't really feel like writing. I've observed many aspects of life here and am hesitant about reacting to them in writing, or expressing definite opinions. The most difficult issue is the group. I dislike saying so, but I think there is a lack of companionship here, especially for me. I hope in time I'll find a compatible group, but at this time the members are not a unified group. They are strangers to each other, and the areas of contact between them are not positive. There is considerable apathy, a lack of responsibility, little or no individual pocket money, and a certain amount of inequality. There is also insufficient economic organization.

Of course the group can't be blamed for everything, nor can any-one be certain that others could have done better, or even as well, under the circumstances. Nor do all of these facts disillusion me in the least. It's just that I want to see things clearly and to help improve matters as best I can.

Possibly my standards and demands are at times exaggerated. Kibbutz life can't be imagined without daily comparison between what it actually is, and the idealistic picture of it and its principles. There is one of two things: either the principles are correct and must be realized—or, to be more exact, become a reality in our daily life—or, on the other hand, if we are incapable of realizing the ideals and principles, it is a sign they are impractical and must be reassessed from a realistic point of view.

I hate the mock holiness that enfolds certain principles and is expressed solely in the fact that no one disputes them—though they don't put them to practice. There is no fixed law in kibbutz life; the struggles of daily life determine its course. But to impose certain rules and conditions and then not follow them—this, as far as I'm concerned, has little value.

Perhaps my original approach—both to the kibbutz and to Nahalal—was too idealistic. There, too, I immediately noticed mistakes and planned to rectify them. It was only toward the end that I realized one couldn't mend or alter things.

Of course this situation can't be compared with that one. Here life is normal and natural, and in the short time I've been here, I've already noticed how much one can do if one is willing and able. I don't really have anything to complain about. One must take life as it comes. I don't feel the least bit disappointed or disillusioned, depressed or frightened. This is simply a detached view of things as I find them.

January 31, 1942

This afternoon we held memorial services for a member of the settlement who was drowned at sea a few days ago when his boat capsized in a storm. This was a warning for the future. The sea is a merciless, cruel tyrant, and it demands, and will continue to demand, sacrifices from those who want to conquer it. This was simply expressed in the service today, and thus deeply moving.

I work in the laundry all the time; in fact one day I even worked outside the settlement doing laundry in a private home. Viewed from a distance (I worked there several days ago), it's difficult to describe my feelings. At first I felt some trepidation, simply because of the hard work entailed and the responsibility. Then I felt strange because of the nature of the work, and also because I was serving in a private home—and as a laundress at that, the meanest of all forms of housework. I thought of Mother and my home and felt a certain pride. Why? After all, I'm quite aware that thousands of girls have had to leave well-to-do homes and do hard work. But they were forced to do so by circumstances beyond their control, and constantly attempt to improve their situation. But we, at least, have the satisfaction (which may be entirely imaginary) of freedom of choice, idealistic justification, and a goal. At any rate, my fears were unfounded. Though it certainly wasn't an easy day's work—eight and a half consecutive hours of washing—they were satisfied with my work and very kind, and paid me 35 *grush*. I was in a wonderful mood all the way home, singing and laughing. There was a feeling of enormous satisfaction in knowing that if I must I can do even that.

Of course that was just one day. I couldn't possibly do such work indefinitely—physically or mentally. Working in the laundry here is less unattractive, and I can't say this kind of work gives me any special satisfaction. After work I'm tired and either have visitors, or eat in the dining room, which leaves little free time for reading and writing.

This evening I'm in charge of the children's building, thus have time to write in my diary and perhaps to add a bit to my play, which is progressing slowly. During the day I sometimes think, how shall I cast Yehudit? What do I do on stage while she's off stage? But all this is pushed aside by workday preoccupations.

I think a lot about my brother and about Mother. I have a dreadful fear I'll never see them again. Or if I ever do—when? At such moments I feel an overwhelming obligation to the Land, to do

something great and important for it, for the kibbutz, in order to justify, in some measure, the sacrifice of having left my family.

February 4, 1942

I've just returned from a short visit to Caesarea. It was my second
time there, and I was more impressed with the site than ever. The
infinite horizon, the sea.... As one sits by the sea one thinks of the
world's past and contemplates its future; one's scope broadens, one's
determination to achieve something great and beautiful strengthens.
For various reasons the atmosphere of the group there is now much
more intimate and unified.

In the morning I strolled among the ancient ruins, in the afternoon in our fields—or, to be more exact, where our fields will eventually be. And when I watched the waves storming the coast with
foaming fury, and then saw how silent and placid they became when
they broke on the beach, I thought, perhaps our enthusiasm and
fumings are no different. When the waves pound in they are full of
virility and vigor. When they reach the shore they are broken and
tamed, and play in the golden sand like good little children.

February 9, 1942

I made a mistake. I spoke up at several general meetings and discussions. Now I'm very sorry. I'm sure most of the members see this as
a desire to be conspicuous, which won't make my acceptance by the
group any easier. It's always more difficult to mend fences than to
break them.

It seems that estimations of my character pass through three phases:
the first impression is very good but entirely wrong. In this one I
include all superficial acquaintanceships and unwanted visitors. In
the second phase the impression takes a turn for the worse, and in
the third phase they get to know me as I really am. But not many
get that far.

Here in the Land, only Miryam really knows me. Here in the settlement, I think I've reached the second phase. It's hard to explain

the basis for my feelings, but I sense a coldness and a lack of trust. The cause is obvious: either they think I'm very naïve, or take me for a chatterbox who arrogantly talks big about things she can never realize. They think my initial enthusiasm and activity will wane as I encounter reality. Naturally, no one has said any of this to me, but I'm sensitive enough to feel it. How shall I react to all this? I've decided to be careful what I say, otherwise to do nothing. Eventually people will get to know me as I am, and will judge me accordingly— neither for better nor for worse.

Sometimes I ask myself whether I care what the people here think of me. But what is of paramount importance is that my estimate of myself be clear. As far as I'm concerned, I really know all my faults and inadequacies. Of course I'd be lying if I said I was not aware of my good traits as well. The words of Ady, the great Hungarian poet, ring in my ears: "I'd love to be loved." The second half of the line— "to belong to someone"—there is no question of at all. I still don't see anyone.

Today I washed a hundred and fifty pairs of socks. I thought I'd go mad. No, that's not really true. I didn't think of anything. I worked automatically, without any regard for time, without a thought in my head. I said to myself a thousand times, "Hannah, you must think. Hannah, you must plan what to do, what to study, what to read." I'd begin to think but couldn't concentrate, and after a few moments my mind would be blank again.

March 28, 1942

I nearly stopped writing recently. The reason is very simple. Lack of time. This means the day has only twenty-four hours, which is just not enough time for everything I have to do. I leave for work in Yagur at 6 a.m., return at 6 p.m., shower. We read a chapter of the Old Testament. Supper. Afterwards a study group, or a meeting, or some form of activity sponsored by the Movement. No books, little time for thought. I must confess that since the seventh grade my intellectual development has stopped. I've acquired experience, however, and perhaps that's more important than reading. But it doesn't really penetrate. Sometimes I feel as light as a soap bubble that gleams colorfully on the outside, is empty inside, gradually expands until if finally bursts, and then reveals it was filled only with air, nothing inside. Nothing at all.

It's horrible that I've lost the habit of reading. I can no longer concentrate on a book, and don't miss it. Only when I talk of books am I aware how I've fallen behind in this area, even more so than the most primitive members of the settlement. This sense of shame prods me to read beyond my need to read. I start reading but soon stop. My thoughts branch out in a thousand directions. When I choose a certain book I feel dissatisfied because I feel tense, and despite it I promised to become a group leader in the Youth Movement. When they suggested this work I happily accepted. I know it's not going to be easy, and it's doubtful I'll succeed, but I feel it's my duty and an obligation. I may fail, but I must try. Youth leadership will offer me a great deal.

About my writing—there's nothing I can say. I've written a few poems while waiting for rides during vacations, as only then do I have some spare time and a few quiet hours to devote to such things. I've stopped work on the play all together. All I can manage to write are a few letters.

I often recall *Tycho de Bracho's Road to God* by Max Brod. I see myself in Tycho's footsteps on this Jewish road, and even if I should prefer Keppler's road—isolation from the world, egotism, and spiritual aristocracy—I could never follow it. For the primary aim and purpose in life is truth—not purely for its own sake, but as it is reflected in our lives. This may be the wrong way. It may be that everyone looking out for his own interests is the natural way. These are dim words, I know. It's true the selfish way is the natural one, but Judaism did not choose the natural way, but the reverse—upstream—and therein lies the difficulty. I recall my talks with Josef. He taught me to see these directions.

My home—it is so distant. Peace—it's hard to even write about it now. We live for each moment. As far as plans are concerned, they are only for after the war. What will happen in the meanwhile? Nobody talks about that.

Enough. I'm tired. I'm going to sleep. Just a word more about the kibbutz. I'm more convinced than ever it's the proper way of life, basically justified. There are many hardships along the way. It will probably pass through many more phases before it can satisfy the broad strata of society. But the framework is sound, and everything else depends upon the people—the value of the content with which they can fill the framework.

April 22, 1942

Yesterday I received a letter from home. It's so difficult.

I work at Kibbutz Yagur. I once began to note this and stopped. Briefly, work is from six to six; at six I return, shower, change. At seven we—a small group—read a chapter of the Old Testament, Isaiah; then, supper. Even if the rest of the evening is free, fatigue precludes any serious activity. The most important work I do in my free time is for the Movement, though I find this very difficult, since I lack experience. But it does a lot for me, satisfies me. This is the first time I've had to deal with something that presents problems: I'm contending with live material and constantly feel a measure of success or failure.

I've given considerable thought to enlistment. The entire country is being asked to mobilize for the war effort, as the war is coming closer. Although I have enlisted in the working front of the kibbutz, and know it is no less important or difficult than the recruitment of girls for the army, I nevertheless feel as if I'm failing to fulfill my duty. Perhaps the reason for this is that on the kibbutz the war effort has not yet reached its peak. In any case, many girls can't join the army. Those who can, who have no family ties, ought to join. I'm thinking of enlisting—not in the British army but in the Home Guard. Though army service is more interesting, what is important at the moment is the assurances that these guard units serve to protect the Land directly; the army can leave the country at any moment.

It's hard to write about everything, as my thinking is still subject to changes, and I still don't have positive opinions about things. It's understandable I have no special inclination for army service, but that's not the issue. I'm positive I ought to enlist. If I were engaged in some form of work connected with the war effort—farming or war production—I might feel otherwise. But presently my work offers little in this respect.

May 16, 1942

Since my last entry, a few changes have taken place concerning my status in the group. First, in connection with the draft: they've elected me to the group's Recruitment Committee. But even more important, I was proposed as a candidate for recruitment in the Palmach.[57] Of course I proposed my own candidacy, but everyone was ready to agree to it in terms of my suitability. They objected only to the fact that I was so new to the settlement. Besides, they wanted me for another job.

After a long debate they elected me supply officer of the kibbutz as well. At first I objected strongly, but in the end I had to agree, and they convinced me, to some extent, that I should at least try. I don't know myself whether I'm suited to this work, but I'll see. I'm starting together with another girl, and hope we'll make a go of it together. I discovered two things during the election: (a) there is a lack of girls on the settlement, (b) the decent behavior of the settlement toward me, or, to be more exact, that the members trust me. This pleases me very much, of course.

Now I'll have more time. I'll continue working for the Movement too. I find the work very rewarding.

June 2, 1942

Just a sentence from *Broken Grindstones* by H. Hazaz: "All the darkness can't extinguish a single candle, yet one candle can illuminate all its darkness."

July 6, 1942

There are days when the end seems imminent—the end of all our work. The question is, how will we end? How will we sign off? The

Germans are at the gates of Alexandria. Why and from where these false hopes of mine that we'll escape? Nevertheless, I can't believe that everything around is doomed to destruction. And not because I feel so deeply, internally bound to the Land, but because I see a healthy nucleus amid all the confusion. And it's impossible that there can be total destruction, that it can all end. Perhaps this will only be a fire to purge dissension and disunity....

Aged twenty-one, August 22, 1942

"I'm well, only my hair has turned a bit gray," Mother writes. It is obvious between the lines why her hair has turned gray. How long will all this go on? The mask of comedy she wears, and those dear to her so far away? Sometimes I feel a need to recite the Yom Kippur confession: I have sinned, I have robbed, I have lied, I have offended—all these sins combined, and all against one person. I've never longed for her the way I long for her now. I'm so overwhelmed with this need for her at times, and with the constant fear that I'll never see her again. I wonder, can I bear it?

October 1, 1942

I've skipped some dates. I've been in the Land three years. It's Rosh Hashanah. I've stopped for a moment to contemplate these three years, to dwell upon the past year and think about the coming one. But it is difficult to summarize it all on paper. I'm indifferent to everything that is happening around me because of my ignorance of fact. I mask this with a cloak of silence. I'm often illusioned about myself, which outwardly appears as great self-confidence. In addition, I have a good share of stubbornness and willpower. Even as I write this, and despite everything, I feel a sort of positiveness that for me there is no other way—that even if I wanted things to be different, this way of life is the only one for me.

Actually, this past year I've become more certain than ever that this is right for me. But the question remains, what will Sdot Yam and the group here offer me? During the holidays I was formally accepted as a member, though I had already been included in all matters before that. But the members are still strangers to me, and who knows when this will change? On the whole, I'm contented. But so far I haven't found any true friends, people I feel really close to. Perhaps this is my fault. And who knows if I will ever find the right group of friends? As far as I recall, I never did, and the only really close friends I've ever had were perhaps G. abroad, and Miryam here. So in this area I don't have much hope.

The question is—will I ever find "the right one?"

Were someone to walk in now and sit beside me, I'd hardly be able to see him in the weak light filtering through the tin cover of the kerosene lamp. We couldn't even talk because my two roommates are already asleep. It's nearly midnight, but it would be nice to talk to someone, to know there is someone. I don't understand myself. I'm looking for something; yet, what I have I push away. I'd best stop. I'm beginning to be afraid of myself.

Sometimes I feel very tired, as my work in the warehouse and for the Movement demand great exertion. I would like to stop working for the Movement and move to Caesarea as soon as possible. Though I've become well acclimated here, I'm extremely attracted to Caesarea, and it's a pity to waste time here. But with us, things move slowly, and for the moment there is no possibility of a change.

Enough. I'm going to sleep. Tomorrow morning we're going on a hike with the children. I've got to stock up on strength and energy.

November 14, 1942

At the meeting of the Secretariat today my transfer to Caesarea was approved. I accepted the matter with mixed feelings, even though I've been vigorously fighting for the change. I know the difficulties in advance—a small group, completely unsuitable. But I may find my place among them. Anyway, I feel it's my duty to do something worthwhile for the advancement of the place. I still don't have a clear picture of what I'll do, but I'll do my best at whatever it turns out to be.

Caesarea, January 8, 1943

The long pauses between entries are indicative of my situation. Sometimes there's no ink in my pen; sometimes I don't have a light; sometimes it's noisy—there are others in the room besides me—and sometimes I have no reason to write. Sometimes I don't have time to write, and sometimes I don't feel like writing. Not because nothing happens—on the contrary, there has been plenty happening both inside and out. But I've simply been apathetic to everything that's been going on.

I've had a shattering week. I was suddenly struck by the idea of going to Hungary. I feel I must be there during these days in order to help organize youth emigration, and also to get my mother out. Although I'm quite aware how absurd the idea is, it still seems both feasible and necessary to me, so I'll get to work on it and carry it through. For the time being this is but a sudden enthusiasm, a hopeful plan to get Mother out and bring her here at any cost. I spent three days in Tel Aviv and Jerusalem trying to arrange the matter. At the moment chances are slim, but who knows … ?

Meanwhile I've been elected storekeeper. All my protests were in vain. I have no interest in the job, but no choice either. It's a pity to waste more years of energy and strength on something I so dislike doing, and which will hinder my development in other directions.

I'm ashamed of myself for complaining, but can't rid myself of the belief that precious years are being wasted, years that should be devoted to study and self-improvement. I'm confident that if I could study one thing thoroughly, I would be of much greater value to the settlement and also far more contented. Instead, I'm assigned to duties that I carry out with hardly any effort, and to which I can contribute little. Nor do they, in turn, satisfy me, or afford me anything whatever. How long can this go on?

"That's a lie!" cries another voice, "I'm studying, learning about life."

That's not true either. I live in a world of my own making, without any contact with the outside world. I live here like a drop of oil on water: sometimes afloat, sometimes submerged, but always remaining apart, never mixing with another drop.

I visited Miryam a few days ago. We were so happy to see each other. She is really my friend.

But I can think of nothing now but my mother and brother. I am sometimes overwhelmed by dreadful fears. Will we ever meet again? And one question keeps torturing and tormenting me: Was what I did intolerable? Was it unmitigated selfishness?

Once, when I was working in the shipyard, Eli asked me, just like that, whether I'm "good." I pondered the question. Perhaps I'm not good. I'm cruel to those who are dear to me, who love me. I only appear to be good. The truth is, I'm hard-hearted with those I love, perhaps even with myself. I can't go on. My eyes are half shut. Everyone in the room is already asleep. My turn has come.

February 1, 1943

How long can one survive without air? How long without food? And how long without social contact, without books? I'm experimenting with myself. I don't usually miss these things because I don't have time for them. But whenever I have a moment to myself, alone, I miss them.

Why do I stay on here, anyway? I'm trying to prove to myself that it's not merely inertia, that I really want to stay.

Ever groaning. Just a complaint I couldn't tell anyone about (had there been anyone to tell, it might never have existed), so I have no choice but to express it in writing.

Sdot Yam, February 13, 1943

I hear singing from the dining hall, a party for members of the Youth Movement. I have no desire to join them. I've nothing to do there. I don't know what to do when I'm with people.

Nonsense! The same gripe again. I don't know what's wrong with me. Loneliness is difficult, but so is contact with people. I don't like my work, and I'm annoyed that it takes up all my time. It's not worth writing about. If I could only organize my thoughts. But I've stopped thinking.

I often recall Scarlet in *Gone with the Wind*. At difficult moments she would stall until "some other time." I'm that way. I'll consider what life is about, the value of society, the purpose of man, the future—at some other time. At present—much work and little satisfaction. The place is beautiful, magnetic. I feel as bound to it as is possible in the short time I've been here. But I wonder—is that enough? I'm fearful of the moment my reserve will run out—my reserve of initiative, strength, and the will to give without receiving anything in return. I wonder if the kerosene lamp beside me can provide enough light? There are some bodies that radiate light without receiving a single ray from an outside body. Can I be like them?

If only I could see Mother and Gyuri. If only.... Who knows what I miss? Perhaps it's only fatigue, moodiness ... It's a pity to waste paper on them....

Caesarea, February 22, 1943

How strangely things work out. On January 8 I wrote a few words about the sudden idea that struck me. A few days ago a man from Kibbutz Ma'agan, a member of the Palmach, visited the kibbutz, and we chatted awhile. In the course of the conversation he told me that a Palmach unit was being organized to do—exactly what I felt then I wanted to do. I was truly astounded. The identical idea!

My answer, of course, was that I'm absolutely ready. It's still only in the planning stage, but he promised to bring the matter up before the enlistment committee, since he considers me admirably suited for the mission.

I see the hand of destiny in this just as I did at the time of my *aliyah*. I wasn't master of my fate then, either. I was enthralled by one idea, and it gave me no rest. I knew I would emigrate, despite the many obstacles in my path. Now I again sense the excitement of something important and vital ahead, and the feeling of inevitability connected with a decisive and urgent step. The entire plan may miscarry, and I may receive a brief notification informing me the matter will be postponed or that I don't qualify. But I think I have the capabilities necessary for just this assignment, and I'll fight for it with all my might.

I can't sleep at night because of the scenes I envisage: how I'll conduct myself in this or that situation ... how I'll notify Mother of my arrival ... how I'll organize the Jewish Youth. Everything is still indefinite. We'll see what the future brings....

May 5, 1943

Such a long silence. I wonder why. Hasn't anything happened? Or if it has, doesn't it matter to me? And if it does matter, doesn't it demand expression? I have fifteen minutes before work. So I'll write a few words.

My job remains the same. I don't like it, even though I appreciate its importance. After work—a bit of reading, a great void. I miss some good company, or, specifically, a companion. I know—just one bold step and I would find a companion. But not *the* companion. Or perhaps yes. The whole thing is so strange. The boys ... they're all right; yet, the same inner voice says, "Not this one." But does the one I'm looking for really exist? Or is he someone my heart and imagination have invented? Meanwhile, I'll soon be twenty-two, and who would believe I've never kissed a boy? It's silly, especially the way it bothers me. I joke with all of them, but I think I'm cold, heartless. Joking, joking—but something must be missing within me, or perhaps it's buried very deep.

I spent a few days in Tel Aviv and Jerusalem making arrangements for Mother's *aliyah*. There may be some hope. Who knows? I did what I could and am now waiting for developments. I hope at least the two of us will be able to meet. And perhaps even Gyuri.... How far off that possibility seems.

I write very little now, and each time I feel an increasing gap between content and expression. The barrier I'm incapable of crossing is the Hebrew language. At first I made light of this difficulty. I thought I would eventually overcome it. But today I tend to believe I'll never master Hebrew, know it the way I do Hungarian.

Is this despondency? When I walk alone on the beach, I sing; my heart is full and light, my spirits high. All is well, and there is no room for despondency. But there are times when I ask myself, what are you getting out of life? And the answer is, that which you put into it. And while it's not a little, it's not enough. One longs for something more. Not only duty, tensions, ideals—these are not enough. One also needs joy, happiness. There is so little real happiness that I've already forgotten what it feels like.

Yet.... No, no. I can't explain....

May 27, 1943

My entire being is preoccupied with one thing: departure. It's imminent, real. It's possible they'll call me any day now. I imagine various situations and sometimes think about leaving the Land ... leaving freedom ... I would like to inhale enough fresh air so as to be able to breathe it even in the Diaspora's stifling atmosphere, and to spread it all around me for those who do not know what real freedom is.

But these are all positive thoughts about the matter, not doubts. There is absolutely no question but that I must go. The hardships and hazards entailed are quite clear to me. I feel I'll be able to fulfill the assignment. I see everything that has happened to me so far as preparation and training for the mission ahead.

May 29, 1943

I'm waiting to be called. I can't think of anything else. I don't think there is any outer, noticeable change in me. I do my daily work as usual but sometimes feel as if I'm seeing things from a distance. I look at everything from one point of view only: is it or is it not necessary for my mission? I don't want to meet people. It'll be easier to leave if I don't. No. That's a lie. Now, more than ever, I'd like someone who is close to me.

There are some things one can't express. One tends to confuse them and believe that as long as one doesn't find expression for them they don't exist. I pray for only one thing: that the period of waiting will not be too long, and that I can see action soon. As for the rest— I'm afraid of nothing. I'm totally self-confident, ready for anything.

June 12, 1943

The settlement decided to allow me to enlist. I'll soon be leaving for instruction.

Aged twenty-two, August 24, 1943

I'm constantly on the road, or at courses. I'm leaving now for a Working Youth seminar. Sometimes I have doubts: will I fulfill my mission? I try to have faith.

I think I'm in love, but there are many difficulties.

September 19, 1943

I arrived in the Land four years ago. Immigrant House, Haifa. Everything was new, everything beautiful, everything a world of the future. Only one figure takes me back to the past: my mother at the railway station. Four years. I never would have believed the distance between us could ever be so great, so deep. Had I known…. Or perhaps I knew but didn't dare admit it.

There's no sense to all this accounting. I'm now in Bet Ruthenberg, a splendid mansion, spending a month at a Working Youth seminar. Before that, I was at another course. After this—I don't really know. Am I satisfied? It's hard to say. I spent two years in Nahalal, after that almost two years at Sdot Yam and Caesarea. Many struggles and considerable satisfaction, but always loneliness. No friends, no girl friends but for Miryam.

And now I stand before a new assignment again, one that demands great preparation for a difficult and responsible mission. Again a sense of transition coupled with strong emotions, aspirations, tensions. And the everlasting aloneness. Now it's clearer to me than ever that this has nothing to do with outside factors. There's a certain peculiarity within me, and a lack of sociability that keeps me away from people. This is especially difficult where it concerns men.

At times I think I love, or could love, someone. But ... there are many objective "buts" in the way, and I lack the courage to overcome them. Meanwhile, there are a few men who love me, and I'm thinking of Moshe in particular ... about whom I can say only good things. And yet, I can't love him. All right, at least my heart is far from breaking. But even so, there is something that terrifies me: I am twenty-two years old, and I don't know how to be happy. No longer can I recall when I was really happy about something, when I really felt happy, even for a few moments. I have a sort of indifference to everything.

I wear a placid mask, and at times I say to myself, What is this? Is this how my life is going to unfold? It's no longer an external matter but something within me. I have no complaints about life, really. I'm satisfied. I can't imagine a state in which I would be more content. On the contrary. And the assignment that lies ahead draws me on. But I forget how to laugh—to really laugh, heartily, as I once could with Gyuri while wrestling on the couch until we rolled off onto the floor, laughing about nothing but the joy of living, of being young and alive. Are hardship and loneliness to blame for the lack of that particular kind of joy? Or do I bear this sorrow from the time when—at the age of seven or eight—I stood beside my father's grave and began to write poems about the hardships in life? I feel I'm just chattering. However, this is necessary, too. Amid essays, speeches, and silences, it's good to converse sometimes, even if only with oneself.

I had a chance to talk with "him" yesterday ... but I left anyway. I wanted so much to talk to him. I waited all week for the opportunity. We chatted a few moments, and it was up to me to continue. I really had no reason to leave. Yet I did. I could not do otherwise. It's impossible to explain ... but nevertheless, I understand. What a pity.

I long for satisfying work. In the last four years I've done all kinds of work, not always out of conviction, always explaining to myself that it was all necessary, and never gaining any real satisfaction from it. I really wanted to be a teacher. If I had to decide today whether to emigrate to Palestine, I'd do exactly as I did. But I wouldn't go to

Nahalal. Probably directly to a kibbutz. Sdot Yam? Maybe not. The group there is too young for me. I refused to recognize this at first, and now many other factors bind me to it. Or are they imaginary ties? It's so difficult to assess them.

Would I enlist? Of course. Thus, I would do nearly everything over again.

In my life's chain of events nothing was accidental. Everything happened according to an inner need. I would have been miserable following a road other than the one I chose. No, perhaps this is an exaggeration. But had I chosen differently, I would not have been in harmony with myself.

Zionism and socialism were instinctive with me, even before I was aware of them. The foundation was a part of my very being, and my consciousness merely reinforced my instinctive beliefs before I knew their designations or had the means of expressing them. Today, as I read more and more in these areas, their inner sense and logic become increasingly clear to me.

Four years. They are rich with experience. I've learned so much. My present mood—I think it's the same sort of *tristesse* I suffered when I was sixteen and remember it now. I hope it's really that, and nothing more—and that it will soon pass.

October 2, 1943

It's been about a month since I finished the seminar, and I'm home now, in Caesarea. I've worked in the kitchen, the garden, the laundry, scrubbing floors, and now I'm on guard duty. It makes little difference to me what work I'm doing. I'm happy to be home, to see people.

I bathe in the sea, swim out far, climb up on a rock and enjoy sea, air, sand, new and ancient Caesarea. Afterwards I dive back into the sea and feel fine, just fine!

No news from Mother, but new immigrants say the situation in Hungary is still satisfactory. I've stopped writing entirely. The truth of the Hungarian saying, "He who knows no Arabic should speak no Arabic" has become clear to me. In order to write, one must know the language. Today I know that I don't know it. That's one of the things that depresses me. A lack of knowledge, a lack of activity. The thing I need is work I like and could do well.

A minor experience I had with some new members proves to me that the job ahead suits me. But when? Another year or two may pass before I see action.

Among the new members is one named Eli. I spoke with him when he arrived, as I did with most of the others. After a few days I felt he was going out of his way to see me. Today he openly stated he loves me even though he has known me just two weeks. I think if he could be just another member for half a year, without talking about love, and if we would eventually discover we have things in common, I could learn to love him. But when love is the primary topic, as of the first moment—I have no way of establishing rapport with him. He's doubtless an interesting fellow, and I could develop a fondness for him—but this makes it difficult for me to get to know him. Are all men like this? And is this their attitude toward all girls? Or is this blitzkrieg my special problem? Or is it that I, more than others, don't know how to react under these conditions?

January 11, 1944

This week I leave for Egypt. I'm a soldier. Concerning the circumstances of my enlistment, and my feelings in connection with it, and with all that led up to it, I don't want to write.

I want to believe that what I've done, and will do, are right. Time will tell the rest.

Hannah Senesh wrote the following letter in Haifa on December 25, 1943, asking that if she failed to return from her mission it be given to her brother Gyuri upon his arrival in Palestine. Her brother, however, arrived the day before she left for Cairo, and thus she let him read the letter quickly, then asked for its return so as to hide from him the danger inherent in her mission. At that first quick reading, and probably because of the excitement of his arrival and their reunion, Gyuri did not realize the letter's full importance—a letter of parting and apology from one who was leaving, perhaps never to return.

The letter is included with her diary rather than her letters, since it is the only intimation she gives of the nature of her mission and seems to belong here.

Haifa, December 25, 1943

Darling Gyuri!

Sometimes one writes letters one does not intend sending. Letters one must write without asking oneself, "I wonder whether this will ever reach its destination."

Day after tomorrow I am starting something new. Perhaps it's madness. Perhaps it's fantastic. Perhaps it is dangerous. Perhaps one in a hundred—or one in a thousand—pays with his life. Perhaps with less than his life, perhaps with more. Don't ask questions. You'll eventually know what it's about.

Gyuri, I must explain something to you. I must exonerate myself. I must prepare myself for that moment when you arrive inside the frontiers of the Land, waiting for that moment when, after six years, we will meet again, and you will ask, "Where is she?" and they'll abruptly answer, "She's not here."

I wonder, will you understand? I wonder, will you believe that it is more than a childish wish for adventure, more than youthful romanticism that attracted me? I wonder, will you feel that I could not do otherwise, that this was something I had to do?

There are events without which one's life becomes unimportant, a worthless toy; and there are times when one is commanded to do something, even at the price of one's life.

I'm afraid, Gyuri, that feelings turn into empty phrases even though they are so impassioned before they turn into words. I don't know whether you'll sense the doubts, the conflicts, and after every struggle the renewed decision.

It is difficult because I am alone. If I had someone with whom I could talk freely, uninhibitedly—if only the entire burden were not mine, if only I could talk to you. If there is anyone who would understand me, I think you would be that one. But who knows ... six years is a long time.

But enough about myself. Perhaps I have already said too much. I would like to tell you a few things about the new life, the new home, as I see them. I don't want to influence you. You'll see for yourself what the country is. But I want to tell you how I see it.

First of all—I love it. I love its hundred faces, its hundred climates, its many-faceted life. I love the old and the new in it; I love it because it is ours. No, not ours, but because we can make ourselves believe it is ours.

And I respect it. Not everything. I respect the people who believe in something, respect their idealistic struggle with the daily realities. I respect those who don't live just for the moment, or for money. And I think there are more such people here than anywhere else on earth. And finally, I think that this is the only solution for us, and for this reason I don't doubt its future, though I think it will be very difficult and combative.

As far as the kibbutz is concerned, I don't think it is perfect, and it will probably pass through many phases. But in today's circumstances it best suits our aims and is the closest to our concept of a way of life—about this I have absolutely no doubt.

We have need of one thing: people who are brave and without prejudices, who are not robots, who want to think for themselves and not accept outmoded ideas. It is easy to place laws in the hands of man, to tell him to live by them. It is more difficult to follow those laws. But most difficult of all is to impose laws upon oneself while being constantly self-analytical and self-vigilant. I think this is the highest form of law enforcement, and at the same time the only just form. And this form of law can only build a new, contented life.

I often ask myself what the fate of the kibbutz will be when the magic and novelty of construction and creation wear off, when the struggle for existence assumes reality and—according to plan— becomes an organized, abundant communal life. What will the incentive of the people be; what will fill their lives? I don't know the answer. But that day is so far in the future that it is best to think of existing matters.

Don't think I see everything through rose-colored glasses. My faith is a subjective matter and not the result of outer conditions. I see the difficulties clearly, both inside and out. But I see the good side, and above all, as I said before, I think this is the only way.

I did not write about something that constantly preoccupies my thoughts: Mother. I can't.

Enough of this letter. I hope you will never receive it. But if you do, only after we have met.

And if it should be otherwise, Gyuri dear, I embrace you with everlasting love.

Your sister.

P.S. I wrote the letter at the beginning of the parachute training course.

THE LETTERS

Haifa, September 21, 1939

Dear Mother:

I want to write you about my first impressions and about my first day in Palestine.

We landed yesterday about 4 p.m. A man from the Zionist Organization awaited us, took care of my luggage, and settled everything so that I didn't have to worry about anything at all. Of course it took a considerable amount of time to go through all the formalities and to be vaccinated against typhus. (Thus far it hasn't bothered me at all, and in about eight days I have to have another one.) Finally they took me, along with all my baggage, to Beth Olim.

From the first instant everyone was very kind, and I must say it was a most agreeable feeling to know everyone I came in contact with was Jewish. For instance, the driver who took me helped me to send you the telegram, and as I had to pay with Palestine pounds at the post office rather than with British pounds, he lent me the money until I could get some of my own changed.

The house where the new arrivals are taken is on the shore, quite near Haifa, a marvelous city with jolly, delightful people. And all about the city, mountains, the sea, lovely houses. It's all truly wonderful.

Well, to get back to Beth Olim. It's a nice big place, but of course it's not the most comfortable in the world. It's not a hotel, or anything like that, but a "home" where each new arrival can have a little apartment and meals for a few days, without charge.

After supper I visited Ilona (whose address I was given by Artúr Thieben). She's a most charming woman, and I felt completely at ease with her from the very first moment we met, thanks to Artúr's recommendation, and probably because of Father. But aside from this, I think she is friendly and kind in general.

I had to return to Beth Olim by ten that evening, but we decided I would spend one more day in Haifa in order to be able to see everyone, and also to do a bit of sightseeing.

I slept quite well last night, and this morning after breakfast I went by bus up to the Carmel. On the way up we passed beautiful modern shops, attractive buildings. Everyone here wears a skirt and blouse, so that it's almost like a uniform.

I have so much more I would like to write, but I must go now. A thousand kisses.

Nahalal, October 12, 1939

Dearest Mother and Évi![1]

I am so glad I can begin my letter this way, that Évi is already in the city. At least I know you won't be so alone, Mother dear. I received your joint letter today, the one in which Aunt Eliz wrote a few dear lines too. I was so happy to get it.

I'll write a detailed letter now, and hope that despite the existing circumstances you'll receive it in good time. I know, Mother, that all the smallest details interest you, so today's letter will deal with all such small things in order to give you an idea of my life here.

Let's start with the daily routine: the bell rings at 5:30 a.m., my two roommates begin to stir, and I get up as well. We have a wash basin in our room, so I can brush my teeth comfortably; get washed; dress in slacks, boots, blouse, a headscarf—oh, wait, the scarf comes later, since at six there is only class and for that we don't need a scarf. I pull my bedding off the bed—the mattresses are very good, and I sleep wonderfully well, using a sheet and a blanket. That is, at night only a sheet, and if toward morning I feel chilly I pull up the blanket. I haven't bought a mosquito net yet and for the moment don't miss it, since we haven't any flies in our room. But if you can, please send one, as I may need it later.

At six the bell rings again: we have to go to class. So far we've had classes in four subjects: chemistry, botany, general agriculture, and fruit gardening. Chemistry and agriculture are taught by a woman; the other two subjects by a man. How well each teaches I've not yet been able to judge, but I think our classes will be interesting. What I'm now learning in chemistry I already know. It's new to me only insofar as the language is concerned. I'll probably learn a lot of new things in the other subjects. We're about to have our first class in dairy farming, and nutrition (I think this is the best way to translate it) is also included in the curriculum. Of course there's also Hebrew class—and that's all so far. As you can see, it's diversified.

The classrooms are attractive, light, and there are about three or four of them in all. But this is really enough, because there are, all told, only four classes, divided into two each terms, "A" and "B," according to knowledge of the language. I believe I have already written that I am in 1A—that is, in the advanced classes. One doesn't stand up when the teacher enters the room, nor to speak and answer questions.

I've already been to the blackboard once—in chemistry—and once I answered a question in botany from my desk. Though the questions and answers weren't very complicated in either case, from the point of view of language I was pleased I did well. The relationship with the teachers is quite different here. One simply calls them by their first name, and the language lends itself best to "tutoring"; thus, the atmosphere is much more informal. The first class ends at seven, and we go to breakfast. The meals are all first-rate, plentiful, and varied. We economize on one thing only: sugar. For breakfast we have tea, tomatoes, butter, cheese, bread, one lump of sugar for our tea.

This week it's my turn to clean our room, so straight after breakfast I begin. First I sweep (everyone makes his own bed after breakfast), then dust, pick things up, and finally wash down the floor (it's stone). I finish all this by about eight. Then comes the red scarf or a big hat, black sunglasses, and generally I cream my face. Then out to the fruit orchard. The work there varies. In the beginning I picked olives for several days, which is easy but monotonous work. The only thing that makes it a bit interesting is that one climbs the trees. Recently I've worked very little among the olives; instead I've been fertilizing the vineyards. Don't worry, this work is not at all unpleasant. On the contrary. And it isn't even hard to do. I don't say that after I've worked for two hours and done a row and a half my arms don't feel tired. They do. But I haven't had any real muscle pains as yet. In the morning I sort olives for a while, which is easy, and I enjoy doing it. One sits comfortably in the shade, and thus one rests as one works.

We work outside until noon—that is, a few minutes before noon—then go inside. But from eleven-thirty on we ask at least twenty times what the time is, and at noon, hastily washed, combed, and with a hearty appetite—and as far as I'm concerned in the best possible humor (one can't generalize about this)—we sit down to eat.

There are ten of us at a table, each table covered with white linoleum. We have linen cloths only on Saturday. What we have for our noon meal is difficult to say; all I know about the food is that I eat it and like it. Exactly what it is, its ingredients, I really don't know. But, for example, yesterday's dinner consisted of boiled eggs in tomato sauce (cold), then some sort of warm vegetable-like thing with dumplings, a type of salad, and grapefruit. Today, some sort of mixed tomato-egg thing, but entirely different from yesterday's. Then minced meat, a wonderful green salad, a sort of cabbage-noodle— but much better than the Hungarian variety (or perhaps it just seemed so because I was hungry), and a wonderful cold fruit juice for dessert. This is particularly important, since we don't have water on the table, and everyone is rather thirsty.

After dinner one can drink water, but although they say the water is good here, they still advise that in the beginning, until one gets used to it, it's best not to drink too much, and to be careful. We finish dinner at twelve-thirty, and at one-thirty our afternoon work begins. Thus, we have an hour's rest. Yesterday I used the time to wash my hair; today I rested a while, studied, read your letters—the post arrives just at that time. Then at one-thirty, back to work in the orchard.

Today I worked all day in the vineyard hoeing around the roots, and we tied the branches. Believe me, it's a wonderful feeling to look at a completed row of vines, and the work isn't even hard.

It's not too hot now. I came at a very good time, as it's beautiful, pleasant weather. I can't even believe you've already got the heating on while we're still wearing summer clothes, walking about in brilliant sunshine. Only the evenings are slightly cool—as if to remind us that winter is approaching.

We now have lemons, figs, nuts, and a tremendous number of other fruit trees, but the season is virtually over. The real fruit season will come later. Here we eat grapefruit the way we eat oranges at home. We don't make a big fuss about sugar—we simply eat the grapefruit in its natural state, and it's enormously refreshing. I don't even find it bitter anymore.

At three we rush in for tea, because if we're not in by the time the bell rings it's more than certain we won't find a scrap of jam left, as the others will have eaten it all. And this is bad, because all we get otherwise is tea with bread—the poorest meal of the day. At three-thirty classes begin, and until then we shower, change our clothes, clean up in general. For the moment I'm in great shape with my cupboard—I don't know where to knock on wood! I have it all to myself, which is just great, since I have all kinds of room. Here's hoping I don't have to share it with someone. From four-thirty to six-thirty we're free, two hours that we spend in various ways.

Today, for instance, I did some ironing, studied, and am now writing to you. Yesterday, Susan's brother was here. He lives in a nearby village and works in this area building a road. Believe me, he's one of the lucky ones. A great many would be happy if they could do this, but there is a shortage of work. Of course he doesn't have a profession or a trade and doesn't know the language. That's the way almost all of them come, and once here they can't find work. Otherwise he's a nice, pleasant lad, and we've spent a lot of time talking together. If there is any sewing to be done, or more delicate washing, I do that during this period as well. So you see, those two hours are needed.

At six-thirty we have our last class. On the whole, I understand the lessons quite well. I take notes, particularly of new words, and thus things progress. At seven-thirty, supper, which is also good and varied. Afterwards, news on the radio, which I don't often listen to because as yet I don't understand it very well. Only what they say about France and Hungary really interests me, and the local news, of course. Heaven knows Europe is very far from here.

We listen to music, talk, study, and go to bed about nine-thirty. A second later we're asleep.

The reproductions have come in handy. We've made exhibits of them in the radio room. Every week we have a different painter or a different period on display, with a short description. I don't have much time to read. That is, I don't want to read in a language other than Hebrew, and that's still a bit difficult.

I see, Évi, you're completely occupied too, and what you're doing sounds extremely interesting. Letters I send Mother are meant for you as well, of course. Don't expect separate letters, and write when you have time. It would be nice to be able to talk a bit. I really would have a lot to talk to you about now. Even a four-page letter isn't long enough. This is relativity: for us four pages aren't enough; for the censor they are too many. But I do hope you'll receive this soon. I'm sending it by ordinary mail, since airmail is too expensive.

A million kisses for you all (I'm including Gyuri, since you told me you forward my letters to him). Send a good many of the kisses to Dombóvár too.

Nahalal, October, 1939

Dearest Gyuri!

I know Mother sends you my letters, but even so I'll write directly as well, since there is so much to write about.

First of all, I beg of you, even though you write to Mother playfully and jokingly, and embellish your letters, write to me about your life and situation sincerely and honestly, and let me know exactly how things are with you. From your letters I judge that you feel very much alone, Old Man, and that at the moment your life there can't be too amusing. Of course this is easily understandable in the present warlike atmosphere, but just because of that, write the truth about everything. After all, you know how much it all interests me, and perhaps it's good for you, too, to be able to tell someone frankly what you're doing, what you're thinking, what you're feeling.

I see that you too are very concerned about Mother being so alone. You can imagine what an awful feeling it is for me. But despite this, Gyuri, I must tell you Mother will be delighted if you stay where you are and continue your studies.

There is just one thing I want to ask of you, and I know, Gyuri, I can ask it in Mother's name as well. As I believe we discussed at home—don't volunteer for the army. Please. Mother, and I must confess I, too, would not have a single moment's rest if you volunteered, and Mother would never forgive herself for not insisting that you return home. I certainly understand the big difference between being under Hitler in Hungary and fighting against him in France. Even so, Gyuri, as long as there is any way of avoiding this step, do so, for Mother's sake, and for mine and for your own.

A few words about myself: I'm extremely busy. Even now I have time to write to you only because we happened to have a free hour from class. But this is beside the point. The important thing is that I am very satisfied and haven't regretted for one moment that I left home and came here. When one leaves work with a rake or spade over one's shoulder and looks at the Emek, the country's most fertile, beautiful area—thirty years ago all of it a horrible swamp—and knows it is Jewish land, it's a wonderful, wonderful feeling.

But I want to be honest. This work doesn't have just a romantic side. When I hoe, or clean something, or wash dishes, or scatter the manure, I must confess the thought strikes me at times that I could be doing something better. But wait ... I didn't express myself properly. What I actually mean is that now I see, truly, that this kind of work is not as simple as I thought. One needs knowledge of the craft, and above all it is important work. But understand me well, Gyuri: what I'm thinking is that perhaps I could do some other type of work better. But to be quite honest I rarely think this way, for I am well aware that these automatic tasks are only for now, at the very beginning, and that later on the work will be more interesting.

The following letter was written to the "WIZO"[2] Youth Group of Budapest.

Nahalal, October 26, 1939

Dear Friends:

I've been planning to write you for a long time, since I know you're awaiting news from me and also that news about Palestine interests you.

Even so, I find it difficult to write because I think you're expecting a comprehensive, all-embracing report rather than just a personal letter, and that is very difficult to give. Not only because a month is a short time to judge things, but also because in Eretz Israel one cannot generalize.

People, the way of life, regions, destinies … there are probably few places in the world where things—all things—are as changeable. The people … this is where it is least possible to generalize. I must be enormously fortunate because so far, I must say, I have met all very nice, kind people. I don't think this is entirely accidental, because one hears everywhere that even with complete strangers everyone is very kind, and everyone is very hospitable.

The first generation retains the characteristics of its country of origin. Of course customs and cultures vary, but differences don't cause any antagonism. By the second generation all differences tend not only to be ironed out but to disappear. I am pleased I can write you that the things generally said of the new, free Jewish generation here are not merely platitudes. On the contrary. One feels, not only in the sabras but also in all those who have lived here a long time and have appropriated the mood of the country, an air of emancipation. Essentially the majority here work under much more difficult circumstances than they did wherever they came from. But even so, I don't think there are many who would change back to the lives they previously led. Perhaps most of those who would are to be found among the Germans and Hungarians, but of course even here one must not generalize.

I am fairly familiar with many of the modes of life here, though I have not yet seen life on a kibbutz. From what girls from the kibbutzim tell me, it's a very close, pleasant, friendly way of life.

Nahalal itself is a *moshav* (village). They say people work much harder in a *moshav* than on a kibbutz, although there too the work is very serious. On the other hand, the advantages of *moshav* life—at least here in Nahalal—are the charming houses, running water, electricity, intensive and extensive farming and agriculture, and the feeling that it all belongs to those of us who work here. I must note that this feeling of "ownership" can be experienced by almost everyone in the land. On the kibbutz this feeling increases, and it intensifies when one stands on any one of the country's Jewish spots or settlements. In such areas you particularly feel this is our home, our Land—or at least that it will be ours.

Of course, here much less is said about this than was said in Budapest at the Hungarian Zionist Organization meetings, because here it is all taken so much for granted that it's not a matter for discussion, much less for argument.

As I reflect upon my experiences this past month, I have great difficulty choosing what, exactly, I ought to write about. It would have been wonderful if all of you could have disembarked with me in the magnificent harbor of Haifa and marveled, as I did, at the way it is situated, both the modern part of the city and the old. You would have been delighted, as I was, with the Hebrew signs on the stores and buses. You would have boarded, as I did, an Egged Company bus and been driven across the Emek through primitive, makeshift settlements of Arab wooden houses, flocks of straggling sheep, and modern Jewish settlements, past huge cacti and beautiful fruit orchards. And finally you would have arrived here in Nahalal.

Now I ought to lead you, by way of my letter, through the school. Of course this will be very difficult to do quickly, as there are three school buildings with rooms for the students, dining rooms, classrooms, libraries and reading rooms, and countless other communal rooms. So even if you were here, it would take quite a bit of time to show you everything, were we to include all the farmlands and orchards, the garden, nursery, forestry school, dairy, beehives, poultry farm, creamery, the fields and buildings that belong to the main house, such as the laundry and the wonderful kitchen. So you see, I really can't adequately describe all of this by letter.

I would like to write a few things now about the indoor life. We have a tremendous amount to do: six hours of practical and three hours of theoretical work, and preparation for classes. So not much free time remains. But whatever hours do remain after work are always pleasant. (Don't misunderstand. This does not mean that the time spent working and studying isn't pleasant as well.)

The nicest time is Friday evening. Before supper there is an *Oneg Shabbat* with singing and music, followed by a delicious supper. That night the gate is open until eleven, and one spends the evening any way one likes—generally very pleasantly. The Hora and other dances, plus songs, are part of the Saturday program, though at present the atmosphere is not very gay, since there are a great many Polish and German girls here who have had no word from their relatives and family; it's understandable that the general mood is somewhat depressed.

One day movies were shown here, and recently we went to a beautiful performance given by Habima, the national theater. There are also lectures given in the *moshav*, so you see there are ample opportunities to pursue a cultural life.

Sport is represented by a ping-pong table, and we generally play on Saturday. But then we have plenty of "physical activity," if our work can be classified as such. We prefer using our Saturday holiday for reading, resting, and taking walks.

Don't be upset or disillusioned by this letter. Perhaps you expected big words about the adventure of *aliyah*, and instead I've given you particulars about the life, just as they happened to come to mind. But these are exactly the circumstances under which we live here. The Hebrew language, newspapers, the radio, our work, our Saturdays— these are the things that lead us toward the goals we have all set ourselves. That's why I think all this will interest you.

With warmest greetings of Shalom to you all.

November 7, 1939

Dear Gyuri,

I think of you so much; you must feel so alone. You know, even when I was home I knew how very difficult your life must have been—alone in a strange land. But now I understand your situation even better, though I believe it is considerably easier for me. After all, I'm not in a strange land, and I'm not even alone. But even so, it's sometimes difficult, and at such times I always think of you, Gyuri, and that you never wrote about your loneliness, never complained. It can't have been an easy year for you, and you can't be having easy months now. Not even your friends are there, and because of the war, perhaps life has become more difficult from other aspects as well. I have now learned from experience how happy I am when news comes from home, or when I get a letter from you. That's why from this point of view I am not going to be sparing. On the contrary. Particularly as at present I'm financially quite well off. I have nearly five pounds, and besides, I get pocket money from the school. Actually, money is not at all important to me from a personal point of view, but very important in order to get you and Mother here as soon as possible.

You see, Gyuri, I have switched from the most sentimental to the most prosaic material matters. But perhaps it's useless to write about sentimental things. It would be wonderful to sit down for a bit—or for a very long while—and talk. Among the many things we would talk about and discuss would be the things it is so difficult to write about—not only because there are no words for such things, but because one is so stupidly shy that one is ashamed to write about one's feelings, even to those who are closest and dearest. For instance, I am ashamed to write to you that here, beside the typewriter, I've been crying. Though I could not tell you why, because I like being here and am fine, and not disappointed in anything. But I think you'll understand how it is just the same, and that what I really miss is you and Mother. Gyuri, I almost said I miss you even more than Mother because I saw Mother two months ago, and it's been so long since I spent any time with you, for those days in Lyon, although they were beautiful, were too short to really overcome this enormous distance.

Don't be angry, Gyuri, that I'm so selfish, and that I make it easier for myself through you, and thus make your heart even heavier. And I beg of you, don't think I am always in this mood. I'm just taking advantage of you, writing to you now that I feel this way.

Concerning your *aliyah*: I think it can be considered only after you've completed your studies. At that time, however, if your views have not changed—and I heartily hope they won't—you must come. Perhaps life is easier somewhere else; perhaps one must struggle more here to make a living; but whatever one finally does attain here one can freely enjoy. I think with a profession and knowledge of Hebrew, and with a bit of improvement in conditions, it won't be

Hannah at work at Nahalal.

so difficult, and I know that for you, too, other things besides the materialistic factors are exceedingly important.

Nahalal, November 28, 1939

My dearest, nicest Mother:

I'm so sorry I always have to write in English, as it's not easy for me, nor for you and the censor. But what can I do? Please imagine how beautifully I would write all this—and how interestingly—if I were able to do so in Hungarian, and thus be consoled that my letters are so drab.

I received your first letter. It took nearly two weeks for it to reach me; your second letter preceded it! I am always so happy to have news from you, and this time I was doubly pleased, as it brought me news that you've also heard from Gyuri. I'm sure you're more relaxed now.

Here the work continues. This week there are two holidays—which is very noticeable in the food and rest periods. Of course someone always has to work, even on Yom Kippur, as the cows and chickens don't fast! Those who work during the holidays get time off later. Though even I had a day of rest this week, as I had a temperature for a day. No one but I seemed surprised, as they tell me this is quite usual for newcomers and is considered acclimatization. As several of us had this fever, we were in the infirmary and had very good nursing care. I'm quite well now—the fever is gone—and hope there will be no consequence so that I'll be able to continue working. One consolation: while in bed I learned considerable Hebrew. Whenever possible I speak only Hebrew, and some of the girls don't even know I speak German fluently.

Now perhaps I ought to write something about the girls: First of all, Miryam. She is from Bulgaria, twenty years old, and a fervent Zionist, too. She arrived at the school a few days before I did, is very intelligent and kind. She sends you greetings, as she knows you already from our conversations.

Miryam is very thin and small, and appears to be somewhat sad and frightened—and perhaps she really is now, at least until she becomes accustomed to this new life.

Another girl is Judith, nineteen, from Poland, who is always laughing; a very pretty girl. She is like a little mother to me. She came to
see me when I was ill, helped me when I arrived, showed me
around, and so on. She is really very nice.

Then there is another Miryam. Her parents are from Hungary, and
she knows some Hungarian, but she was born here. Her parents live
in a *moshav*, and she invited me to spend the holidays with them. Of
course I couldn't accept, as I don't have holidays yet.

There are girls here from Transylvania, Germany, Czechoslovakia,
Poland, etc., etc. Oh, yes, I ought to write about Hanna, the director of the school. She is a middle-aged woman, and although I was
told she is rather severe, I have found her kind on the several occasions I've spoken to her. Perhaps she'll be severe with me later, but
thus far I've found no evidence of this.

Yesterday I had guests. Some of the girls came running to tell
me I had Hungarian guests from Jerusalem. I ran, as I thought perhaps it was Uncle Mihály Fekete.[3] But no. There were several
boys, and they brought me greetings from Ilonka in Haifa. They
are on a trip through Palestine, and they met Ilonka in Haifa, so
she gave them my address, as she knew they wanted to visit the
school.

A great many people come to see the school, as it's quite famous.
So with the help of one of the girls I showed them around everywhere, including the farm. They liked everything and were astonished at the cleanliness. The kitchen here at Nahalal is famous
throughout the Land for its immaculateness, and it is said there is no
other like it in the entire country. I'm sure the girls who work in it
are less enchanted, for it certainly takes a lot of work to keep it that
way. It is said kitchen work is not very agreeable, and the girls don't
usually like working there.

Oh, Mother, it's all so wonderful! I asked for a holiday, as I heard
new girls are given time off to see something of the Land. Hanna has
given me nearly an entire week off! It will be fine to go to Haifa,
Natanya, and everywhere else (this is somewhat of an exaggeration,
as you can't do much in less than a week). The school is nice and
everything is fine, but a holiday is even better.

Now I must get ready to leave, so I must end this. I send you a thousand kisses and eagerly await news from you.

November 29, 1939

Dearest Mother:

I've not written much about my work lately, as it has changed so from day to day that it would have been difficult to make a detailed report. I'm going to work in the dining room for the next two weeks and can already give an accounting of the first day's work there.

First of all, I must admit that my work now has very little connection with farming. These ordeals are sure signs of worse to come, and the kind of work everyone must do until such time as one is ready for the *haklaut* (farming) fields. So to return to the subject: I leave the breakfast table at seven-thirty, put on an apron and head cloth, saddle myself to the cart (it's like a big tea cart), and first take the cups from nine tables, then the cutlery, then the plates, then the platters, and give them to the girls on the dishwashing detail.

By about eight I can peacefully cast my eyes on the bald tables. But this does not mean they are clean. So I get a large pan of water, soap and a cleaning cloth, and whatever other cleansing powders there are (whose names I don't even know), put them on the cart, and start scrubbing down the linoleum on all the tables. The first three days of this duty I scrubbed three tables each day, from top to bottom, and upside down, including the chairs, and by nine, a prayer under my breath, started on the floor. On the first day I did a terrible job, all streaky and spotty, and didn't mop up the water properly. On the second day they showed me how to do it, and by the third day—today—I am already a master floor scrubber, familiar with all the excitement of floor scrubbing.

For instance, I know how it feels when one wants to walk across the wet stone flooring, or when the mop is wet and one wrings it and wrings it, and by the time one wrings the water out of one end, the other end has slipped back into the bucket. Or when one washes and washes the rag and thinks it must finally be spick-and-span and by the time one returns with fresh water the bucket is filled with the black water from the dirty rags, etcetera. In other words, I have become familiar with all this excitement, along with the wonder and joy one feels when one looks up and down the large dining room and sees it is spotlessly clean and that one has accomplished this miracle oneself. Of course this sensation lasts only a few minutes, whereas the exasperation lasts more than an hour and a half. In view of this, and despite all the beauty and satisfaction attached to the work, I very much doubt I shall make floor-scrubbing my life's work.

As these last operations have been undertaken in a blue apron and red head cloth, around eleven I dress all in white and begin my chores as a housemaid. I set the tables for ninety people, with one or two plates for each, knife, fork, big and little spoon, paper napkin, salt, soup ladle, and a bowl on each table for the odd bits of waste.

Of course this must all be ready by noon, including bread on the tables (someone else slices it at noon) and soup. Then comes the high point of the day: midst the jubilation of the waiting crowd I go to the entrance hall and ring the bell. Whereupon they rush into the dining room and within half an hour they've spilled, soiled, devastated—in short, made a mess of—everything I've worked all morning to clean up.

During this above-mentioned half hour I carry the food onto the tables, and once that's done, sit down to eat the remains midst the havoc. After dinner I discover, much to my sorrow, that every platter has been wiped clean at all the tables—at least all those platters upon which one might like to find something—and thus, with unselfish motives, I begin clearing the tables again at twelve-thirty, expediting the plates to the dishwashing detail. Once again, I wipe the tables, and with murderous efficiency spray the entire dining room with Flit. When I see all the flies languidly lying on the window sills (they have not gone to air-raid classes so have no idea how to protect themselves from such assaults), I put the murder instruments away, indifferent to the fact that within half an hour all the flies, with renewed health and vigor, will once again be walking on the windows, scornfully watching while I have to wash down or wipe off the tables and those areas of the stone flooring that have become muddy in the interval.

In a matter of minutes I put the cups on the tables for tea, spoons for the jam, and finally, with my remaining strength (don't take this too seriously), I slice the bread. This is done with a machine, the kind with which ham is sliced in the delicatessen stores of Europe. Of course I slice the bread somewhat thicker, and about two hundred slices at a time. This is plenty, no matter how much fun it is to slice, and it's very good bread. I must note that I've discovered the secret of slicing. It's actually much easier to do than I've been doing so far. Of course even the simplest work has its technical secrets—which one can't really be shown but must find out for oneself.

By the time all this is done, I've already put in more than my eight hours of work. In fact, it's already a quarter of three. So now I return to the nice new house, take off my working clothes, shower, put on clean clothes from head to toe—the kind you are familiar with at home. This isn't quite true, though, because what I wear depends upon the weather. Today, for instance, it's a beautiful day, so I'm wearing a dark blue skirt, yellow polo shirt, and sleeveless sweater; brown loafers and cotton stockings (silk ones are for Saturday only), and, as it's now much cooler, I put on a leather jacket. But when the weather is bad—wind, rain, cold—either a warm skirt, or heavy slacks, boots, a warm sweater, and a leather jacket. And in the event of rain, a head scarf. Which is certainly not what I can call the "old style," i.e., the way I used to dress at home.

Here the most usual outfit consists of boots, slacks, and leather jacket for men, and the same for women. I must confess at times it's very funny to see an old, fat lady in slacks and boots. At the dentist one has to take off one's boots and walk about in stocking feet. I can't say this way of dressing is exactly an esthetic sight, though on the young with good figures slacks look smart, of course. And as far as the men are concerned, they always bring Hungarian peasants to mind, as they wear the same kind of boots and leather jackets.

The following letter was sent to the Maccabee Society of Budapest.

Nahalal, December 18, 1939

Don't imagine that just because I don't write I don't think of you often. On Tuesday evenings I always think you must all be talking about us, and by "us" I mean those living in Eretz Israel, and it's a wonderful feeling to be able to include myself among them.

I must honestly confess that since being here I am considerably less preoccupied with the history and ideologies of Zionism than I was at home. But, on the other hand, I speak a good deal more Hebrew, and I am much closer to the pioneer way of thinking and living. But then of course this is only natural. At home we prepare for the *aliyah* and construct a foundation upon which we can build when we get here. I feel I brought with me a pretty strong foundation, strong enough to build a good and contented life upon; a foundation that enables me to participate in the communal work.

Perhaps after the tone of our discussions at home you'll feel that my letter is not enthusiastic enough. Perhaps you'll think I am disappointed, or that my idealism has cooled. I am not disappointed in anything, and I have not lost my faith in Eretz Israel. But I now realize that one must not always talk about a dream State when one mentions Palestine, since there are those who imagine the Land to be constantly under brilliantly blue skies, whereas there are days—such as today, for instance—when it's pouring with rain, the wind is blowing, and it's quite cold. On such a day they would feel deeply disappointed in Eretz Israel.

Yes, there is bad weather here too, and there are many economic difficulties and mistakes. But we are at home, free; we have goals; we have a future.

Nahalal, December, 1939

Dearest Mother,

Perhaps so far you've judged my letters to be superficial, Mother dear. After all, I'm almost always writing about what I do, how I live, where I've been. But I am sure you're waiting for an answer to an unasked question. After all, you made a sacrifice when you let me leave home, and I made a sacrifice when I parted from you. And now I'm sure you would like to know whether it was all worth it. Perhaps I don't have the right to answer this question yet. It really takes a good deal more time to make a decision, but I'll attempt to answer sincerely according to how I feel at this moment.

My answer, dearest Mother, is unequivocally Yes. I won't deny that there are times when I would give a great deal to see you all for a bit, or at least to have the knowledge that you're all somewhat closer. But at such times I think that a year or two away from you, spent in fulfilling the very reasons for which I came, is not too long a period, and try to imagine how wonderful it will be when we can all be together again.

It was worth coming for the sensation of feeling that I am the equal of all men in my own country (at the moment this last is merely a feeling, not a fact), for that peaceful feeling with which one can walk down the street without wondering whether the person coming in the opposite direction is a Jew or not, and for the knowledge that the smallest matters are not decided by the criterion of whether one is a Jew or not.

However, this factor—that there is no anti-Semitism—may not even be enough of an answer. The most positive answer is that a healthy, new Jewish life is developing here, which one can best express by stating that in the Diaspora Jews were sad if they had no particular reason to be good humored, and here, on the other hand, people are good humored if they have no particular reason to be sad—as people are in most lands.

Nahalal, January 10, 1940

Dearest Mother,

My work is smashing! When dressed in trousers, boots, or rubber apron, I wash down the cows. (I'm not a bit afraid of them. In this I'm not your daughter!) I think of my old classmates at home and how they would turn up their noses at such work, which to me now seems absolutely natural. If at times a cow, regardless of all the nudging and pushing, refuses to stand up or lift a leg, or is reluctant to fulfill any other of my wishes, I take advantage of the opportunity to speak Hungarian, a language not often understood in this area, and wish the cow that which in Hebrew I don't know anyway because as yet I haven't learned to swear in the language! But fortunately the cows don't understand either, and thus the relationship between us is most peaceful.

Today I really goofed with the calves. When I went to clean out their stalls I had to take them into another barn. Two people, I later learned, always do this work so the little calves won't stampede or run amok. But I, unaware, opened the gate and began driving them ahead. In one second the five little calves ran to five different corners of the barn. You've never seen such mad running about. It took my roommate (who is also working there now) and me at least ten minutes to round them up and get them into their proper stalls, both of us running around like mad. We really worked up a sweat, but it was actually great fun.

It was less fun, however, to trundle the manure "trolley." (Though this is a sensational contraption, equipped with carts suspended from a cable running from each of the three large barns, carrying out the manure directly to the cement-lined manure heap. Everything works automatically: tracks, switches, the emptying of the cars. But even so, quite a bit of work remains for us to do.) In other words, as soon as we got to the dung heap I sank so deep into it that I could barely pull my boots out.

There are three barns built of concrete: one small one for five cows, and two big ones for both the cows and calves—seventy head of cattle in all. Naturally everything is concrete, the walls half of slate, everywhere drains and conduits, automatic drinking troughs, so that it's relatively easy to keep things clean. And of course everything is so sparkling clean that it could hardly be more so in one's own dining room. Anyone who knows anything about dairy farming will understand what this means: we wash down the cows every day, and before putting down clean straw we clean the stalls so thoroughly that you can't find a single blade of straw. Every other day we scrub the feeding troughs, and the walls and floors are scrubbed daily. Of course there are faucets and rubber hose everywhere, so it is really very modern, attractive, and hygienic. Of course this cleanliness can only be attained in a school, and in the daily routine on a farm there are a good many things one just can't do every day. But anyone who has been trained this way, and grown accustomed to doing this in this manner, does attempt to continue doing so after leaving here.

I am enclosing a flower with this letter, sending it not only because it's already spring here, but also to take the place of that flower I would ordinarily take to Daddy's grave at this time of year if I were there. On the eighteenth[4] I'll be thinking of you, dearest Mother, even more than usual, if that's possible.

January 13, 1940

Dear Mother,

I want to write you about the last excursion, which was fabulous. The entire class left at six-thirty in the morning, singing, playing harmonicas, headed for the open field beyond. The good earth of the Emek had not yet forgotten the big rains of two weeks ago, so we had to walk through considerable mud. But this did not spoil our fun one bit or interfere with our enjoyment, and we unanimously agreed that this was a typical European "spring" excursion. The Emek is beautiful at such times, and we really walked through a considerable part of it until finally, at ten-thirty, we arrived at our destination, Mishmar Haemek, a very lovely and interesting kibbutz. The most outstanding thing to see there is the big Central Institute of Education, where the ten- to eighteen-year-olds from all the kibbutzim of the Shomer Hacair are brought up.

The children are entirely independent from the kibbutz. In fact, they have an autonomous world, with their own economy, dwellings, separate kitchen and dining room, and of course the school. The teaching method is entirely modern, and they lay enormous stress upon working independently. There are between ten to fourteen pupils in each group, guided by an instructor; the teaching is in the form of seminars based upon what they have studied and read alone.

They are studying subjects about on a par with work done in a lyceum, and also do agricultural work. Of course certain subjects are omitted. The smaller children, boys and girls together, also work an hour or two a day in the fields, and this increases according to age. The older ones work half a day and attend classes half a day.

We inspected the kibbutz, too, and I was most impressed by the children's house. One day when I am not so busy I'll write about it in detail. We ate our dinner (which we took along) with healthy appetite, and returned to Nahalal by way of long rows of Arab and Jewish settlements, making a wide, roundabout circle in order to get to them. It was interesting to see Arab and Jewish life side by side, and to see mainly that essential difference between them that stems from training in earliest childhood and from native environment. Or, to be exact, the lack of training of the Arabs as compared with the visible training and preparation of Jewish youth for the rigors of life.

It was completely dark by the time we reached home, and we were relatively tired. But it was a beautiful, interesting excursion.

Nahalal, February 28, 1940

Dearest Mother,

Distant ... far away.... One can no longer use old words. They have acquired new meanings with the new times. Today, when worlds separate next-door neighbors and the world's oceans are spanned by the love of united peoples—today one must be careful of the word "distant."

Perhaps the distance is great in miles, and borders have become insurmountable obstacles, but if I look at myself in the mirror and see my tangled hair I can actually feel your disapproving gaze upon me. If I meet someone for the first time, the thought flashes through my mind, "What would Mother think of him?" If I do something I know is right, I know you, too, would approve, and I feel that our thoughts are meeting somewhere, perhaps midway above the sea. I feel how strong and resilient is this unseen thread that binds us, and I feel how unnecessary it is for me to write about all this, for you actually know about everything anyway.

So is it possible to say we're "far" from each other?

What am I sending you for Purim? Just these lines. And the fervent request to heaven: Let the time come as quickly as possible when we will again be together, and letters and words will be unnecessary.

Nahalal, March 31, 1940

Mother Dear,

In a letter he wrote some time ago, Mike asked a question that I don't want to leave unanswered. But I don't want to write a separate letter, so, dearest Mother, it must be included in this one. Mike was shocked by the lack of religion among the youth here and asked why fathers don't take their sons to religious services. The question is extremely complicated. First of all, I must report that there is a religious element here. But let us speak of the irreligious. Under no circumstances can the fathers take their children to services, as this is the very generation whose only religion and only God is work, and this is its strength as well.

Perhaps this generation was also influenced by the agnostic or atheist movement of Europe, and instinctively cast off everything that reminded it of the Diaspora and of the outer manifestations of religion. Besides, according to the national structure the observation of religious laws is more difficult here than it was in the Diaspora, where, if necessary, there was someone to take over duties and to do the work when there were Jewish holidays to be observed.

Thus, the fathers are the ones most to be blamed for the lack of religious training. But now I must say that they themselves feel this drawback, and even the youth seems to be a little in search of religion. Thus, there is hope that between the two extremes the pendulum will find a healthy medium at which to stop. As far as I'm concerned, this should not be left to chance. There should, instead, be a complete revision of the religious laws. But to achieve this, someone should be appointed who has great religious authority, who could find the middle road between orthodoxy and complete atheism, and whose decision would be acceptable. As far as I can judge, the present form of religion is not observed on all points, which makes life here much more difficult.

An example: I heard about one of the Mizrachi[5] kibbutzim, where over a long period they dumped hundreds of gallons of milk on Saturdays because the cows had to be milked, of course, but according to the religious laws the milk could not be used. They no longer do this, yet no one from that kibbutz will travel on a Saturday, though they have no other holiday, which means being totally tied to the spot. Even if they did spend a Friday evening and Saturday in Tel Aviv, they couldn't go anywhere if they wanted to because theaters, cinemas, museums, etc. are all closed, and buses don't run on the Sabbath, either. Thus, they would merely waste an entire free day, which they certainly would not be pleased to do, no matter how great their religious belief.

Nahalal, April 5, 1940

Dearest Mother,

We have just completed a magnificent excursion, and I want to write you about it immediately so that I don't forget a single thing.

Last week I was restless and so decided to go to Haifa to visit Ilonka and the family on Saturday. Miryam could not come with me that morning, so I went up to the road alone, where a lot of my classmates had already met and joined forces. We waited a while, but nothing came. That is, nothing in the direction of Haifa.

Suddenly a beautiful car approached, going in the opposite direction. On the spur of the moment I decided to wave it down, and the car stopped. It was on its way to Tiberias, so three of us got in. We had barely recovered from our joy and wonder when we were already speeding toward Tiberias. I could write pages and pages about that drive, or I wish a fine impressionist painter would immortalize the constantly changing vistas that emerge around each bend, each hilltop. Here and there it is only an enlarged splash of color: wonderful green, blue, brown; in another place a tiny detail, a miniature, with little dolls' houses, fruit trees, gardens. We three happy passengers constantly exchanged glances, wondering whether or not to believe our eyes as the incredible beauty of the panorama intensified. Then suddenly Nazareth appeared. Blinding-white monasteries,

churches, old stone houses, Arabs, monks, nuns—this is the superficial picture one gets of Nazareth, and beyond this we saw nothing,
since the car did not stop.

We continued the journey toward Tiberias along winding roads,
up and down. That is from Nazareth to Tiberias up, and then all at
once, after a sudden bend, a wonderful blue springs into view: Yam
Kinneret, the Sea of Galilee. And on its shore the town, sparkling-
white.

Then from the hill a sudden descent: Tiberias, which lies below
sea level. Our driver (an Englishman with whom we exchanged
barely a word) put us down, and we would gladly have run right into
the lake, whose color, situation, surrounding hills, and vegetation
reminded me of Garda. We ate in a park, even bought ice cream,
oranges, and very fine white twist bread—all for about a *piaster* each.
After stuffing ourselves we decided to see everything worth seeing.
An elderly Jewish police "type" was standing in the road. We
approached him and asked what was worth seeing, and whether it
would be all right to walk about the Arab section—whereupon he
offered to act as our guide. Of course he was off duty, or perhaps he
was not even a policeman. At any rate, that's of no consequence. The
important thing is that he knew everything and everyone in town,
and proved to be a wonderful guide.

First we went down to the lake by way of the Arab quarter, and
that's a chapter in itself. It is composed of narrow, dirty streets lined
with balconied stone houses so close together they practically meet
overhead. The houses all have deep hollows and recesses where mer-
chants have settled in—though one sees rather attractive modern
shops as well. Still, it was strange to hear a popular English tune coming from a café at the end of a narrow alleyway. The same mixture is
visible as far as the people are concerned: modern European dress
alongside ancient Arab garb, and in most places the two completely
mixed.

Our guide took us first to an Arab-Christian cloister. But more
interesting than the houses and furnishings were the Eastern faces. I
have rarely seen as many wrinkles on a face as I did there, wreathed
in white hair and long beard. All this, along with the habits, makes

an exotic picture for me, though it is certainly not very unusual here.

After that we went to the Eastern Jewish quarter (don't think of this as Eastern European, but as the quarter of those who have come from East of Palestine). Outwardly it is a little more orderly than the Arab quarter, though here, too, there is plenty of scattered orange peel decorating the streets, but the streets are wider than those in the Arab quarter, and the houses roomier. Nor is the entire quarter as old as that of the Arabs. The inhabitants dress in European clothes but speak Arabic. Hebrew is used only for religious ceremonies, though naturally the children already speak Hebrew.

We also visited the synagogue. It is very interestingly furnished, square-shaped, benches placed along the walls and covered with all sorts of colored and checkered pillows and armrests, in true "oriental" comfort. In the front section there is an attractively decorated Torah shrine, in the center the dais for the rabbi, which differs from the European only in workmanship. There is no balcony for women, since only men participate in the services. After that we went to see the Ashkenazi synagogue, which, on the other hand, is exactly the same as, let us say, the one in Dombóvár. That is to say, nothing unusual. There was what we imagined to have once been an interesting beautiful synagogue, but it is now only a ruin (a few years ago it was destroyed by floods, as was a large part of the lower town); only a few columns, bare walls, and the Torah shrine remain. We could imagine the whole only from the carvings on the columns and the Torah shrine.

We didn't even begin to see everything of interest in Tiberias. But we didn't dare go any further, since we had wandered so far from Nahalal (about an hour's ride by car) and had to think about getting back. For a while we hung around the park in the hope of seeing the car we had come in, as its owner said he would be returning to Haifa and had told us to watch for him. But we waited in vain. My two classmates were beginning to get extremely worried, but I refused to be upset, and sat in the shade and sang. Perhaps this contributed to the ill humor of the others! However, the whole atmosphere changed in a flash when an attractive little car appeared around the bend with a young man at the wheel. My two classmates began waving at the poor thing, whereupon he fearfully stopped and opened the door. I then jumped from my hiding place and in a moment we had installed ourselves in the three remaining seats. The poor fellow hardly knew where to put his brand new hat, which had been on the seat beside him. He hurriedly slammed the door, afraid someone else would appear, but we assured him there were only "three little girls."

Our driver turned out to be quite a decent chap. We even stopped once in the Balfour Forest and had a little walk, then sat down, and looked down into Ginegar, which is just beneath the forest and is Jewish territory. The sheaves of wheat seemed very far away, a large part of the grain meant for fodder already gathered and stacked. After the romantic beauty of the Kinneret, the Emek stretched before us with its great fertile fields. Its beauty seems forever new, forever a thing of wonder to behold.

Nahalal, May 6, 1940

Dearest Mother,

I ought to give you the smallest details about a most beautiful and highly successful holiday, but because of lack of time I can only sum it up briefly.

Thursday afternoon I went to Haifa, visited a friend on the Carmel, spent the night there, and in the morning at about nine went down to the highway just under the Carmel that leads toward Tel Aviv. I quickly got a lift to Tel Aviv in a nice private car, the driver a most sympathetic gentleman who has lived in the country for a long time and was extremely interesting to talk to. Thus I arrived safely and continued my journey to Jerusalem in much the same way, all the way to the home of Uncle Mihály.

Uncle Mihály and his family received me most warmly, and we spent the afternoon and evening talking, with new people constantly dropping in, joining in the conversation, as the Fekete house is most hospitable.

The following morning we went with friends to see the Old City. I'll describe it for you in detail another time. In the afternoon we went to one of the city's suburbs with friends who have a car, and spent the afternoon and evening visiting. The next morning they took me through the university, and in the afternoon I went to Givat Saul to see friends, who then insisted I stay for supper. After supper we went to town to dance, and that was very pleasant too. Monday morning we went to the Bezalel Museum, where, apart from the usual Jewish historical items, there was a most interesting Chinese-Japanese exhibit. In the afternoon we went to Bethlehem to visit a very lovely old church.

Next morning I went to see the Tnuva Dairy Center. It was so interesting to see everything we do in such a primitive way being done by modern, sophisticated methods. Machines do everything, so one rarely sees a human being around. From there I wandered along to Keren Kaymet Hayesod, the beautiful modern building of the Jewish Agency, which I investigated inside and out. Then onto the garden of the King David Hotel—and nearly turned to stone in wonder, as I have never in all my life seen such a beautiful garden. But then the entire hotel isn't bad! In the afternoon I attended the conferring of doctorates in the amphitheater of the university, and afterwards went walking in the grounds of the Hadassah Hospital, at the same time inspecting the beautiful, modern building.

In the evening I went with Uncle Mihály and his family to a lovely concert given by the Palestine Orchestra. Wednesday afternoon we visited Rockefeller Museum and went once again to the Old City. In the afternoon there were visitors, and then a film. And Thursday morning I came home.

Nahalal, June 29, 1940

Dearest Mother,

Everything is fine with me. Sometimes I am even surprised that the day's tiny events continue to interest me. At the moment, farm work chases away all one's dark thoughts. I'm working in the hay press, gathering the fodder, and so on. I'm brown as a berry, and the pitchfork feels as comfortable in my hand as the pen once did. The best parts of the work are the overture and finale: driving back and forth to the fields in the tractor. But the work itself, with its monotonous rhythm, is good and not hard. The mule-stubbornness of the horses sometimes disturbs the monotony, plus a thousand small details about which I just don't have the patience to write now. Today's happenings do not encourage one to write about the little things in life. And about the big things it's hardly necessary to write.

I ask only one thing, Mother dear: be very skeptical of the things you hear—or will hear—about Palestine. So far there is the most absolute peace here; yet, one already hears entirely different news from the outside about us.

Nahalal, July 22, 1940

Dearest Mother,

In connection with my birthday, you ask whether I am more satisfied than I was this time last year. If I discount the most difficult factor, which is that you and Gyuri are so far away, I can safely say yes. I feel I have learned a great deal this year, even beyond school. And if I had to make a decision about school and *aliyah*, I would do exactly the same thing. I'm happy I can live here, and now I know that when I called Eretz Israel "home" I was not just using a hackneyed phrase.

Nahalal, August 12, 1940

Dearest Mother,

What the exact situation will be with the work and profession of farming, I don't know as yet. For the time being I can only generalize concerning the simple, physical labor, the village life in connection with farming.

Let me itemize: in the first place, concerning the physical labor itself, I have a new attitude. Instead of the statement I made at home before coming—that anyone could do the work as well as I—I now see that conversely, I can do the work as well as anyone else. I don't say this work absorbs me. Primarily (because the work is almost completely mechanized) I notice that while working I generally think of something completely removed from what I am doing. Naturally, this is not possible if I am doing some sort of absorbing work. But there are mechanical tasks that certainly allow this. On the other hand, lately even the simplest tasks have been able to completely hold my attention, and I am pleased if I complete my work well and fast.

The only reason I mention all this is because I think it is a sign that I'm attached to the work and interested in it, not doing it solely because I must in order to complete the work expected of me in an allotted time. Physically I feel strong and quite up to the work. Thank goodness I was not ill a single day this year, which is something few here can say. (Of course I must immediately knock on wood!)

Despite all this, and even though I see that physically and emotionally I am quite capable of doing this primitive sort of work, I am positive that over a long period of time it would not satisfy me. For this reason I am going to make every effort to familiarize myself with as many subjects as possible, and to acquire as much professional training as I can in connection with the general curriculum.

For the time being, I think my main subject will be poultry farming, which I'll study next term. The old dream—that perhaps there is a possibility of teaching in this field—remains unchanged. Of course I have no concrete conception, and these days one really can't make exact plans.

As far as country life is concerned, I like it very much. I like the peacefulness, the uniformity. The one thing still lacking is an intimate, satisfactory social life. As you see, I don't miss city life one bit. During the long vacation I didn't put my foot into the city, even though all my acquaintances are there. As a matter of fact, we led a sort of country life even in Budapest. As far as the city was concerned, i.e., life in Pest, we were barely aware of it in Buda.

I consider farming one of the most important occupations in Palestine, though there is need for well-trained craftsmen in all fields. But the country is basically so much more adapted to agrarian pursuits than to manufacturing, and because of its natural endowments has such enormous agricultural potential that one must consider it primarily an agrarian state, an industrial country only secondarily. As far as I can see, even manufacturing must be in conjunction with its agricultural possibilities.

Nahalal, August 15, 1940

Dearest Mother,

Day before yesterday I started working in the bakery. It's very interesting, nice, and quite difficult work. One can learn a great deal, and it's a joy to work there. We knead by hand, bake in electric ovens, and use either 65 or 130 pounds of flour daily (the latter if we bake for two days at a time). Two girls do the work, and we're relatively independent, though of course the supervisor, Lea, is present for the most important tasks, particularly when one is rather new. But even so, we're much freer and can make our own working arrangements.

Apart from learning Hebrew and baking, we are now engaged in preparing a performance (actually a sort of celebration for the recently graduated class), which is a lot of trouble, and as usual I'm involved in it. Gyuri is right when he says anyone who spends time doing this sort of thing is mad. It takes a lot of time, and I'm afraid produces few results.

Saturday afternoons we have basketball matches; in the evenings we go for walks, sometimes talk with Hungarian boys in Nahalal; but I don't spend much time with them because they always speak Hungarian. Now and then, just to please me, they try to speak Hebrew, but for many it's still too difficult. Occasionally we arrange big debates, they on the offensive, and me trying to parry the attacks. They are dissatisfied with a good many things here. They expected and imagined things would be different because they are the victims of the romantic Zionism of the Diaspora, in which much was promised to the immigrants and nothing demanded of them.

Here, on the other hand, life demands a great deal more than it gives, at least according to the vocabulary of Budapest, and he who constantly compares and weighs, who wants only to receive and not to give, finds it very difficult. These boys are now working for the peasants in the village, without pay but with keep, until they learn farming. This is satisfactory during *hachshara* (training), and I think after six months they are already paid a wage. If they find work, that is. The important thing is for them to remain farm workers in the villages, but of course many decide to go and live in the cities.

Nahalal, August 20, 1940

Dearest Mother,

Let's start with the work in the bakery. As I've already written, it's most agreeable. We start sometimes at six in the morning, sometimes at seven-thirty, depending upon the work. We roll out the dough prepared the previous evening, all the while working up a proper sweat as it's not easy to roll out nice, smooth dough from 65 pounds of flour in all that heat. While the dough is rising we prepare the molds, clean them, and grease them. Then comes the most exciting part: the shaping of the dough and pouring it into molds, which has its own technique and is not at all easy. (But by the third day it really went quite smoothly, which is pretty fast.) After that Lea lights the oven. This is the only thing we don't do ourselves, though of course she helps us in other things if we need help. But for the most part the two of us can do everything ourselves. We have a sensational electric oven, and while it's heating and the dough is rising in the molds, we do the necessary cleaning up. Then, with a huge shovel, we expedite the molds into the oven, which is presently my province. (As this is my second week in the bakery, I'm the one "responsible.")

While the bread is baking we continue cleaning up, and if all goes well we can even dispose of the "floods" without too much trouble. This is a repetitious, natural catastrophe. We first pour a quantity of water over the paved floor; after that we utilize every possible rag, broom, and vessel to scoop up the same water, all the while vigilantly watching to see that the water doesn't run from wet to dry parts (to achieve this one must be extremely familiar with the exact geography of the rooms, their hills, valleys, and channels). In other words, this is an extremely complicated operation, but at least the consequence is that the floors are eventually very clean.

Meanwhile the bread has been baking for an hour, which, during the summer, is quite a while. We finally take pity on it, and with the aforementioned huge shovel I extricate it from the oven. Once the fresh, brown bread is out—thirty to thirty-two loaves on the shelf—we carefully inspect each loaf, and if they have really turned out well it's a grand feeling. Of course if we bake in both ovens, the entire work is doubled.

The bakery's outstanding achievement is the *plecele*. This is Lea's specialty, and already a tradition. It is prepared from the ends of the dough, and consists of the aforementioned dough, oil, onions, and salt. The bakery girls eat the *plecele* while they're fresh and generally still warm!

Yesterday we prepared dough for zwieback, which is made of very fine, twist-type dough. Today we dried it, and now I finally know what makes grass green—i.e., how zwieback is made.

In the evenings, immediately after dinner, we have to prepare things in the bakery for the following day, which generally takes about a half hour. This is my work for the time being, and I'm really sorry I have bakery duty only for two weeks.

Nahalal, September 1940

Dearest Mother,

A year has passed since I left. Do you remember, Mother dear, at the station? That was a very difficult moment. I couldn't think of the future, of my plans; all I could see was you, and felt I was being enormously selfish and extremely self-indulgent. Perhaps these two statements are contradictory. But I was filled with contradictions. One thread pulled me here, before I was actually here, and the only other, but enormously strong thread, tied me to you. And if I didn't believe even now that despite all hardships and seemingly insurmountable obstacles we will all three eventually meet here, it would be very difficult for me.

It is not easy to discuss these things, and almost impossible to write about them. It's as if I wanted to justify myself to you, even though I know there is no need for me to do so. I know if there is anyone who understands me, who approves of my decision, if there is anyone who excuses me, it's you, dearest Mother.

But despite this, I still must, after a year, thank you for your courage and self-sacrifice, both of which made it so much easier for me to attain my goal. I don't know what to write, darling Mother. I would just like to kiss your hand.

Nahalal, September 30, 1940

Dearest Gyuri,

This is a rather disproportionate correspondence, as I write and you don't answer. But if at least I knew that you receive my letters, I wouldn't mind too much or begrudge the time. I would like so much to have news of you, to know how you're getting along, what you're doing. Write me about yourself, Gyuri, as everything you do interests me. And above all, is there any hope of your *aliyah*? Please don't lose your incentive or perseverance, despite the difficulties involved. True, this is easier said than done, but I know what a strong character you have.

But instead of asking questions, I'll try to tell you about myself. After being here a year, I can safely state I'm satisfied with the road I chose, and if I could see you and Mother here already, I could not wish anything better for myself. This statement is the result of many details, but the nucleus is that I see an objective, and a definite reason for my being here. I lose this feeling of confidence only when I think of the difficult year Mother has had.

I know the way I write about things makes everything seem almost too simple. But the truth is I find great joy in the language, and I've learned a great deal more of it this past year. Another thing: I've learned to really work. I doubt there is any kind of work in the world about which I could now say, "Under no circumstances will I do it." I've tried just about everything, from scrubbing floors to carrying manure, and nothing has happened to me.

However, it is now about time that I began working in my special field, and it bothers me a great deal that they've not yet assigned me permanently. On the whole, the school leaves much to be desired, though from the point of view of learning things, indubitably one learns a great deal. But as a boarding school it's like something out of novels written for girls of the past century. (Of course this doesn't tell you much, as you've never read any of them!)

As far as sports are concerned, there are only swimming and gymnastics. Here I'm considered a good swimmer, though the sabras swim quite well, particularly those who grew up along the seacoast.

I write about the foolish little things, as it is so difficult to write about the big, important matters. Thus far there is complete calm and security here in Nahalal, though in the cities one is more directly aware of the war. Despite this, I keep thinking that perhaps it would be best if Mother came out here. As far as an immigration certificate is concerned, I think it's easier now than it was before. What do you think about this?

Nahalal, October 25, 1940

Mother Dear,

I want to write you about my work. After all, I've barely accounted for it. At the moment six coops are entrusted me (there was a time when I took care of eleven), fifty to sixty hens in each. There are larger coops, made of concrete, but mine are very cleverly constructed wooden coops, the invention of our instructor. They are easy to take apart, to move around, to keep clean, and require barely any work.

In the morning I give the chickens fresh water—of course I first wash the pans—feed them (I think it is unnecessary to say with what and when) and leave them in peace to walk about and to scratch in the yards. I always find something to do—there is never a lack of work—until nine-thirty, when we prepare a mixture for them all (hens, pullets, and roosters), and amidst the greatest imaginable excitement I begin distributing it. I can hardly walk among the jumping white feather balls, since each would like to be the first at the feeding trough. By the time I finally distribute all the feed, it seems as if their necks are nailed to the troughs. They stand in double rows and won't move until every speck of food is gone. Meanwhile I fill the water dishes, gather eggs, and get extremely irritated because despite all my efforts they barely lay, since at the moment they're molting.

We keep an exact record of the eggs, a separate one for each hen house. We stop working at eleven and at two-thirty start all over again—feeding, watering, gathering eggs. The little chicks are fed greens, and since this is their favorite food, they nearly eat me along with it.

At four-thirty our work is done. Apart from the daily routine out-
lined above, once a day we prepare the feed, sometimes carry out the
manure, take care of the gardens attached to the poultry yard, and
attend to whatever other work there is about the place. We've already
started the incubation period—for experimental purposes rather
early in the season.

The following letter was written to her cousin, Évi Sas.

Nahalal, October 30, 1940

Recently we celebrated the first anniversary of my arrival. Based on
the foundation of affection and enthusiasm I had for the Land even
before coming, during the year I've been here, slowly, imperceptibly,
a true love has evolved, and I now feel completely at home in Eretz
Israel. I have grown to love the country, the people, the way of life,
the language, and village living. I see now that actually even at home
I was not at all a city person, lived in Buda as if it had been a village,
and for that reason even here I've missed nothing of city life.

Just what it is I love most here is difficult to say. Perhaps the endless variety of the country. There is not a plant, a hill formation, a
color that you can't find here. Beginning with the tropical world, to
the world of the Galilee, or to the completely European characteristics in certain regions of Jerusalem, you can see and experience
every shade and nuance here in a few hours of travel.

This doesn't apply only to the Land but also to the climate.
Besides, the air is very clean, the atmosphere clear, and it is possible
to see far into the distance. From Jerusalem one can see the Dead
Sea, and from every hill the view is fabulous.

The people? I don't want to write about the city dwellers, as I
don't know them. And besides, it's my impression that they are the
same as people are in all the cities. But let's take those who live on
the kibbutzim or the *moshavs*. Outwardly they are completely simple
and easy to communicate with. There are not too many "pleases" and
"thank yous"—or let's just say no courtesy. But there is a great deal
of kindness. Actually, they don't even feel it's kindness, but find it

absolutely natural that if you go to a kibbutz you'll stay and eat there, even if they never saw you before. You can stop anyone in the street, and he'll show and explain everything to you, whatever it is you want to know or to see.

Of course this kindness is not the same everywhere, nor with everyone. Don't imagine them as dear people forming an ideal social life. But I, from personal experience, have enjoyed so much kindness and hospitality from relative or complete strangers that I am forced to generalize a little.

But this is not the only good characteristic. One can say, primarily about the young, that they are healthy in body and mind. It's difficult to write about these general standards, as I'm afraid it sounds like propaganda or distortions about this new generation. As I write I can see my classmates—good-natured, charming, decent, intelligent girls—or I can hear the young people from the kibbutzim and the *moshavs* as they travel about, jammed into trucks, going on excursions, singing, or dancing the Hora; or I see them at a performance, and can honestly say I think they are healthy in body and spirit. But words on paper paint a rather platitudinous picture.

The interests of the young here are entirely different than ours were. The best example of this is Friday evening, when there is generally a concert on the radio. Boys and girls from the *moshav* are in the garden, dancing and singing to music played on harmonicas, while in the radio room, listening to the concert, the girls, almost without exception, are from foreign lands. We, of course, eventually join the singing and dancing sabras, but they rarely come inside to hear the concert, even though they are very fond of music. Many among them sing beautifully, and they all like to sing. Often during the summer we get together and have a song fest. There are very lovely Hebrew folk songs, and if anyone knows a new one he's the hero of the evening.

But they are not too fond of the so-called serious music. This applies mostly to the children of the *moshav*. On the kibbutz they are given a more general musical and cultural education, not to mention those who are city bred and trained. There is, of course, great interest in cinema and theater. For performances of the Habima Theater, the Community Center is always jammed to the rafters. The young are interested in the movies, older settlers much less so.

The most general cultural medium is, of course, the printed word. Everyone reads a lot and, for the most part, only in Hebrew. Thus they can become familiar only with that foreign literature which is translated. They are not too inclined toward philosophy, and ideological discussion they leave to us, the foreigners. But if one does chance to enter into debate or discussion with them, their opinions are most interesting. They have a definite point of view that they don't generally discuss. This "we"-"they" differentiation is entirely technical, and I use it only in order to highlight the differences. But in truth, we mix exceedingly well and as a rule are good friends. All gatherings are completely mixed. In many of the kibbutzim, the combining of sabra and foreign groups has been very successful. All of which proves that although the difference is considerable, there is absolutely no antagonism.

I like the democracy that, outside of my school, manifests itself almost everywhere. As a matter of fact, in the kibbutz and the *moshav*, democracy is not the right expression, because this is only possible where there are different classes. In the *moshav* there is no higher rank than *chaver* (comrade). Others who live here, i.e., teachers, doctors, and so on, are also *chaver*, considered in the same category. That there is no difference in the kibbutz is natural, as there is nothing better or worse than that which exists: total equality. Everyone lives in the same conditions, the only difference being the kind of work one does. But that, for one thing, frequently changes, and for another does not decide one's place or station in the hierarchy of the kibbutz. Naturally, even within the kibbutz there is a leadership, but this only differentiates responsibility and influence and has absolutely no personal advantage.

In the cities the differences are greater, and communication between the various social classes less frequent. This division is for the most part only on an economic level, as otherwise there is absolutely no difference between a capitalist and a laborer. More often than not they are intellectually and culturally equals. (The exceptions are Oriental Jews, who have become much like the Arabs and comprise the labor stratum. They are, unfortunately, extremely inferior culturally.)

The raising of the cultural level is a very difficult question here, and the supposition in the Diaspora that in Eretz Israel one must go about with a lantern in order to find an illiterate is, unfortunately, a myth. As there is no state school system, and no money for one, the matter of education is among the most important social questions.

Nor are the existing schools always on the level one would imagine. Of course there are first-rate schools too, lyceums in the cities, and in the villages good district schools. There is a very interesting and well-tested type of school here that parallels the lyceum and includes ten- to eighteen-year-olds. The curriculum consists of a combination of theoretical studies and agricultural work, in the upper grades equal amounts of time spent studying and working.

The lot of the teachers is hard in all the schools, as in many places there is no grading, and if there is it's not taken seriously. The children are afraid of absolutely nothing and no one, and thus the only influence the teacher has on his pupils is his own personality. There is little or no respect for authority, and many say the children of Eretz turn liberty into libertinism, self-confidence into arrogance, and candidness into impudence. I am not so pessimistic about things and think the foregoing judgment is extreme and superficial, the result of particular incidents.

I've really made great progress with the language and have had, and have, a good deal of joy from it. I am beginning to know Hebrew poetry and have been reading the poems of Rachel, Chernickovszki, Simonovits, Bialik, and Sneur. I had no idea Hebrew literature was so rich. The most valuable, however, is the Tanach (Bible) with which I was not at all familiar until now, and must seriously tell you it is most enjoyable reading. Perhaps it means more in the original, and it is also important to note that here the Bible comes to life. The Land, the people, geographical names—it's all in daily use, so one does not have the feeling that it dates from ancient times but that it is part of the present.

Of course all this is the shining, attractive part. That there are times when it's not all so nice and easy, you can imagine. But that is all fleeting, and the work helps one overcome the rough spots. You've probably heard from Mother how delighted I am with the work in the agricultural school. But I still maintain, or at least want to maintain, that I would like best of all to combine the work I am now doing with teaching children. My table of values is the following: I am interested in plants, but more so in animals, and most of all in people. I believe my thinking is quite realistic, because aside from the aforementioned schools, there are many institutions where children are taught farming, and boys and girls study agricultural pursuits.

When I begin writing I find a great deal to write about—but enough for today!

Nahalal, December 17, 1940

You're right, Mother dear, the longer I spend learning my profession the more interesting I find it. For instance, at first poultry raising seems very simple. You give them water, distribute the feed, gather eggs, and clean the roosts. What, you wonder at first, is there to learn? But gradually you become acquainted with the problems, possibilities, and reasons, and naturally you develop a different relationship to your work.

My two class- and roommates are following the same profession, so our room is called "Kukuriku."

We're getting ready for the WIZO celebration. I have a rather important part in the play, despite my Hungarian-accented Hebrew. Actually my accent isn't really too bad, and there have even been occasions when people couldn't guess my origin. But generally, after two sentences, Hungarians can be identified, and some can be placed even after just a single word or two.

As in Hebrew, the accent is at the end of the word, i.e., *ani RO-ca* (I want) and our Hungarians (those who are incorrigibly deep-rooted) pronounce it *ani roca*. This causes considerable amusement. As in my case the Hungarian intonation is not as pronounced, I was given a part in the play.

Concerning my first Hebrew poem—you see, Mother dear, you must learn Hebrew if you want to understand it. I showed it to my Hebrew teacher, who liked it very much and could not even find a linguistic error.

Hannah at Kibbutz Sdot Yam.

Nahalal, January 28, 1941

How can I explain to you, Mother dear, that there is nothing as fantastic or remarkable about my accomplishments as you seem to think. There are hundreds, even thousands, who take the same route I'm taking—a route that is, in many aspects, easier for me than for many others. I don't feel any self-sacrifice is involved because what I am doing gives me a great deal of joy, and at the same time few can say they live in such calm and pleasant circumstances as I do.

Perhaps for the time being I don't even have the right to discuss everything, as the school is still far from the typical life in Eretz, and it is possible that the years ahead will bring many hardships. But I am not afraid of them.

This past week I've been working alternately in the truck garden and the bakery. I've been replacing our supervisor in the bakery, as she has been ill. It's very pleasant to work independently like this, but still, working outdoors is better. Though at present farming is not too interesting: weeding, hoeing, picking and gathering cauliflower, cabbages, carrots, turnips, beets. These are the seasonal vegetables, along with many others. In fact, nearly all the vegetables are ready for gathering now. But whatever the work, it's nice to be outdoors, meanwhile thinking about whatever one likes. Even if one is ill tempered when one begins working in the morning, by the time one returns from the fields one feels fine, and everything is in order. (Or almost everything.) As if the earth and air drained away one's ill humor. Of course, all this magic lasts until one works six or eight hours, but I suppose it would disappear if one were driven and harassed.

Nahalal, March, 1941

Dearest Mother:

I know that during the eighteen years I lived in Budapest I was very contented and didn't long one bit for country life. True, I never did take advantage of the so-called benefits of city living, outside of going to an occasional concert or theater, or some other performance. And

I would be less than sincere were I to say I could not, for anything in the world, live in the city, or that if I did I would feel like a stranger and be unhappy. But this much I can say: when I'm in Haifa or Tel Aviv on holiday (I can't say anything about Jerusalem, as I was there only once and enjoyed myself enormously), I didn't feel unhappy, but certainly have no desire to live in either place. I have come to enjoy the vista when I look out the window, the quiet and peace, the uniformity and simplicity of country living, and I feel this way of life would completely satisfy me if I could have the right kind of people around me.

However, this is perhaps not a decisive point. The second point is the question of work. What I thought of in theory two years ago is now justified by practice: the basis of Eretz is farming. And I also see that there certainly is need of educated people. The concept at home— that if someone knows nothing better or wiser to do he should become a farmer—is completely erroneous. But I don't want to put the question from the point of view of "How much am I needed here?" or else you might think that I see a gap somewhere and am doing all this against my will.

Don't worry, Mother dear, from time to time I pose the same questions and seriously weigh them: Did I choose the proper profession? Will it satisfy me when the novelty has worn off? Will it satisfy my nature and fulfill my capabilities? And thus far I have always reached the conclusion that I chose properly.

I don't know in exactly what direction I'll continue, but I'm sure I will find the most satisfactory solution, because I'll look for the best possible way and won't be satisfied with a compulsory solution, or second-best. Of course, this depends also upon whether I'll have the possibility of looking for the right direction and of experimenting for a while.

In short, I feel bound to the work, and it would be very difficult for me to renounce it. Of primary importance however, is the third point: after a brief period here I discovered that the social structure of Eretz has many facets. From the point of view of origin and education there are no fundamental differences, or even if there are, this is not what causes the division. From the very first moment I naturally felt closer to the pioneer element, as from the point of view of mentality and manpower I find their way of life and their concepts clearer, more straightforward, and sounder than my earlier judgments of things in general.

It would take much too long to write about everything, but in brief, I would like to choose a road for the future that would bind me to this pioneer element. At the moment I've been thinking a good deal about joining a kibbutz. But if later I'm convinced that the kibbutz would not be satisfactory for my disposition, there are still many other possibilities that would enable me to remain among this element.

At the moment I'm working with little chicks. Yesterday, Saturday, I was entrusted with two thousand of them, but ordinarily I have only about four hundred to look after. Of course, taking care of this number doesn't fill my work day, so I have considerable other work as well. It's possible that now, besides working with the chickens, I'll start carpentry. Our instructor knows I would like to do this kind of work, as it's often essential and one can't always be running off to look for someone who knows how to do it, so he has promised to teach me.

December, 1943

Darling Mother,

I want to write about something important without any preamble. At the moment there is a real possibility for you to come and join me. I have taken all the necessary steps, and it's likely the journey can be arranged within weeks, perhaps even days.

I know, my darling, that this is very sudden, but you must not hesitate. Every day is precious now, and there is a growing likelihood that the road will be momentarily closed or that other hardships will suddenly arise. Gyuri will be here in the nearest possible future, too. I don't know whether there is any need for further arguments.

Mother dear, be brave and quick. Don't allow material questions to stand in your way. In today's world that must be your last concern, and you must have confidence in us that here you won't have any financial worries.

I'm sure, my darling, there is no need for further discussion. I don't want to ask you to do this for us—do it for yourself. The important thing is for you to come. Bring what you want to if you can do so without difficulty, but don't let such things stop you even for an instant. I just can't write of anything else now.

I kiss and hug you. With inexpressible love.

The following letter was written to Professor Mihály Fekete.

January 15, 1944

Dearest Uncle Mihály,

I know you don't approve of what I have done, and it is very difficult for me not to be able to explain in detail the reason I did it. But I hope you will still maintain the old friendship for your "soldier-foster-daughter."

My plans concerning my mother have not changed. On the contrary. My new situation will create certain opportunities that I will naturally attempt to take advantage of as quickly as possible. I hope, meanwhile, that Gyuri will be here too. However, it's quite possible that I will be leaving the country. Don't think for a moment, Uncle Mihály, that I am taking this question lightly. You know how I have been awaiting the arrival of Gyuri and Mother. Even so, I would like to believe I have done the wise thing. Perhaps upon another occasion I will be better able to explain the reasons.

I would like you, Uncle Mihály, to be familiar with the financial situation so that should I not be here when Gyuri or Mother arrives they will be able to have access to my money without having to wait for me. The amount that has been in my name up till now, according to the enclosed receipt, is at the Keren Hakibbutz, from where it can be taken whenever Gyuri or Mother present proper identification.

I have one more thing to tell you in case I am not in the country when my mother arrives, or am unable to get leave immediately: the Mazkirut Hakibbutz gave me their most solemn promise that when my mother arrives they will assist her in every possible way, either to get settled, or to find work, or in whatever way necessary.

And if by any chance I don't write—which I hope will not happen—only they can give exact information concerning anything to
do with me.

I would like you to know there is a suitcase at K's that may be of
some use to Mother, and another suitcase in the kibbutz (Caesarea)
with Daddy's books and a few specific personal belongings.

Please don't be surprised by the "testamentary" tone of this letter,
but since in the foreseeable and immediate future I shall be in Egypt,
I don't want Gyuri or Mother, when they arrive, to be totally without information about these matters, which, when one first reaches
Eretz, can be important.

Please forgive me for burdening you with so many things. I have
become accustomed during my four years here to turn to you,
Uncle Mihály, and you have really spoiled me with your kindness
and willingness to help.

Warmest regards, and deepest gratitude.

Cairo, January, 1944

My Darling Gyuri,

We arrived safely after an approximately ten-hour ride by car. The
drive was pleasant, since I came with a group of good-natured people. We sang, talked, and even slept (of course this last is not a sign of
good spirits, but it made the trip pass more quickly). I drove a part
of the way, though of course not all the way because there were three
drivers beside myself. I had plenty of time to think, and thus naturally thought about you. Again and again I thanked Providence that
we could at least meet, even though only for such a very short time.

You can imagine how interested I am in your first impressions of
the Land, and of the kibbutz. You don't have to hurry too much in
forming opinions; try to know the country first—which will not be
an easy achievement. (I'm not thinking of knowing it geographically,
but its way of life and its society.)

At the moment it is difficult for me to write because everything
is considered a "military secret" and I'm afraid the censor will delete
something. In short, I am well; there are a lot of soldiers (boys and

girls) here from Eretz among whom I can find a good many to be friendly with. During the day I'm busy; at night we go to the cinema, or I stay home and read. Fortunately I am not in the barracks but in the city, so I can take advantage of my free time.

Gyuri, please write about everything. You know how much it all interests me. Did you send Mother a telegram? I will try to write more in the immediate future and will send a picture as well.

A million hugs.

Cairo, February 27, 1944

My Darling Gyuri,

The only fortunate thing is that there are so many soldiers here from Ma'agan and that one by one they take trips home so I can send you a letter, and along with this one a little gift. I would like to send you every nice thing I see, to make up for the many years I could send nothing. But I don't know what you need, and of course I am not exactly wealthy, so my gifts are not very impressive. I am also sending you my fountain pen, as I have been given a new one.

I received your first letter with the greatest possible joy. It took about a week for it to arrive, which is not terribly long. But send one back with Yona, and that way I'll get it even more quickly.

Not long ago I talked to someone who has just returned from Turkey and asked for news of Mother's arrival. He said everything possible has been done, but that so far there has been no sign that Mother has even thought of *aliyah*. Of course one does not know anything to the contrary, either. I hope my letter, which Mother probably received, has convinced her of all the advantages of coming as quickly as possible. That it's impossible at the moment to come through Bulgaria is a great obstacle, but there is some hope that there will be a new way soon.

As for me, there is a good chance we will soon be leaving here, and in that case I will be writing shorter letters. But in any event I'll make every attempt to keep you informed of my well-being. I'm preparing several letters for Mother that you'll have to send her later. She must not know, under any circumstances, that I've enlisted.

I hope you're guarding those addresses I gave you in connection with matters to do with you and Mother. You can use them safely at any time should you have need of them.

I hug you. With everlasting love.

Cairo, February, 1944

Dear Gyuri,

Today I went on an excursion again, this time to the royal graves of Luxor. They are interesting, monumental creations. But as a matter of fact I don't have the patience for such things now. As far as I can see, we're moving on next week, and I am tensely awaiting the new assignment.

Should Mother arrive during my absence, you will have to explain the situation. I know, darling, this is a difficult task for you, and I don't know if Mother will understand what I've done. I can't find words to express my pain at the thought that once again I am going to cause the darling so much worry, and that we can't be together. All my hopes are that you two will soon be united.

Unending love.

The following letter was written to the secretary of the kibbutz, who arranged her mission.

Cairo, March, 1944

Dear Braginsky,

Before my departure, I would like to send you a few words. This is not good-bye; we already said good-bye in Eretz. But I feel the need of saying a few words to you, my close good friend.

I know that uncertain situations can arise. To be exact, difficult situations which can affect our fate. I know in that event you will ask yourself certain questions—and I want to answer them beforehand. Not on behalf of others, only on behalf of myself, even though everyone feels as I do.

I leave happily and of my own free will, with full knowledge of the difficulties ahead. I consider my mission a privilege and at the same time a duty. Everywhere, and under all conditions, the thought that all of you are behind us will help.

I have something to ask of you that it is perhaps unnecessary to ask, but I must. We have grown used to the fact that a lot of comrades know about our affairs, since we all live our successes and difficulties together. But you must be aware that in fulfilling the curiosity of those who are interested in knowing our fate, we might well have to pay a very high price. You know how much all information or disclosure of fact can mean. I don't want to multiply these words.

Before my departure I must express my appreciation for your help, for all I've received from you, and for the friendliness you always extended to me.

We will talk about everything else upon my return. Until then, warmest regards from Hagar.[6]

The following four letters were sent from Yugoslavia. At the time her whereabouts were a military secret; even her brother did not know where she was.

April 2, 1944

Dear Gyuri,

As I thought I would, I left my former place. I am well and like my work, which is all I can tell you now. I know this laconic communication doesn't say much, but you, darling, can write to me about everything. How are you fitting into the new life? It should be easier for you to judge things, now that you have had time to become acquainted with the good and the bad. I think the people are quite decent there, which helps considerably to create a feeling of being at home.

I don't envy you the approaching summer. One doesn't exactly freeze in the Emek Hayarden. But Kinneret is close by, and that's not exactly bad! Any news from Mother?

My darling, a thousand hugs.

May 10, 1944

Dear Gyuri,

Though airmail traffic is not too good, I've received three letters from you, and I am so happy I've finally had news. It makes me feel well to know everything is in order and that you're content. I, too, am well, but it hurts that we are so far from each other. I've enjoyed some fine and interesting experiences, but we'll have to wait until I can tell you all about them.

Darling, I am as concerned about Mother as you, and it's terrible that I can do nothing for her. Without knowing any of the details, I can envisage the horrible situation. You can imagine how much I think of both of you, and more than ever before of Mother.

Forgive this brief letter, but by now you must be used to these succinct messages. Some day I will make up for all the omissions.

Thousand kisses.

May 20, 1944

Gyuri Darling,

Again a short letter so you'll know everything is all right with me, and that's all. I have a suspicion all my friends and acquaintances are annoyed because I don't write. Perhaps they are even angry with me. Please try to explain the situation, and if you can't perhaps they'll forgive me later.

I don't write to Mother at all, so your letters will have to take the place of mine. In fact, I even give you permission to forge my signature with the hope that you won't one day take advantage of this to "extort large sums."

It is unnecessary to tell you how much I would like to see you, talk to you, or at least be able to write in more detail. I hope you know all this anyway. Your letters arrive with great delay, but sooner or later they do get here, and I am always so happy when I have news from you.

A thousand kisses, and warmest regards to our friends.

The following letter was written the day before she crossed the Hungarian border.

June 6, 1944

Darling Gyuri,

Once again I'm taking advantage of an opportunity to write, even though I have nothing to write about.

The most important thing: most heartfelt wishes for your birthday. You see, I was so hopeful that this time we could celebrate it together, but I was mistaken. However, let us hope we can next time.

I would be very pleased, Gyuri dear, if you would write a few lines to M. at our kibbutz. It has been a long time since I wrote, but I think a great deal about all of them. I am well. I have reason not to write to them at this particular time.

Any news of Mother? I beg you, please write about everything. Your letters reach me sooner or later, and I am always so happy to read them.

My darling, I wish you the very best of everything. A thousand kisses.

This letter was written to her comrades in Caesarea an hour before she flew from Italy to Yugoslavia.

March 13, 1944

Dearest Comrades:

On sea, land, in the air, in war and in peace, we are all advancing toward the same goal. Each of us will stand at his post. There is no difference between my task and that of another. I will be thinking of all of you a great deal. That's what gives me strength.

Warmest comradely greetings.

This letter was written the day she parachuted into Yugoslavia and was received by her mother very much later; it was forwarded by an unknown route.

March 13, 1944

Mother Darling,

In a few days I'll be so close to you—and yet so far. Forgive me, and try to understand. With a million hugs.

THE MISSION

THE LAST BORDER

I had the privilege of serving with Hannah during World War II, slogging through the land of the Yugoslav partisans for months until the terrible day she crossed the Hungarian border and fell into Nazi hands.

I first met Hannah when the paratroopers convened to plan their mission. I was a soldier at the time, and because I knew Yugoslavia well I was invited to talk to them, advise them, tell them where I thought it best for them to land in order to avoid capture. During my sessions with the group, a girl—the only girl in it—attracted my attention by her alert participation. It didn't occur to me at first that she was one of the paratroopers; I assumed that she, too, had been called in to give information about one of the countries the mission was heading for.

Several weeks later we met again in Cairo, and Hannah implored me to join the group. I distinctly remember how much she impressed me. I still didn't know her well, nor did I understand what motivated her. She was happy, cheerful, joked with all of us, including our Arab driver, yet never took her mind off the mission. Her changes of mood astounded me. One moment she would be rolling with laughter, the next aflame with fervor. I felt that a kind of divine spark must be burning in the depths of her being.

Hannah was delighted when it was finally decided to send me on the mission too. I'll never forget the way she helped me overcome my enormous psychological tension during our training. Hannah seemed utterly fearless. During those dreadful, difficult moments before jumps when my heart would pound with trepidation, I would think of Hannah, her comforting words of encouragement, and feel relaxed, reassured.

The way things turned out, we left for Yugoslavia together. One

223

night all five members of our mission were flown to Bari, Italy, accompanied by Enzo (Hayim) Sereni.[1] We reached the Italian coast after a thirteen-hour flight and spent the next day in a village near the city. Sereni breathed more easily in his native land, felt free and stimulated. He chatted with everyone he met, played with the children, patted them, gave them sweets. From time to time he would return to report what he had seen and heard. That evening he and Hannah had a heated argument. Hannah could not accept his forgiveness and tolerance toward the Italians after their cruel bombing of defenseless Tel Aviv, which was still fresh in her memory.

The next day we set out for the nearby city to make final preparations for our departure. I'll never forget the discussion on the way between Hannah and Enzo on the subject of whether or not there is a God. Enzo was an extremely astute man, a student of philosophy, and he fervently postulated God's existence. Opposing him with clear, penetrating logic was twenty-two-year-old Hannah. Observing her forcefulness, determination and passion, I began to wonder whether I would be able to work with her. How does this young girl, still so inexperienced, have so much self-assurance? Where do her fortitude and the courage of her convictions come from? I was convinced that she would be stubborn and hard to work with. I told Sereni how I felt, and he answered, "She certainly won't be easy to work with, but believe me—and don't ever forget—she's an unusual girl."

That was true. She was fearless, and none of us was as positive as she that our mission would succeed. Never once did she consider the possibility of failure; never once did she allow us to become dispirited or discouraged. She would explain with iron logic how we could extricate ourselves from any predicament, and her inner conviction would reassure us. Of course, she experienced moments of discouragement, but renewed strength constantly welled from the depths of her being. When, on the night of March 13, 1944, we were told to get ready to leave, she was overjoyed. She sang the whole way back to the village where we were quartered, and made us sing along with her. That song, in the course of our mission, became our group's theme song.

But I was not in the mood to sing. The hand of fate felt heavy on my shoulder. I had been informed the day before that my father and older brother, neither of whom I had seen in nine years, were in a concentration camp near Trento. I had hoped to have some time to visit them, but our orders kept me from doing so. Again it was Hannah who understood—and how well she understood—my feelings, and tried to prop up my spirits and comfort me. At the airport we met the officer in charge of our operation. Despite his British reserve, he couldn't restrain his surprise at seeing a woman among us. The British boys working in the large parachute storeroom where we were taken to put on our harnesses couldn't take their eyes off Hannah, nor hide their amazement. The Scottish sergeant who helped me into my parachute said simply, and with considerable emotion, "I can't believe it. I've been working here a long time, and I've fitted hundreds of parachutists, but never a woman among them." And he added, "If I told it to my Jewish friends in England they wouldn't believe me."

A group of paratroopers, evidently Americans, were equally surprised but assumed she was a paratrooper's wife who had come to see him off. When they met us again, just before we took off, they were shocked to see her, and one of them, extremely moved, walked over to her and wordlessly shook her hand. Hannah didn't understand the handshake, but her charming and simple reaction threw the astounded American completely off balance. In the last moment before takeoff we wrote final letters to those we held dearest. Hannah, too, wrote several, including one to Caesarea.

Finally it was takeoff time. We parted warmly with dear, good Enzo Sereni, embracing him (I can still hear his parting words: "Remember, only he who wants to die, dies!"), and climbed aboard the plane in sequence so as to facilitate jumping. Hannah and I were to jump first—I ahead of her. Y. and A., and the accompanying Britisher, were to follow on the second pass over the target. We sat inside the crowded plane, parcels all around us, some for the partisans, some for us. We felt weighed down. What with the harness on our backs, the weapons, and our heavy winter clothes, we had almost no freedom of movement at all.

The roar of the engines made conversation impossible. I studied the faces of my comrades, all deep in thought, and felt our hearts must be pounding in fateful unison. My eyes rested on Hannah. Her face was aglow, and she exuded happiness and excitement. She winked at me and waved her hand encouragingly, and a delightful, impish smile enveloped her features. Below her paratrooper's helmet her face seemed smaller, her expression almost elfin, and her luminous smile reminded me of a little girl on her first merry-go-round ride. Her excitement was contagious; we were all infected by it. Gradually tension relaxed, and the air seemed lighter. Fears and black thoughts receded, finally disappeared, and we began feeling peacefully confident. Time ticked by. Fatigue and tension had taken their toll; blessed sleep embraced us, one by one.

We awoke to find the crew tossing parcels out of the hatch, and the plane circling its target. I'll never forget the moment I made that jump, Hannah standing by, so slim, her face wreathed in a huge smile, her expression calm, happy, thumbs up—her favorite victory sign. I jumped ... and she was right behind me. A few moments later we were on the soil of Yugoslavia, land of the partisans.

We wandered across that land together for months, witnessing the cruel yet wonderful, ferocious partisan battle for victory and liberty. We saw incredible heroism, victory, tragic defeat. We saw destruction—entire towns and villages in total ruin, flames consuming the labor of generations. We encountered attacking as well as retreating forces, joined up with caravans of brave, simple people escaping from the relentless enemy, or returning to repossess their hills, fields, villages. Everything we saw touched us deeply: the cruelty, the terror, the humanity and tenderness. Our goal lay further on ... our mission was to try to save at least some of our brothers.

A great number of people—partisans and civilians—were fascinated by Hannah, the young British officer, smart in her uniform, pistol strapped to her waist. She fascinated them. They had heard about her before our arrival, and she became something of a legend. When she encountered members of the high command she aroused their respect, and although the Yugoslavs had taken women into the army on an equal footing, and partisan women marched into battle alongside the men, there was a special, mysterious quality about Hannah that excited their wonder and respect. Hannah was to continue on into neighboring Hungary, but we encountered a wall of reality at the very outset. We had to reach the Hungarian border on foot, and the partisans informed us that there was no possibility of crossing, because the Germans had recaptured the border region. "You'll just have to wait," they said. A few days later we learned that the Germans had occupied Hungary as well. It was catastrophic news for all of us—and it was the first time I saw Hannah cry. I thought she was crying solely because of her mother, whom I knew she adored, and to whom certainly anything could happen now. But amidst her sobs she exclaimed, "What will happen to all of them ... to the million Jews in Hungary? They're in German hands now—and we're sitting here ... just sitting."

Her conscience knew no rest. It was as if the earth beneath her were on fire. She constantly sought ways to cross the border, but we were entirely dependent upon the partisans, and our objective was foreign to them. Meanwhile we roamed that beautiful land of mountains and forests beset by rebellion and battle, awed by the magnificent landscape. We lived through amazing experiences— some disillusioning and depressing, others encouraging and inspiring. Our emotional fare was certainly varied. One evening we were invited to a partisan festival. Men and women in uniform, fully armed, thronged the town, their laughter and loud voices adding to the festive bustle. As we—four members of our group—entered the hall, the crowd cheered us as representatives of the British Empire. We felt sad that we had to keep our true identities secret, that we could not share with them the full purpose of our mission.

By then we were well known among the high command. The colonel asked Hannah to come forward and speak. This she did, with me acting as interpreter. Her every sentence was greeted with appreciative, cheerful enthusiasm, and afterwards the crowd formed circles and danced. The joyful gusto that filled the hall was as compulsively exciting as the beat of the music; it was exhilarating to watch the men and women dancing, rifles strapped to their shoulders, hand grenades swinging from their belts. Hannah slipped into the main circle, quickly adapted to the beat, and danced for hours.

We also endured fearsome, endless days under fire. In our wanderings we joined a partisan unit and found ourselves in a village near the border, within enemy territory. There was a surprise attack, and a hail of bullets burst upon the village. The partisans retreated, seeking shelter wherever possible, and the majority escaped. The villagers ran about in total confusion, sliding down the hillside or sheltering under rocks. We were completely alone, cut off, surrounded by the enemy. We slid down a rope and continued running in an open valley, entirely exposed to the firing from the encircling hills. We tried desperately to catch up with the retreating partisans. All around we heard cries of fear from clusters of bewildered civilians who stumbled along, clutching pathetic belongings, their children, driving their thinning herds of cattle. The cries of the wounded and the groans of the dying filled the stillness; people dropped like wounded birds. All about us there was horrible panic. In the mad race to save my own life I forgot everything. Suddenly I stopped, horrified at the thought that I had been cut off from Hannah. I turned, saw her running behind me, breathing wildly, gasping for breath. Her instinct for self-preservation, goaded by the firing and sounds of battle, spurred her on. With our last ounce of strength we reached the forest and, we hoped, protection from enemy fire. We fell to the ground, exhausted but safe. For a short while we lay silently in the bushes, clutching our rifles, listening to the incessant tattoo of bullets, the moaning of the wounded. Suddenly a group of German soldiers came into view, and my finger tightened on the trigger. But Hannah, calm, in control of her senses, stopped me. Firmly, quietly, she said, "Stop it! Don't shoot!" Her eyes reminded me of that which I had forgotten in all the chaos: our goal was to rescue our brothers; shooting at the enemy could only jeopardize our mission.

I vividly recall another memorable occasion. Four of us were lying alone, cut off in a thick forest, hidden behind tree trunks, our guns aimed. Our nerves were at breaking point. At the edge of the forest the Germans, shooting wildly in all directions, were so close they could have stepped on us. I'll never forget Hannah's amazing composure. I would glance at her from time to time, lying there, pistol cocked, a heavenly radiance on her face. I was literally overwhelmed by wonder for this unique girl. Her remarkable strength of character, her courage, her integrity and unwavering dedication to our mission aroused my utmost admiration and respect.

One evening we found ourselves in a village under the command of a woman partisan. When she stepped into the room where we were seated, I was astounded. I knew her! We had been childhood friends, had lived in the same district, had played together in the streets of the capital. The years of terror had left their mark on her face, and despite her youth her hair was streaked with gray. In the course of conversation it turned out that all of us in the room were Jews. We became very excited by this discovery and felt united by an almost sacred bond. She revealed the horrible suffering of the Jews in the Diaspora to us, who had been so protected in Palestine, and we, whom she had thought to be British officers involved only in military affairs, told her about Eretz and the homeland we were building. Hannah was deeply impressed by this encounter. A couple of days later she handed me the four-line poem "Blessed Is the Match," which revealed the passion within her.

At long last the day Hannah had been hoping for arrived—the day for her to cross into Hungary. It was June 9, 1944. At the end of a four-hour trek, we reached a village near the border and found members of our unit sitting in the room of a little house with two Jews from the Hungarian underground and an escaped French prisoner of war. We were making our final preparations, and I, to be quite truthful, felt uncomfortable. I was not satisfied with the arrangements. But by then it was quite impossible to restrain Hannah. She absolutely refused to wait another day, another hour, and all my efforts to persuade her to wait a trifle longer were in vain. She had firmly decided to cross over without further delay—if necessary even without an escort. That was that. The matter was settled. Hannah, in high spirits, joked with everyone, teasing the British officer in our unit. But beneath her banter there was a sharp edge, a steady note of earnestness. We had an early supper, and the minute we finished Hannah asked me to come outside with her. In the yard we discussed necessary details of her assignment and arranged about future contact. We walked in the orchard near the house and painstakingly reviewed all the possible means of communication, contact, codes, and so on. We finally agreed on a key to our secret code: United Kibbutz Movement Sdot Yam Caesarea. She begged me to give her a cyanide pellet, but I refused. I knew it was my duty to increase her self-confidence, to encourage her, to remove all doubts of her success.

She asked me not to accompany her to the border, since she did not think it wise for us to enter a danger zone together unless absolutely necessary. One of us, she said, ought always to be relatively safe so our mission could continue if one or the other were captured. At seven o'clock, the head of the partisan group assigned to accompany Hannah and her comrades to the border came into the room and said they would be leaving in fifteen minutes. Hannah was extraordinarily cheerful during those last minutes, radiant, the epitome of a free soul. She was bubbling with joy, forthright, impish, and amazingly carefree—yet, at the same time, alert, self-assured.

She recalled some funny incidents that had happened to us in Yugoslavia, then she created a dream for the future, for the day we would all return and meet in Eretz Israel. "We'll rent a big bus," she said, "and drive up and down the country. First we'll visit all the settlements that sent members on this mission. Then we'll arrange celebrations in those settlements, and we'll tell them everything that happened to us, and spin tall tales. In addition, we'll visit the entire country, from Dan to Be'er Sheva. We'll spend a month traveling."

We left the house together but walked in the opposite direction from the border, just in case one of the villagers was watching. We shook hands and thanked each other for shared experiences. She said, "Till we meet again—soon, I hope, in enemy territory." I watched her march confidently toward her unknown fate, and at the bend in the road she turned and waved farewell. I didn't know I would never see her again.

Reuven Dafne

How She Fell

Leaden clouds covered the sky as our car skidded along the rain-drenched desert road. Only the skill of our driver kept it from rolling into the ditch. My bones ached from sitting so long, and the desolate view tired my eyes, dulled my brain. The cold increased, penetrating my very soul. An unpleasant shudder of foreboding passed through me. I struggled to stave off the nagging thought that things were beginning badly. The superstitious fear of ill omens—acquired during my time at the front—overwhelmed me from time to time, no matter how hard I tried to resist it.

We sped on toward Tel Aviv. The pouring rain cloaked everything in sadness, and as we neared the city my depression increased. Fragments of thought flashed through my mind: I'm going to paratrooper's training school ... tomorrow or the day after I'll jump from a plane for the first time ... the parachute won't open ... it won't open ... it won't open ... I'll drop down ... down ... down. And this time I won't wake up, as I did from those childhood nightmares in which I jumped—always waking up in the nick of time, before my feet touched the ground, my heart pounding, but alive, alive!

I knew I could never tell anyone about my fear, and that there was no way out. I was no longer my own master. I had been entrusted with a mission. If I failed, we would all be put to shame and we would all suffer. And who knew where that might lead? I feverishly repeated to myself, "It won't open ... it won't ... I must jump! I'll jump and be smashed. Then they'll get someone else for the job, and it won't be my fault...."

The car wove its way through the streets, its wheels splattering mud on passing pedestrians. The flamboyant Hebrew city did not receive us with a smile. I greeted her disconsolately, as a stranger, without the joy I had always felt before when returning from afar. I

was allowed a half hour's respite before resuming the journey north-
wards to the school, and decided to visit Zvi and let him know I was
back. Tired, dejected, I groped my way up the dark stairway. A
strange girl was sitting in the darkening room. I asked for Zvi, and
she said, "He'll be right back."

I lit a cigarette, watching her out of the corner of my eye. There
was something enchanting, captivating in the way she sat, her long,
pretty legs crossed, her hands resting gracefully on the little table. She
was a soldier in the British Air Force, and the blue-gray of her uniform matched her blue eyes. Her light brown hair flowed in soft
curls around her refined, elongated face; there was something
delightfully harmonious about her. I liked her at once, without being
able to determine exactly what it was about her that had charmed
me, or why she was so completely pleasing to the eye. The door
opened and Zvi entered. He bombarded me with questions. When
did I get in? How long was I staying? Where was I off to?

The girl suddenly stood up, her face aglow with a wonderful
smile. "Are you Yoel?" she asked. I looked at her again, finding her
even more attractive than at first glance, and was struck by the
thought, "That's her! Of course!" And with the same note of surprise
in my voice said, "And you're Hannah!" Zvi asked in amazement,
"What, you haven't met?"

The day's oppressiveness lifted at once. I answered with a broad
smile, "No!" and my "no" blended with hers. Our handshake became
a prolonged handclasp as our eyes met and held. This wonderful girl
who had captivated my heart at first sight mystified me. A torrent of
questions came to mind, and I felt sure there was much that she too
wanted to say. Yet, I knew then, as I was sure she knew, that our bond
was not one of love but rather the deep covenant of those engaged
in war against a common enemy, the unvoiced pact of fellow soldiers.

"I have so much to ask you. Are you spending the night in Tel
Aviv?" she asked. It was only then that I remembered that the car was
waiting for me. I had to move on, to paratrooper's school. "No," I
answered hesitantly. "I have to leave at once. I'm going to learn how
to jump."

Apparently she sensed my fear, perhaps even noted a tremor in my voice. "I've just finished the course," she said. "It's nothing. You go up in a plane, you jump, and you're right back on the ground. I'll never forget how Nahalal looked from the air. It was a great experience. You'll love it." She spoke as naturally and plainly as if she were describing what she had had for breakfast that morning. I was ashamed, feeling that if this girl could jump, then I could too. All the same, I suspected she was putting on a show for my sake. I was sure that she had also been afraid, and if she could be afraid, so could I! I went on my way in high spirits. The rain pattered on the car roof and washed its windows. It was good to know that she would be there with me on the long, hard road ahead.

It was the eve of departure. We were all tense at the thought of leaving Eretz; everyone wondered whether he would ever see the Land again. It was a silent parting, one that neither relieved tensions nor lightened spirits. We had to avoid arousing curiosity and questions. The mission itself was a silent one; no one must know that we were going armed with a sling to do battle with the powerful enemy. Behind us lay days and nights of tense preparation, including endless discussions with ghetto fighters. We had studied conditions, countries, roads, carefully preparing for all eventualities.

Whenever we went out together, Hannah always proved a cheerful and charming companion. At such times we would try to divert our minds from the mission that lay ahead, but of course it was difficult. Hannah's face would occasionally turn sad. Once she told me that her mother was still living in Budapest, alone, and that she was supposed to come to Eretz. Hannah was frightened that she would arrive when we were who knows where and that there would be no one to meet her. She also told me about her brother, who was due to arrive any day, and probably would—straight after our departure. She said she had written him a letter in which she tried to tell him about the Land and guide his first steps. In fact, the very day the car came to take us on the first leg of our mission, the news reached her that the ship *Nyasa* was due in port, with her brother on it. Hannah became extremely emotional, and I hardly recognized in her the strong self-assured young woman I had come to know so well. Tears

flowed from her eyes. With difficulty I managed to obtain tickets for
Haifa, and accompanied her there to see if her brother had arrived.
He had, and after an enormous amount of maneuvering we were
able to spirit him out of Atlit camp, even though the usual procedure
was to detain immigrants for as long as two weeks. We managed to
postpone our departure for twenty-four hours to enable Hannah to
spend a little time with her brother. Whoever reads her diary and
senses the uniquely deep brother-sister relationship will be able to
appreciate the remarkable willpower it must have taken her to fore-
stall any further delay.

All too soon we were driving southwards. The sparkling white
houses in the Jewish settlements gave way to drab Arab villages. We
all felt the seriousness of the moment, but probably no one more so
than Hannah, who was leaving such a complex personal issue
behind. But she said nothing as we sang, joked, and planned all kinds
of projects for after our return. We decided that at the end of the war
we would return in a big bomber, and each of us would parachute
into his own settlement. There were five of us in the car, plus two
British drivers, to whom we paid scant attention. We were soldiers,
arrogant and ill mannered, and we failed to take the Britishers' feelings into account. But Hannah did not, and she was careful to translate all our jokes so they could laugh with us, understand our silly
plans, feel involved.

After we crossed the southern border, she declared suddenly that
she wanted to learn to drive! We protested vigorously, saying she
would endanger our lives. But she insisted that it was as good a time
as any to learn. She slid behind the wheel, listened as one of the drivers explained what was what, and began driving. After a few hundred yards of careful, if at first unsteady, progress, she accelerated,
evidently feeling entirely secure and at ease. We begged her to drive
more slowly, to let the driver take over. But she ignored us and sped
on furiously through the desert. Whenever another car approached
we all trembled, and more than once I closed my eyes, expecting the
worst. But she was having a wonderful time with her new toy. We
soon realized she knew exactly what she was doing, that she had a
firm hand on the wheel—and we all relaxed. She drove for hours on

Hannah and Gyuri in Tel Aviv, two days after he arrived in Haifa from Spain and one day before she left for her mission. It was the first time they'd seen each other in almost five years, and it was their final meeting.

end, without tiring, and only handed the wheel back to the driver when we reached the Suez Canal.

A difficult period lay ahead. Our departure was delayed from day to day, from week to week. There were rumors that Rumania and Hungary were on the point of surrender. It was of the utmost importance that we reach them before this happened, or at least immediately after, so that we could save as many of our people as possible. But this was of no concern to the Allies. We knew that the British were attempting to protect us, but in so doing they were preventing us from helping our people, and naturally there were endless arguments—even serious clashes—between our British sponsors and ourselves. Hannah was the chief rebel. And she was not always right. On the contrary. More often than not, she was wrong. She was totally unconcerned about her own safety. We argued constantly. Sometimes I wondered how I would ever be able to work with her once we were in enemy territory. She didn't appear to be sufficiently cooperative; she seemed concerned only with her own goals; she was totally lacking in caution and refused to accept discipline. She insisted that we divide up the fields of activity in advance, so we would not have to waste time on such matters once we were dropped. She wanted to be sure she got her share of the action, that she would not be left out. Apart from Hannah, we were all products of youth movements, and accustomed to certain methods and routines of working. Being unfamiliar with these, Hannah was afraid she would be brushed aside. As things turned out, she was fated to precede me. Our parting was rather emotional and eased the tension that had gradually been built up between us. "See you in Budapest," I said when we parted, and to the surprise of those of my comrades who knew how strained our relationship had become, remarked later, "She's really a good kid ... I'll miss her."

Several months later, Hannah and I met again in the forests of Yugoslavia. We had changed, and so had our plans. The Germans had occupied Hungary; we knew only too well what that meant for the last great Jewish community in Europe. We had become accustomed to marching for forty-eight consecutive hours without rest, without food, in rain, through swamps, under enemy fire; we had witnessed acts of heroism we were never to forget. In the partisans' eyes we represented a great empire, and we learned to protect its honor.

Hannah was unmistakably our leader. She was the only woman who had ever parachuted into Yugoslavia from a friendly country, and she knew how to talk to a general as well as to a private. Her reputation preceded her; everyone was familiar with her progressive views. She did more for British propaganda in Yugoslavia than all of Churchill's announcements, and even more than the inferior weapons the Allies sent to aid the partisans. Thanks to Hannah, we learned to control our desire for revenge when confronting the enemy. It certainly was not easy for us to hold our fire when we came face to face with the Nazis. But she always said, "That's not what we came for. We must save ourselves for our mission, not place our lives in jeopardy." And we always bowed to her wisdom. Hannah's eyes no longer sparkled. She was cold, her reasoning now razor-edged; she no longer trusted strangers. She suspected that the partisans were reluctant to help, that they were misleading us. We argued with her about this, but she was adamant and finally succeeded in making us suspicious as well. Only weeks later did it become clear how right she had been. The partisans regarded us as allies, but they didn't trust us. And if Hannah was difficult to get along with before, she was ten times more so now. At first she had only sensed the forces that lay dormant within her, but now she was fully conscious of them and had unlimited faith in herself.

Just what brought about this change in Hannah is difficult to say—perhaps the German occupation of Hungary, or being so often under enemy fire—but whatever the reason, her missionary feeling intensified. She was impatient and unwilling to delay, no matter how sound and reasonable the advice. She had her own theory: "We are the only ones who can possibly help; we don't have the right to think of our own safety; we don't have the right to hesitate. Even if the chances of our success are minuscule, we must go. If we don't go for fear of our lives, a million Jews will surely be massacred. If we succeed, our work can open great and important avenues of activity. Thanks to our efforts, multitudes will be saved." I felt that she was wrong. If we crossed into enemy territory and failed, the entire operation would be ruined—as had already happened in other lands. But it was impossible to oppose her.

One night we went to a field to await an airdrop of supplies. I looked at this amazing girl who could be so feminine but who was now dressed in her gray uniform, an automatic strapped to her waist. We marched out of step, battling mud, discussing this and that. She told us about the secrets of the poultry trade, and we debated political issues in Eretz. From time to time we would pass a partisan sentry, and she would respond to his salute with a curt yet charming motion, always turning her head to look straight into his eyes.

It was a cold, clear night; the partisans had made a bonfire. They began to sing a wild song, their voices expressing the anguish of an oppressed people. That night we liked the partisans very much. They were simple people, most of them illiterate, but they had learned the truest, most profound lesson a nation can learn: the need to live as free men and to be willing to sacrifice their lives for liberty. A pretty blonde girl of about seventeen sat facing us. We knew her well. She was an upper-class city girl to whom we had often spoken. Her English was fluent. She fell asleep, her head resting on the shoulder of a partisan. He, a simple man of the forest, did not move for hours so as not to waken her.

Suddenly Hannah got up and asked me to walk with her. As we walked side by side in the still, dark night she poured out her heart, saying many of the things she had said before; only that night she spoke differently. She was no longer the stubborn young officer who was unwilling to accept another point of view, but a sensitive young woman, perceptive and tender. She said she was overwhelmed by her inner turmoil, that although she knew she was not always sensible, ours were not sensible, reasonable times. She felt incapable of waiting on the sidelines while thousands were being slaughtered. "It's better to die and free our conscience," she said, "than to return with the knowledge we didn't even try. Each of us is free to act as he thinks best, and I quite understand the way the rest of you feel about discipline. But for me this is not a question that can be decided by authority." She was right, even though her opinion ran counter to logic. I took her hand and said, "Let's go!" Happy that I understood her, she began describing to me the things she had imagined, the things she hoped would happen. She drew imaginary portraits of Jewish partisans sitting around campfires, singing songs of Eretz, the forests of Europe echoing with the sad songs of Jewish freedom fighters.

I left her the next morning. We had decided to go separately so as to open up different routes of escape and rescue. I sensed the fatefulness of our parting—but we had made up our minds, come what may, whether or not the road seemed right. That was May 13, 1944, the very day—as I learned later—that the expulsion of the Jews from most of Hungary's cities had begun. But of course we were unaware of the situation and agreed to meet after the Sabbath service at the Great Synagogue in Budapest. And if Jewish services were no longer being held there, we would meet on the same day, at the same time, at the Cathedral.

I waited in vain for her at the Synagogue; I looked for her at the Cathedral. When I was thrown into jail, battered and broken in body and spirit, I kept thinking, it's a good thing she doesn't have to suffer all this. Who knows whether she could have stood it ... it's a good thing she isn't here. She probably turned back for some reason ... crossed later ... when she comes she'll succeed where I failed ... and the world won't be able to say there is no way of helping, no way of saving Jews. She'll succeed, she must succeed....

One of the guards took pity on me and came into my cell to console me. He told me it would soon be over, that they wouldn't torture me indefinitely, that in a few days I would be transferred to another prison, that no one would bother me any more.

"No," I replied. "They'll just hang me!"

"What are you talking about?" he said. "We don't hang people so easily, don't worry. There was a girl here from Palestine, a few days ago, and she was only sentenced to five years."

I was shocked. I guessed that the five-year sentence was something the guard had just invented, but not the girl from Palestine; I knew she must be Hannah. So Hannah and I were both under arrest. Who knew when Peretz's[2] turn would come? Even if he managed to avoid them, he would still be forced to flee. He would be unable to do anything because the police would be on to him. I felt completely helpless. The moment I was arrested I knew my life wasn't worth a jot. But we were responsible for far more than our own lives. And we had both failed: I, the careful one, the one who had wanted to preserve my life, not only because I had no wish to die, but also because it was no longer mine alone but dedicated to a cause—and Hannah, who had been so ready, so willing to sacrifice herself, who had looked forward consciously to that moment when she would proudly face the enemy, the murderers.

One day in the Gestapo prison I heard a loud voice calling "Hannah Senesh!" And then I thought I heard her answer. She was in the same prison! I frantically pounded on my cell door with my fist, kicked at it, stormed and raged. The door opened and the warder asked gruffly what I wanted. I pushed him aside and rushed into the corridor. No one was there. Had Hannah been there a moment before, or was I dreaming? The question troubled me all that afternoon and night. The next day I was again taken for questioning, and in the van that took us to headquarters I met other prisoners. I asked if they knew anything of Hannah, or had heard of her.

"What a question!" one of them said. "She was with us yesterday. They took her up for questioning. A remarkable girl. She is always talking about the Jewish problem, and tells everyone about Eretz Israel. She really gave us hope." The prisoners told me she was in solitary confinement three floors above my cell. I tried in vain to attract her attention all the next day. The following morning, sitting in the sunlight, it occurred to me that I might be able to flash signals with my mirror onto the ceiling of her cell. That afternoon, when the sun was on her side, she flashed an answer. Thus we established contact. In the course of the next six weeks we held many short "conversations" in this way, and so each of us always knew what was happening to the other. This means communication was much too difficult to use for "friendly chats," but I learned from other prisoners that she was in good spirits, that she accepted her fate valiantly, and was utilizing every minute to encourage others.

She found an ingenious way of communicating with prisoners whose cell windows faced hers by cutting out large letters and placing them, one after the other, in her window to form words. In this way she introduced herself to the prisoners, learned their troubles, gave them information about happenings outside the prison walls, and also told them about Palestine and kibbutz life. Her window became an information and education center, and from morning till evening prisoners looked toward it for news. Opposite her were some members of the Zionist Movement who had been arrested for underground activities and were awaiting sentence. She gave them new heart.

Her behavior before members of the Gestapo and SS was quite remarkable. She always stood up to them, warning them plainly of the bitter fate they would suffer after their defeat. Curiously, these wild animals, in whom every spark of humanity had been extinguished, felt awed in the presence of this fearless young girl. They knew she was Jewish, but they knew also that she was a British paratrooper who had come to fight them. Having been taught for years that Jews never fight back, that they will accept the vilest treatment, they were taken aback by her courage. The warden of the prison, a notorious sadist who was credited with the death of many he had tortured with his own hands, considered it a privilege to visit her cell daily to argue with her fearless criticism of German rule and her prophecies of an allied victory.

Those were days of change in internal Hungarian politics. The government the Germans had set up after occupying the country was thrown out; the new government was preparing for the surrender. The Nazis tried to continue deporting Jews, but the new Hungarian government intervened—not because they had any love or pity for the Jews, but because they wanted to show the Allies their good intentions. The time had come for decisive action. With the agreement of the political prisoners with whom I shared a cell, I sent a secret letter to the Hungarian regent, Admiral Horthy, describing our situation. I stressed that if anything happened to us, even at the hands of the Germans, he would be held responsible. The reply was not long in coming, though in an unexpected manner: on September 11 a warder ordered me to pack my belongings. He informed me I was being handed over to the Hungarians. My heart pounded. Evidently liberation was near. I knew what it meant: Hungary would surrender to the Allies, and we would be taken to a safe place out of reach of the Germans.

I was standing at attention in the corridor, my face to the wall (the customary procedure in Nazi prisons), when, out of the corner of my eye, I suddenly saw Hannah. She looked young and lovely, though very pale. She skipped lightly down the steps, wearing a raincoat and carrying a black case—as if she had just returned from a journey and was stepping from the train—then paused beside me. We clasped hands for a moment, but a Gestapo officer roared at us, drew his pistol, and cocked it to prove it really was loaded. We were herded into a closed van generally used for transporting dangerous criminals. It was divided into compartments, and I was put into one directly next to Hannah's. We communicated by tapping quietly on the partition. I was happy we were together, that she was alive and evidently in good health, and I was confident we would soon be freed. It was good also to see Peretz's face peering from a compartment opposite. He signaled, "Where to now?" We were led, two by two, through the latticed entrance of the Hungarian army prison. This was the building where I had been tortured during my previous interrogations. But this time, though still a prisoner, I felt superior, as if I were entering as a guest of honor, positive I would soon be able to avenge myself upon my torturers. All the prison officers stood on the stairway, shook hands with us, and received us as friends. Everyone wanted to show his goodwill, hopeful it would stand him in good stead after the surrender.[3]

Taking advantage of the relaxed conditions, Hannah and I sat down in the corridor and held a lengthy conversation, a continuation of the one we had had in the middle of that field in Yugoslavia near the campfire. It was to be our last. We told each other what had happened since that night. Happiness and deep sorrow were mingled in our talk. We were all too aware of the mistakes we had made; we had learned from experience. She told me the shocking story of her capture, and only then did I come to know why she had been unable to keep our rendezvous at either the Synagogue or the Cathedral.

We had already known that the border runners were in everyone's employ, including the Germans', and could no longer be trusted. Then one day Hannah came across a group of refugees who had escaped from Hungary. Among them were three young men who were willing to join the rescue mission—a non-Jewish Frenchman and two Jews who had been planning to reach Palestine. All three agreed to go back into Hungary with Hannah. The four set out, and although the area was unknown to them they nevertheless decided to cross into thickly patrolled enemy territory, a map and a compass as their only guide. I still don't understand how, in the circumstances, they managed to reach their goal—a Hungarian village—without encountering German patrols. But somehow they did. Hannah and the Frenchman hid among some bushes on its outskirts, while the other two went into the village to contact friends who had permits to travel to the capital. The police stopped them. Instead of trying to bluff their way through, or using their guns against the few police-men, one of the boys shot himself instead. Then farmers told the police that the men had been accompanied by another two partisans whom they had seen hiding in the bushes. The next thing they knew, Hannah and her companion were surrounded by soldiers. She suffered dreadful tortures that she wouldn't talk about, but her miss-ing tooth provided mute testimony. I heard from others how they had tied her, how they had whipped her palms and the soles of her feet, bound her and forced her to sit motionless for hours on end, beaten her all over the body until she was black and blue. They asked her one thing, only one thing: what is your radio code? Yes, the code was important to them, for they had found the transmitter she hid just before she was caught—and now they wanted to use it to send out false information, to mislead bomber squadrons so that they could be greeted by fighters and anti-aircraft guns. Hannah didn't reveal it. When she was being transferred to Budapest she tried to kill herself by jumping from the window of the train, because she didn't know how long she could hold out. But she was caught in the act and beaten even more. "You don't have the right to destroy your-self," her guard told her. "You are state property; we'll do away with you when we no longer need you, not before." But her most awful test was yet to come. They brought her to Budapest and there, to her horror, she found her beloved mother. She hugged her and could find only the words: "Forgive me, Mother, I had to do what I did."

The Germans knew their business. They threatened that if she did not reveal her secret, they would torture her mother before her eyes and kill her. Still Hannah would not yield. I was completely shattered on hearing her story and stared at her in astonishment. How could she have remained so resolute and calm? Where did this girl, who loved her mother so much, find the courage to sacrifice her, too, if necessary, rather than reveal the secret that was not hers, that affected the lives of so many? As it was, Hannah's fortitude saved her mother. Had she broken down, they would doubtless have executed her immediately and sent her mother off to the gas chambers of Auschwitz. But the Germans didn't give up. They kept Hannah and her mother in the same prison, believing that prison, hunger, and the fear of death would humble her. Friends in the prison—there were some prisoners who had known the family before the war, or had heard of them—did what they could to make things easier for them, and even managed to have mother and daughter transferred from their separate, distant cells to nearer ones, thus making it possible for them to meet. Once or twice a week prisoners were allowed to stroll in pairs in the tiny prison yard, the eyes of the SS guards fixed firmly upon them. Every snatch of conversation was firmly punished. To mark her parents' twenty-fifth wedding anniversary, Hannah sent her mother some gifts—a beautiful vase she had fashioned from an empty can and silver foil, some colorful paper flowers, a poem. She improvised dolls and other toys from paper and rags, and those prisoners "in the know" provided her with the raw material. Whenever possible she would pass a note to her mother. But these, together with the poem, were destroyed by her mother for fear of searches and retribution.

All this I learned as I sat with Hannah in the corridor of the Hungarian military prison. The next day we were taken to different prisons. Hannah was dropped off first, at Conti Street. She stood at the gate, looking so young, so brave. As the van moved off, she put down her bag and gave us an encouraging thumbs up sign, her lovely face wreathed in a smile. It was the last time I saw her.

I don't know what happened to her between September 11, the day we parted, and October 28, the day of her trial. I later placed inquiries in the newspapers, hoping to find people who had been in prison with her during that period. Only one man responded: he had been a court official and had seen her just once, but she made such a deep impression on him that he himself had wanted to know about her last days. I found out only that after Mrs. Senesh was released, she had gone to see Hannah, who had requested one thing: a Hebrew Bible. Her mother searched all over Budapest for one, without success.

On October 28, 1944, Hannah was brought before a military "court" in Budapest. We know very little about her trial. There are people who were present at the time, but they were taken from the room at the most dramatic points, leaving her to face her judges alone. We know that she admitted her "crime." But she explained boldly what had brought her to Hungary, analyzing in a penetrating way the political-moral decline of Hungary during the preceding years. And she stressed—in the very midst of Fascist rule—the great crime in which the Hungarians had participated, concluding that those responsible would pay for their actions, as would those who could have prevented them. She admitted that she had come to save Jews, not to save Hungarians from suicide. But insofar as it would have been compatible with her task, she would also have saved Hungarians—and to a degree, the Hungarian nation—from the heavy blame that now lay on their heads. There is no doubt that in closed session Hannah insulted the judges even more brazenly.

In the corridor outside stood Hannah's black-clothed mother, awaiting news of her daughter's sentence. Those were times when Jews were not allowed on the street, but she had come. While the court was in consultation the defendants had been taken out into the corridor. The Hungarian sergeant assigned to Hannah turned a blind eye as mother and daughter embraced and had what was to be their last conversation. Hannah was confident of victory. "Why worry about a sentence when we'll all soon be free," she encouraged her mother.

Hannah was right. The judges were taken aback, both by her character and by her convincing words. A death sentence might mean that one day they would face judges whose judicial powers and views of justice were quite different from their own. An unprecedented action was taken; the court announced that sentence would not be passed for eight days—until November 4. By then, the judges calculated, the verdict would be made for them. American bombers had been pounding the city, and Russian cannon could be heard booming on the outskirts. The news spread like wildfire. Before the defendants had reached the prison corridor we all knew of the strange decision and had understood its significance. They did not dare to execute her, and they did not have the courage to pronounce any other sentence. They were afraid. Not a bad sign! We all felt much more optimistic.

The days that followed were difficult. We heard continually about the progress of the Red Army and of its powerful attacks, but no one knew exactly what the situation was. Confusion reigned. The judges who had tried Hannah fled the country, so there was no one left to try Peretz and me. Prison boilers became pyres for court records that had been kept since the beginning of the war. The thunder of the artillery increased hourly, rattling the windowpanes. Then came the news that Conti Street Prison had been evacuated and that Hannah was among the last prisoners transferred to Margit Boulevard Prison, where I was. We had two fervent wishes: that they would not move us before the Russians arrived, and that they would bring us food. We suffered desperately from hunger. Because of the frequent bombardments we were sometimes given soup only once a day, and in the penetrating cold of late autumn we trembled with hunger and increasing weakness. It sometimes seemed that even if we were lucky enough not to be moved, we would starve to death before the Red Army broke through.

November 7 was a dark, cloudy day. We sat around quietly, leaning against the wall, huddled together in an effort to conserve the little body heat we had. Suddenly we heard shots. We looked at each other, frightened and bewildered. What had happened? Had someone been executed? Impossible! This was not their method. Last respects were always paid. There was always the marching of the firing squad, the reading of the sentence, prayer and a bugle call accompanying the dark moment of execution in the gray courtyard beneath our cell window. Someone climbed up to the high window and, looking down, informed us that he could see a table with a crucifix on it, but no sign of an execution. At the same moment we heard voices in the courtyard—an order to rearrange the straw. Apparently a guard had fired a bullet by accident, and the reverberation had amplified the sound.

That afternoon one of our cellmates went to the doctor. Every day one of us would go for treatment or a pill because the clinic served as a center of information and communication. The return of that "patient" was the most important event of our day. That afternoon we waited even more eagerly than usual for our cellmate's return. He was back within half an hour, pale and shaken, as if he really were ill. He leaned against the wall for support, removed his hat, and announced in a faint voice, "They've executed Hannah." We were stunned. Hannah? Executed? No! Impossible! Why Hannah? Why not us? "It's a mistake … a mistake…." After the first wave of shock I was sure my cellmate had misunderstood. I mumbled over and over again, "It's a mistake … a mistake … a mistake…." until the Frenchman imprisoned with me at the time gripped my hand and whispered, "Calm down, control yourself."

We pounded on the door until the guard came and asked what we wanted. "We want to know who was just executed."

"What do you care? Shut up!" he shouted. We pleaded with him, and for the first time since we had come under his protection he heard from us the official formula prisoners were ordered to use when addressing a guard: "We respectfully request…." The guard sensed that we were frightened, and he consoled us: "Don't worry. She wasn't one of yours. Just some young girl … a partisan, they say … a British parachutist. But that's surely a lie. Whoever heard of a young girl being a British officer?"

So it was Hannah after all. Wonderful, sparkling Hannah, who had been so sure we would return to tell our comrades of our exploits, to spin tall tales. I felt I had to speak. But the words strangled in my throat, left me stuttering. I saw them all staring at me, and I managed to utter, "She was the most wonderful person I ever knew." And they repeated after me, as in prayer, "She was the most...." We rose and stood in silence for a long while, honoring her memory the only way we could. Then we just sat down, speechless, stunned. Tears would not come. I couldn't find anything to say. All I could hear were my cellmate's words over and over again, "They executed Hannah ... they executed Hannah...."

I spent seventeen more days in that cell. It slowly emptied until there were just two of us left, the Frenchman and myself. When you are in prison for a long time, the quiet becomes unbearable. You feel as if you are trapped in a cemetery; you have to make noise—talk, sing, do something to disrupt the silence. Yet, during those seventeen days not a sound was heard in our cell. One by one we parted, and although we knew our parting might be final, still we shook hands in silence. I parted from Peretz, never to see him again. No one dared disturb the silence of that cell. It was as if the silence were Hannah's monument, a constant reminder of the terrible fact that she was gone.

About two months earlier, at the clinic, I had fallen into conversation with a young man who was accused of betraying his country. He had tried to convince his friends that it was their duty to rebel against the German invaders. During our conversation he mentioned that he lived at 30 Bimbo Street. Amazed, I recalled Hannah's words at the entrance to the prison as we parted; "If we get out, look for me at my mother's house, 28 Bimbo Street." I asked him if he knew his neighbor, Mrs. Senesh. "Of course," he said, "For many years." "And her children?" He knew them, too, and told me enthusiastically about both of them, about the son who was in France and about the daughter who had gone to Palestine. He told me all this at length, for they had been childhood friends. He was shocked when I told him he was mistaken, that Hannah was not in Palestine—that she had returned on a mission and was now in prison.

That young man served as a prison orderly (most of the menial tasks were done by prisoners), and in fact he was the last person to see Hannah alive. He was on cleaning duty immediately outside her cell—Cell 13, the Condemned Cell, where she had been taken on

November 7—when the prosecuting officer, Captain Simon, entered. It is from him that we learned about Hannah's stand in her last moments.

Simon began tonelessly: "Hannah Senesh, you have been sentenced to death. Do you wish to ask for clemency?"

"Sentenced to death? No, I wish to appeal. Bring in my lawyer."

"You cannot appeal. You may ask for clemency."

"I was tried before a lower tribunal. I know I have the right to appeal."

"There are no appeals. I repeat: Do you or do you not wish to ask for clemency?"

"Clemency—from you? Do you think I'm going to plead with hangmen and murderers? I shall never ask you for mercy."

"In that case, prepare to die! You may write farewell letters. But hurry. We shall carry out the sentence in one hour from now."

Motionless, Hannah sat alone in her cell, her eyes fixed to a point on the wall. What she saw there, what she was staring at, we shall never know. Perhaps her mother's face. Perhaps the scenes of her childhood—the sea, the sand, the places and the people so dear to her.

She asked for paper and pen and wrote letters to her mother and to us. No one besides Simon ever saw the contents of those letters, for they never reached their destinations. In the letter to her mother I imagine she explained why she had chosen the path she had. She wanted her pardon and knew she would obtain it only if her mother understood that her conscience and way of life had compelled her to take the steps she had … that ideals and a sense of moral obligation had prompted her actions.

The letter she wrote to Peretz and to me—a letter that was probably intended for the entire pioneer movement—also failed to reach its destination. It disappeared, along with all the other files on Hannah's case. But after her death, Captain Simon told the Seneshes' solicitor, "Hannah Senesh remained rebellious till her last day. About to die, she revealed that evil purposes had directed her steps. She wrote to her comrades: 'Continue on the way; don't be deterred. Continue the struggle till the end, until the day of liberty comes, the day of victory for our people.'"

At 10 a.m., the same officer stepped into her cell a second time and silently signaled her to follow him. Two soldiers escorted her into the courtyard. Next to the gray brick wall, near the little prison church, stood a wooden sandbox. They drove a post into the sand, tied her hands behind her back, and strapped her to it. Hannah observed all the gloomy preparations with wonder. She looked straight into the eyes of the officer, who stepped toward her with a blindfold. She shook her head defiantly and lifted her blue eyes to the cloudy, foreboding sky as the three rifles spat. Hannah was buried in Budapest's Jewish cemetery, in the Martyrs' Section, among the many anonymous victims of the Germans. We don't know who brought her body there. The Jewish Burial Society was functioning no longer; Jews were not allowed to leave their houses. Perhaps an admirer did her this final kindness.

I've tried to trace her family and her home. The mystery of her personality, the riddle of her life, has increasingly baffled me. The more I discover about her background, about the scenes of her youth, the less I understand her. I saw how she had lived—the villa in a wealthy neighborhood, the huge country house where she spent half her childhood, her family respected in Jewish and non-Jewish circles alike. I don't know what compelled her to go to Palestine. Whether it was the anti-Semitism she encountered at school, the discussions she had with a girl from Palestine, or some other unknown factor. Only when she reached Palestine was her character finally shaped. For this reason, Hannah's death symbolizes a great deal for those of us who continue to live there, but not only for us. She was the product of an assimilated Jewry that had long turned its back on Judaism. With her sacrifice, she lit the way toward a new era.

Yoel Palgi

Hannah Senesh's coffin arriving from Hungary at Israel's port in Haifa in 1950.

MEETING IN BUDAPEST

From the autumn of 1939 to the spring of 1941, there was a steady flow of cheerful, reassuring letters from Hannah in which she described, in minute detail, her work and life in Palestine. These letters helped in some measure to fill the great void left by her absence.

Our correspondence continued uninterruptedly while Hungary remained neutral. But after November 1940, when Hungary joined with Germany, Hannah's letters arrived with decreasing frequency; those I did get were brief and heavily censored. Then, after the summer of 1941, her letters ceased entirely and were replaced by occasional twenty-five-word Red Cross communications. But I was not at all worried. On the contrary. My gratitude that Hannah was in the safest possible place, and happy, grew apace with the increasingly rapid gathering of ominous clouds over Hungarian Jewry. By then my fears and anxieties were entirely centered on Gyuri, who disappeared from France without a trace in the winter of 1942. My letters to him were returned unopened. Then, at the end of January 1944, a telegram from Hannah informed me he had arrived in Palestine. I was happy and grateful that my children were safe and together at last, and excitedly I prepared to join them.

I had received word from Hannah in December 1943, through secret channels, advising me that I should prepare to leave at a moment's notice. The president of the Zionist Organization, who intimated the same thing, had also contacted me. But the deadline for Hungarian *aliyah* was fast approaching, and the anxiously awaited immigration certificate failed to arrive. Then March 19, 1944, greeted us—the day of the German occupation of Hungary. All the humiliating, discriminatory, annihilating laws it had taken the Nazis years to institute in other countries were put into effect and enforced in Hungary with fantastic speed. The compulsory wearing of the yellow star struck us with paralyzing force; there were those who would not under any circumstance be seen wearing it in the street. Arrests, house arrests, evictions, deportations, suicides marked each day of German domination. Visiting my relatives in the provinces was no longer possible, and by May I heard they were all in the ghetto. Then rumors spread that Jews in the ghetto were being transported by freight car to unknown destinations. And a few days later, Jews in Budapest were ordered to move into yellow star–designated houses. I, too, packed a few essentials, ready for any eventuality, but was uncertain what to do, how to proceed.

Old friends—a husband and wife—tried to convince me not to move into one of these houses but to obtain false documents stating I was Aryan. They wanted me to escape with them to Rumania, assuming that it would be easy to make our way from there to Palestine. I thought the plan unfeasible, even absurd, yet out of desperation agreed and obtained the forged papers. But I had not as yet reached a definite decision.

For the past several years I had been renting part of my home to Margit Dayka, a popular actress, who, in those tragic days, demonstrated infinite sympathy for those of us who were being hunted, and was unfailingly helpful and kind. On the night of June 15, Margit remained home with me. Perhaps she was aware of how completely dispirited I had become since the disappearance of my relatives, or perhaps she didn't want to leave me alone, knowing that only a few days previously the Gestapo had come to requisition a part of the house in which I lived, and had only been prevented from doing so by her heated intervention. She made me promise that I would not, under any circumstances, allow anyone to enter the house during her absence. The following day we agreed that she should go to the Housing Authority and demand that the part of the house in which I lived be placed in her name too. "And of course I'll take care of your things, Catherine," she said, "so you'll find everything intact and in perfect order when you return." She was touchingly gentle and understanding.

I slept little that night. Not only was I exceedingly troubled, but I was on air-raid duty as well. Next morning, June 17, I got up at about eight and began dressing. The bell rang. I hurried to the window and saw a stranger who, on catching sight of me, said, "I'm looking for Mrs. Béla Szegö."

"She doesn't live at this address," I answered.

"Of course she does," he insisted, taking a slip of paper from his pocket. Then, "Oh, wait a minute. Not Szegö … Senesh. Mrs. Senesh is the name of the woman I'm looking for. I'm a state police detective. Please open the door."

I showed him into the entrance hall. "You're being summoned to the head office of Military Headquarters as a witness," he said. "Please come along."

"Witness for whom? In what matter?"

"I don't know," he said, shrugging.

It was beyond my comprehension. Certainly I knew no one in the Armed Forces, and Jews had long since been drafted into the Compulsory Labor Forces. The thought flashed through my mind that the summons might have something to do with Gyuri, who was of military age. However, he had left the country six years previously with permission from the proper authorities. I wondered whether his escape with false documents from France to Palestine, by way of Spain, had something to do with the summons.

I asked the detective to wait while I finished dressing, and rushed to wake up Margit. Hearing what had happened, she threw on a dressing gown, rushed downstairs, and asked the detective to be seated in the drawing room. She tried to find out why I was being taken for questioning but could obtain no information either. Before leaving he assured us both that I would be back home very soon. Even so, I had the presence of mind to give the forged papers I had acquired for the planned escape with my friends to Margit.

The detective took me by tram to the military headquarters in Horthy Miklos Boulevard, which was half an hour's ride from my house. What did I feel? Perhaps curiosity as much as fear, since I could not imagine why they wanted me. But in those days, arrest without reason was a daily occurrence, and there were few among us who were not afraid of being picked up and taken to the police or military headquarters for questioning. We began to accept the disappearance of relatives, friends, acquaintances; our ranks were thinning daily. The only thing of great importance was the safety of both my children—and that was assured. Whatever happened to me did not matter.

Those were the thoughts that raced through my mind as I chatted with the detective about Margit. He was interested in her career, in the plays and films she had starred in, and in the theatre in general. He was really quite courteous, even considerate, and immediately agreed when I asked permission to telephone Margit. It seemed even more important now to have the house put in her name, and I wanted to remind her about it. I stopped at a tobacco shop to make the call, but when I began dialing, the proprietor shouted, "What's the matter with you! Don't you know anyone wearing a yellow star is forbidden to use a public phone?" I really hadn't known, but neither had the detective; he said I could use the phone in his office.

When we arrived at the military headquarters building, we walked up to a second-floor office, where two policemen were having their midmorning snack of smoked bacon and green peppers. The detective went to announce my arrival and, when he returned, asked the police to leave. He also allowed me to phone Margit and, after I talked to her, asked whether I had any children. When I replied in the affirmative, he asked where they were. There happened to be a large map on the wall, and I smilingly pointed to Palestine. A very tall civilian of military bearing entered the room. His name, I soon learned, was Rozsa. He indicated a chair and settled himself behind a typewriter. The interrogation began. After taking down the usual data concerning family and background, he first questioned me about Gyuri, as the eldest, but quickly turned his attention to Hannah. Much to my surprise, he questioned me endlessly about her, stopped the pretense of typing, and asked what specific reasons she had had for leaving home. "I can understand a boy leaving home: to see the world, to complete his studies, to prepare for his career. But a girl … why should a young girl want to leave her home, her mother, her friends?"

"For the very reasons you mentioned," I replied. "Jewish youth has no future in Hungary, no opportunity of making a living. And much as it hurt me to part with her, particularly after having had to part with my son, I'm happy she's not here now to see and experience the terrible suffering of the Jews."

A scornful smile spread over his unpleasant face, and the interrogation continued. The majority of questions revolved around what Hannah had been doing during the past few years, where she was at present, what she was doing now, and, above all, how, from where, and how often I received news from her. The thought struck me that perhaps one of her letters had been intercepted and contained something that displeased the censor. But there was no time for conjecture, as the interrogation intensified and its tempo increased, the snapped questions becoming more incisive. What had Hannah done before leaving Budapest? Who were her friends? Her teachers? What had she been interested in? With what had she primarily concerned herself? What profession had she thought of following? What were her ambitions? To all these questions I simply answered that she had always hoped to be a teacher and had studied with that end in mind. There was further questioning in the same vein, which I finally put an end to by saying, "Perhaps you'll construe this merely as a mother's normal pride in her child, but I can tell you my daughter is an unusually gifted girl and in every respect a very remarkable young woman. You need not take my word. You can question her teachers, who will, I am sure, verify my statements."

He was finally satisfied with the interrogation and instructed the detective to type a summary of what I had said. He then warned me I would have to swear under oath that my testimony was the truth, and sign it. I summarized my statement, and the detective typed it on a long sheet headed "Hannah Senesh." We had barely finished when Rozsa returned, carefully read it over, made me swear to its veracity, and sign it. "Now then," he said, "where do you really think your daughter is now—this minute?"

I repeated that to the best of my knowledge she was on an agricultural settlement in the vicinity of Haifa.

"Well, if you really don't know, I'll tell you. She's here, in the adjoining room. I'll bring her right in so you can talk to her and persuade her to tell us everything she knows. Because if she doesn't— this will be your last meeting."

I felt as if the floor were giving way under me; I clutched the edge of the table frantically with both hands. My eyes closed, and in a matter of seconds I felt everything—hope, faith, trust, the very meaning of life, everything I had ever believed in—collapse like a child's house of cards. I was completely shattered, physically and spiritually. The door opened. I turned, my back to the table, my body rigid.

Four men led her in. Had I not known she was coming, perhaps in that first moment I would not have recognized the Hannah of five years ago. Her once soft, wavy hair hung in a filthy tangle, her ravaged face reflected untold suffering, her large, expressive eyes were blackened, and there were ugly welts on her cheeks and neck. That was my first glimpse of her.

She tore herself away from the men and, rushing to me, threw her arms around my neck, sobbing, "Mother, forgive me!" I felt the pounding of her heart and her scalding tears. At the same time I noted the expectant, avid expressions on the faces of the men as they stared at us—as if they had been watching a scene in a play. Again the floor seemed to sway, and it took all my strength to maintain my self-control and remain silent.

Rozsa said, "Speak to her! Use your maternal influence and convince her she had better tell us everything, otherwise you'll never see each other again."

I had not the faintest idea what was happening. Not even in my wildest imaginings would it have occurred to me that Hannah, the fervent pacifist, was a volunteer in the British Army. Nor did I know that a woman could become a member of the British Armed Forces. What puzzled me was how she had suddenly been catapulted from the far distance into the hell that was then Hungary. Certainly no one told me anything, or explained anything, and I could not possibly have guessed the truth. But of one thing I was absolutely certain: if there was something Hannah did not want to reveal, she had good reason, and under no circumstances would I influence her otherwise.

"Well," Rozsa snarled, "why don't you talk?"

My voice sounded strange when I answered, "There is no need to repeat yourself. We both heard you."

"All right, but talk to her. We'll leave you alone for a while."

They led us to facing chairs and then left the room, only the detective remaining. We couldn't find words. Then suddenly it occurred to me that Hannah, upon hearing about the horrible things happening to the Jews in Hungary, might have volunteered for a daring, even reckless mission in an effort to rescue me. I was only too familiar with her extraordinary courage, willpower, and perseverance when faced with seemingly insurmountable obstacles. And regardless of the considerable distance that had separated us, I was always aware of her love and constant concern.

"Hannah, tell me, am I the cause of what's happening here? Did anxiety about me bring you back?"

She quickly reassured me. "No, Mother! No! You're not to blame for anything. Not anything at all."

"But how did you get here? I received a telegram not long ago to say that Gyuri had arrived in Palestine. Isn't he there now either?"

"But of course he is, darling. I sent the telegram myself. You needn't worry about Gyuri, believe me. He's fine."

I noticed one of her upper teeth was missing, obviously a result of the same beating that had produced the welts and bruises on her face and neck. The presence of the detective inhibited our conversation, but despite him I said, "Of course your tooth was knocked out here."

"No, not here," she answered.

Seeing her in such battered condition was heartbreaking. I stroked her hands; the nails were broken, the skin like sandpaper. The purple-black bruises on her face were like knife wounds in my own flesh, and I leaned over to kiss her. The instant I embraced her the door burst open and Rozsa rushed in with his four henchmen. He had evidently been spying on us. He pushed us apart and said, "Whispering is not allowed here! Anyway, that's enough for today." After they took Hannah away, Rozsa turned back to me. "I could detain you as well, but I'm taking your age into consideration. Go on home! If we have further need of you we'll telephone. Of course everything depends upon her. If she refuses to confess at subsequent interrogations, we'll probably have no further use for you. But I warn you, you're not to tell anyone anything that has happened here today. Not a word! Not even that you've set foot inside this building. Understand?"

"Yes, I understand. But someone already knows that I'm here."

"Who?" he asked in astonishment.

"Margit Dayka, the actress."

"How is that possible?"

"Mrs. Senesh is her housekeeper," the detective interrupted. "She was there when I picked up the witness."

"Will she ask questions when you return?" Rozsa demanded.

"Undoubtedly. After all, she isn't accustomed to seeing me hauled off by a detective."

"If she asks you anything, just tell her you've been forbidden to say one single word. Remember that! Not a word. You can leave now."

He left the office, and the detective, seeing I was barely able to move, said, "Rest a moment. We don't have to leave immediately."

His kindness gave me courage to ask what was going on. But he protested that he didn't know, and at that moment several policemen came in, saying the room was needed. The detective accompanied me down the stairs and attempted to comfort me. "Don't take the threats too seriously. Things don't happen quite that fast around here. Everything will be straightened out—you'll see."

In any event, it was reassuring to know there was someone left who behaved like a human being. I stumbled home. It must have been about one in the afternoon. A few neighbors and acquaintances were waiting in front of the villa, together with Margit. They ran toward me, clamoring to know what had happened.

"It was all a misunderstanding," I told them. But immediately after Margit and I were alone in the house, I said, "It wasn't a misunderstanding. A horrible thing has happened, but I'm not at liberty to tell you about it. Perhaps I won't be able to keep it to myself, but at the moment I can't possibly tell you."

The bell rang. Margit ran to open the door. I heard voices. I went to my room, but Margit followed. The producer of her recent film had come to take her to the studio to see the rushes. "But I don't want to leave you alone now," she said. She told my sister later that I had changed so incredibly in the short time I had been away that she had difficulty believing I was the same woman who had left with the detective that morning. Of course I didn't know my appearance had been so affected, and when she insisted on staying home with me it required superhuman effort to control myself. All I wanted was to be left alone. I begged her to leave and promised that if anything happened I would somehow get word to her. She returned the forged documents I had entrusted to her that morning, and finally left.

But I wasn't alone for long. There was a knock on the door, and the caretaker led in the husband of the couple who wanted me to escape with them to Palestine. He had come to see how I was getting on with my preparations, since the attempt had to be made in the next day or so. In answer to his repeated questions, I told him firmly that after giving the matter most careful consideration I had decided not to leave Budapest. He attempted to persuade me, to convince me that so far as he could see it was the only step for me to take. Once again he detailed the bright prospects of life in Palestine. "We have neither friends nor relatives there," he said, "but even so, we feel it is the only place for us to go. You, on the other hand, have two children there. If there is anyone to whom it's worth the risk and the gamble, you're certainly the one. And don't forget the efforts Hannah has made to obtain an immigration certificate for you."

While he talked I considered the advisability of telling him what had happened. I felt as if Providence had sent him. I so desperately needed someone to confide in, to consult. And if he and his wife ever reached Palestine, they could at least tell Gyuri what had happened. I knew him to be a serious, levelheaded man who could be trusted absolutely, and finally I decided to tell him everything.

He listened with rigid attention and then spoke. "I hardly know what to say. This is really a catastrophe, and of course I understand now why you don't want to leave. It's difficult to find an explanation for what has happened. I promised not to betray your confidence, so of course I won't tell a soul, but I don't agree with your decision to maintain complete silence. On the contrary, I think you ought to confide in those who might possibly be able to help you. First of all, I think you ought to tell Margit, who probably has connections in military circles."

I accompanied him to the door, and we were standing in the entrance hall, saying our good-byes, when the bell rang. I looked out of the window and saw a closed car surrounded by SS men. One of them rasped, "We are looking for Mrs. Senesh. Please let us in."

"I'll get the key right away," I stalled. I ran into the living room, quickly gathered up the forged documents, which were still lying on the table, and hid them in Margit's cupboard. Then I ran to unlock the front door. My friend wanted to leave, but one of the Gestapo men (whose name, I later learned, was Seifert) scrutinized him and, barring his passage asked, "And who are you?"

"Mrs. Senesh is a close friend of my wife. I came to inquire how she was, and I was just leaving." Seifert debated whether to let him go. We waited tensely, knowing that those who happened to be in the company of someone being arrested were often taken to prison as well. Finally Seifert let him go and then entered with the four others, saying, "Come along immediately for interrogation."

I was alone in the house. The caretaker, who lived in a flat at the side, had gone shopping. I desperately wanted her to witness my departure. Then if I failed to return, she would tell Margit, who would, in turn, notify my sister. "I can't possibly leave now," I said with assumed naïveté, "since I'm entirely responsible for the house and personal belongings of Margit Dayka, the actress, and she's not at home."

"But you'll be brought back straight after the interrogation," Seifert promised. "Just get ready to go."

I went to my room slowly, Seifert on my heels. I tried to decide whether to tell him I knew why I was being taken for questioning, or whether to feign ignorance. Remembering Rozsa's threatening tone, I decided to say nothing. Seifert began inspecting the house, strolling from room to room, shouting out questions about the furniture, the contents of drawers and cupboards, finally demanding to know which of the rooms were mine. I replied that the actress occupied all the rooms but one. He then asked about the front door and all the other doors in the house. Of course I was aware there would be a thorough search of the premises as soon as I left. Suddenly Seifert held a photograph directly in front of me and asked, "Do you recognize this girl?" It was a picture of Hannah looking the way she had that morning.

"Who is it?" I asked.

"Have you a daughter, Hannah Senesh?"

"Of course," I answered, "but if this is supposed to be a picture of her, she's unrecognizable. Where did you get it?"

Instead of answering, he urged me to hurry, ordered me to lock all the doors, and asked who had keys to the house.

"Only the actress and I. There is a separate entrance to the care-taker's quarters."

"When will the actress come home?"

"Probably by evening."

Fortunately the caretaker returned, and I was able to exchange a few words with her. I gave her Margit's number and asked her to telephone immediately after I left. She, on the other hand, knowing I had not yet eaten anything that day, rushed to the kitchen, prepared a few sandwiches, and slipped them into my large handbag. We left the house, and I locked the front door. Whereupon Seifert asked, "Why are you taking the key along?"

"Didn't you say I would be back before evening?"

"Of course, of course," he answered hastily, aware he had betrayed himself. "Take the key."

We climbed into the police van and in a few minutes arrived at the prison. Only after we got out did I realize how close it was to my house. The car had stopped at the freight entrance of the Budapest County Department of Justice building, which led directly to the German Police prison. Seifert got out with me but spent some time taking leave of the others, exchanging jokes, discussing Saturday night plans, and wishing them a happy weekend. Then he conduct-ed me to an upstairs office. All this took place at about five o'clock on a Saturday afternoon. Seifert asked for and examined my identi-ty papers in the presence of a gaunt, fearsome-looking young SS man with a Death's Head[4] badge on his cap, a young German sol-dier, and a middle-aged, corpulent civilian. He put my documents in a dossier marked "Very Urgent," asked for my house keys, and left.

The young Death's Head man, whose face resembled his badge,

took over. He asked for all my personal belongings, examined my handbag, and turned it inside out. He confiscated my money, fountain pen, watch, and wedding ring. He asked whether I had any more money. I wore a little bag around my neck in which I carried the maximum amount of money Jews were allowed. After an instant's hesitation, I handed it to him. The reward for the momentary delay was a powerful slap across my face. I spun completely round on my own axis but strangely enough didn't feel the blow at all. After that morning's encounter with Hannah I felt nothing—as if a stranger had taken my place, or a mechanized puppet. But the young soldier was embarrassed, and the corpulent civilian repeatedly blinked and motioned me to disregard the abuse. (I learned later that the civilian was a Jewish prisoner, formerly the general manager of an important firm, who had been drafted for office work in the prison.) A meticulous record was made of the objects and the amount of money taken from me, and the small change was returned. Death's Head told me that when I was released (if ever), everything without exception would be returned to me. He then gave the soldier the number of the cell to which I was assigned: 528. As we were climbing the stairs the soldier asked if I had anything else concealed on my person—because, he warned, I would be searched, and he wanted to spare me a repetition of what had happened downstairs. I assured him I had nothing more but the clothes on my back and my handbag with its innocent contents.

Two Swabian women guards searched me carefully before one of them conducted me to a wide corridor on the fifth floor. A heavy steel door creaked open, and I stepped into a surprisingly spacious, bright room. With its six white iron beds it looked (apart from the bars on the window) more like a hospital ward than the prison cell I had imagined. A number of inquisitive-looking women turned expectantly toward me, but I soon learned they always did this—and so would I—upon the arrival of a new "roomer." One of them jumped up and ran toward me, and I recognized her as Baroness Böske Hatvany, divorced wife of Baron Lajos Hatvany. Some of the women were seated on two of the beds, playing bridge, though like any kind of activity it was strictly forbidden. Baroness Hatvany had cleverly drawn numbers and figures on bits of paper and made playing cards. The women killed time this way, since from five in the morning until bedtime they were officially supposed to sit on the benches placed around the table in the center of the room, doing absolutely nothing. From time to time the matrons observed us through the peephole in the door to see whether we were breaking the rules. Despite this, we took turns to lie on the beds, but even in our dreams we heard footsteps and automatically jumped up and ran to the table.

When I entered the cell the women surrounded me and questioned me about events on the outside. Böske made the introductions: Mrs. Eugene Vida, wife of the only Jewish member of Parliament, whose ex-butler had denounced her for making an allegedly anti-Nazi remark. Countess Zichy, of Jewish origin, who was arrested while attempting to hide valuable paintings; the widow of Lehel Hédervary, accused of collaborating with the Allies; the sister of Jacques Mannheim, the Parisian banker. These are some of the names I still remember. They all wondered how I came to be among them. After all, I was not a member of the moneyed aristocracy, nor politically involved. It was also generally known that since my husband's untimely death I had led a most retiring life. Of course I didn't dare reveal the reason for my imprisonment. It was getting dark, and I had eaten nothing since the night before. I was famished. I found the sandwiches I had brought with me and bit into one of them. Twelve pairs of eyes fastened upon me. Hungry as I was, the mouthful caught in my throat. I handed the small packet of food to Böske, who carefully divided it. She seemed to be the "officer in charge."

Later that evening a heated argument developed concerning next day's cleaning of the room and adjoining toilet. It was Countess Zichy's turn, but she protested violently, stating that she would not under any circumstances clean the toilet—not only because she had never performed such a task, but because she hadn't the faintest idea how to go about it. Someone offered to do the work for her, but Böske insisted that no one could be exempted from the work detail for any reason but illness. She then explained the use of the brush, disinfectant, and scrubbing powder. Everyone joined in the debate, pro and con, and had the situation been less tragic it would have been extremely funny. Because of my state of mind, I was not yet able to make contact with prison life; my thoughts were certainly elsewhere. I crouched in a corner and remained silent.

After a completely sleepless night I was rousted out of bed at five. Sunday was a day of rest even for the Gestapo interrogators, but as my dossier was marked "urgent," the consensus of opinion was that I would be taken to Schwab Hill for questioning early the next morning. Worry and uncertainty weighed so heavily upon me that I could no longer stifle my secret. I told Böske everything that had happened. She listened in shocked silence and promised to tell no one. Whether she did or not, I don't know. But that Sunday evening, Clara Zichy apologized to me for making such a fuss the previous evening, and all the others seemed particularly kind. I observed them through a haze, my thoughts wholly centered upon Hannah, wondering whether she was still alive. Certainly she would never divulge what they wanted to know, and they would show no mercy. What use was there in my going up for interrogation the following morning? I shuddered at the thought of being questioned, and decided it was senseless to endure further torment. Even if Hannah were alive, I could be of no help to her whatever while imprisoned.

Small shelves, which prisoners used to keep toilet articles on, had been fixed on facing walls of the cell. There were not enough of these for everyone in the overcrowded cell, so those who had been imprisoned the longest had prior claims on them. One of the few things one could do to pass the time was arrange and rearrange the little odds and ends sent in the fortnightly parcels prisoners were allowed. Clara Zichy said that among the things she had received, the most useful was a razor blade that served as a knife, pencil sharpener, and scissors. I glanced at it out of the corner of my eye as it lay temptingly in view on the left side of her shelf. That night, while everyone was absorbed in the complicated business of placing mattresses on the floor (it was roomier and more comfortable sleeping that way than sleeping two in one bed), I managed to take the razor blade without anyone noticing. Since I lay directly next to the open window, I was able to hide the blade on the outside ledge.

The light switch was in the corridor; because the guards never bothered to turn it on, we all went to bed as soon as it grew dark. That night, when everyone seemed to be asleep, I tried to put an end to further misery and suffering. Locating the main artery in my wrist I slashed it and felt the blood flow—but it did not gush forth as I had expected. My neighbor sat up, and for a while I feigned sleep. Then, after a considerable interval, I tried once more. But again there was only a trickle of blood. Before I could bring myself to make yet another attempt, the prisoners began stirring. Böske, an alert woman, looked toward me inquiringly and noticed something wrong. Fearfully she rushed over and grabbed my wrist. While tightly binding it with two small handkerchiefs, she berated me, saying that what I had foolishly attempted could have gotten them all into serious trouble. She advised that when I was taken for questioning I should wear my long-sleeved raincoat in order to hide the bandage.

At seven o'clock a soldier appeared and read my name from a list. A cellmate immediately gave me my day's ration of bread; they all knew from experience that during the morning-to-night interrogation on the Hill I would be given nothing to eat. However, hungry as I was later that day, the bread was so moldy I could not eat it. Prisoners rounded up for questioning were made to assemble in the second-floor corridor and ordered to face the wall. The slightest movement, gesture, or even flutter of a hand in attempted salutation was forbidden. About forty of us were crammed into a huge police van and transported to the Gestapo headquarters. The van was windowless, but there were a few narrow air vents near the top. When we were under way I noticed that postcards previously written and addressed were collected and slipped through the vents in the hope they would be picked up by people humane enough to forward them.

I sat all day in a crowded waiting room for women. During the morning a woman deliberately squeezed in beside me and began asking questions, whereupon a prisoner across the aisle gestured and placed a finger across her lips. Later she explained that my inquisitive neighbor was an informer. I was not questioned that day. That evening I was handed a postcard and told that this would be my one and only opportunity to notify someone of my whereabouts and to ask for food parcels, clothing, and toilet articles. Packages were accepted every other Wednesday morning, from ten until noon, and delivered to the prisoners immediately. It was already Monday evening, and I wondered if the card would be delivered in time. Nor did I know to whom I should send it. I was afraid of sending it to my closest relatives, and I did not want to involve Margit by writing her a card from a Gestapo prison. After considerable speculation I addressed it to the hairdresser in my neighborhood and asked her to please give it to the lady who lived in my house.

On parcel-day there was tremendous excitement in the prison. Although consignments could not be distributed until after ten in the morning, the tension of waiting and expectation began early in the morning—not only because of hunger but because the awaited package was the only means of communication with the outside, the only link between the prisoners and their families or friends. Every parcel was carefully examined and thoroughly pilfered. Paper and string were confiscated, and what finally remained was distributed. There were those who received two or three parcels, and those who received none and were consequently panic-stricken.

By noon that first Wednesday I had given up hope of receiving anything, concluding that the card had arrived too late or had not been delivered. But at the last moment a parcel arrived, apparently delivered by taxi. There was a jar of soup in it, still steaming, and everything else was fresh and wonderfully appetizing, particularly after the inedible prison fare. I was surprised, however, that most of the clothing Margit had sent consisted of worn things I no longer used and had put aside to be given away. I learned later that the room I had indicated to Seifert as mine, and which did in fact contain most of my clothes, had been thoroughly searched and subsequently sealed by the Gestapo. Thus, Margit was compelled to send whatever she could find in the mending room, plus some of her own things.

Every day, after the midday meal, we were allowed a ten-minute walk in the prison yard, along with prisoners from cells on either side of ours. This exercise period was the highlight of our day. Though conversation was forbidden, we managed to exchange bits of news, which amazingly enough filtered into the closely guarded cells. One soon came across forgotten acquaintances, and from day to day, as new prisoners arrived, friends and relatives one hoped had managed to escape joined the ranks. Gradually the number of inmates grew, and before long there were about twenty in our cell, which was not intended for more than six. But prisoners also left. On the morning of June 23, Böske Hatvany and Mrs. Vida were taken away. Where, no one knew. It was rumored that there were twice-weekly deportations, as well as twice-weekly selections for shipment to the Kistarcsa internment camp in the suburbs. To be ready for any eventuality, we all packed little bundles each morning, since one had to leave instantly if one's name was called.

The morning Böske was called I was summoned again for inter-rogation. When I followed the soldier down the stairs to the second-floor corridor to join the assembled group, a young prisoner who was scrubbing the floor whispered, "Auntie Catherine, Hannah is here, too. I talked to her last night." I could barely control myself. I glanced at Böske and longed to run over and tell her, but she, like everyone, was facing the wall, and I was only too well aware that talking was strictly forbidden. That day Seifert, who was in charge of my case, interrogated me. He questioned me for hours on end, lingering interminably over the slightest detail. Though his interrogation was infinitely more thorough and painstaking than Rozsa's, Seifert's manners and method were more polished and courteous. Because of this I had the temerity to ask, "Won't you please tell me what has happened? What the charge is against my daughter?"

He weighed my questions silently, and finally, instead of answering directly, said, "According to my interpretation of Hungarian law, your daughter's life is in no danger. German laws are more stringent." I breathed more easily.

That very evening Hilda, a Hungarian prisoner of German origin, and the prototype of German beauty, unlocked the door of the cell and in a sharp, strident voice called my name. Because of her beauty and fluency in German, she was exempted from physical labor and assigned primarily to office work and errands of considerable responsibility. Now and then, when the matrons were at meals or busy elsewhere, she was even entrusted with keys to the cells. When I stepped into the corridor and the door of the cell was closed behind me, she whispered that I was to stand by the window of the cell and look across. Looking out of the window was generally forbidden, but then so many things we ventured to do were forbidden that I did as she bid. At the window directly across the yard, and exactly opposite mine, I saw Hannah. She smiled and waved. Early next morning I stationed myself in the window again, and after a brief wait she appeared and wrote huge letters in the air, carefully outlining each with her index finger. I answered the same way. Knowing that we might be watched, we were exceedingly careful and "talked" only of inconsequentials—at least in the beginning.

It seemed strange that Hannah's window was so different from the others. It was immediately beneath the ceilings, horizontal, and considerably smaller than ours. I was told that all prisoners in solitary confinement had such windows to prevent them from looking out. How she managed to look out of hers we couldn't fathom. My cell-mates stood beside me and watched our "correspondence" with great interest. Hannah noted the yellow star on our clothes and asked what it signified. I explained and inquired whether she was excused from wearing the discriminatory emblem. She answered that she was no longer a Hungarian citizen, thus not bound by such "laws." One of my companions wrote in the air, "You're lucky not to be branded." Whereupon Hannah drew an enormous Star of David on the dust-coated window, and there it remained until weeks later when the window was washed. As soon as she had drawn the Star she disappeared from the window, and although I watched for her all day she did not appear again. The next evening the beautiful Hilda again called me sharply. In the corridor she whispered that I could talk to Hannah for a few moments in the bathroom nearby.

At last I could hold her close, kiss her. Hannah hastily explained that she was a radio officer in the British Army and had volunteered for a mission that "unfortunately I could not complete." She continued, "I'm reconciled to my fate. But the thought that I've needlessly involved you in all this is unbearable." I convinced her that I was perfectly all right, and the one consolation in the entire tragedy was that

I could be close to her and could see her now and again, even talk to her. Had I been allowed to remain free I would probably not have been able to obtain visiting privileges, and there could even have been the horrible possibility of deportation and separation forever. She smiled sadly and looked almost like her old self. The visible marks of the beatings had healed. Her hair was clean and well combed, her expression calm. But the gap in her mouth disturbed me. In answer to my question, she said she had taken a course in parachute jumping while still in Palestine and had lost the tooth completing a jump. Obviously she did not want me to know the truth, and sensing my doubt she smiled and said, "Dearest Mother, if all I lose during this venture is a single tooth, we can both be really grateful."

I asked if she had been tortured, and how severely, beyond the obvious. "Believe me," she answered, "compared to the mental and emotional anguish, the physical suffering is negligible." She related that before she and her companions were charged with anything, the sudden suicide of one of the boys in her group triggered the catastrophe that caused them all to be arrested. Consequently they were searched, and the radio earphones were found in one of the boys' pockets. At this point Hilda knocked, and we said good-bye.

During the following days I hardly saw her; in fact, there were days when she did not appear in the window at all. I learned that she was taken to the Hill daily for interrogation and did not return until nightfall. She became acquainted with several of my cellmates, either in the police van or else in the waiting room. From them I discovered that she had parachuted into Yugoslavia and had lived for months with the partisans there. Occasionally she appeared at the window for a few moments early in the morning. She cut out huge paper letters and held them up to form words, but often she would duck down suddenly in the middle of a word or sentence. I learned that she could reach her window only by putting the table on her bed, and on top of the table a chair. Since the chair was used as a washstand, and she had only a short time early in the morning to use it, she would quickly jump from her perch when she heard the guard returning for it.

On the rare days when there were no interrogations, I could stand at my window and watch her walking in the yard after lunch. Or, to put it more accurately, I could watch one corner of the yard, for as the line turned I could catch a momentary glimpse of her in that corner. The prisoners walked in pairs, but she brought up the rear alone. As a prisoner in solitary she was forbidden to have direct contact with anyone. She knew I was watching her, and each time she reached the corner she would look up. On one occasion our groups chanced to be in the yard at the same time. By then the majority of the inmates knew us or had heard about us. Consequently, everyone who was aware of our relationship watched excitedly to see if we could manage a meeting, an exchange of words. It seemed hopeless. I was at the head of my double column, she alone at the tail end of hers. The matron stood in the center of the vast yard, watchful; the armed military guards were stationed at various points.

Hannah continually stepped out of line, evidently troubled by her shoelace. Meanwhile the line kept going ahead, and she kept taking a step backwards each time she stooped, until we were side by side. My partner stepped back, and Hannah slipped into her place. It was done so smoothly, so effortlessly, one would have thought it had been carefully rehearsed. We chatted softly, but I kept my eyes on the matron. Whenever her gaze caught mine I became silent, whereupon Hannah said, "Listen, Mother, we're in the greatest possible danger here anyway, so we might as well talk freely. We've nothing to lose."

She told me that a day or two after our first meeting, Rozsa had wanted to interrogate me again and had telephoned my home while Hannah was in his office. Margit had answered and obviously told him I had disappeared. When, upon further questioning, she could not give him the information he wanted, he became furious, slammed down the telephone, and raged, "That damned Jew hireling! She's probably got her hidden!"

July 17, Hannah's birthday, was drawing near. I wondered what little gift I could send her. I had already shared my lot parcel with her, but had providentially put aside a jar of marmalade. When my cellmates saw me preparing the carefully guarded bottle, they contributed gifts from their own precious stores: a handkerchief, a sliver of soap, a sponge—in prison each a cherished, rare possession. One of the matrons agreed to deliver the gifts. That afternoon she summoned me to the peephole and dropped in a piece of paper upon which Hannah had written a few lines to thank us for our thoughtfulness and generosity. She said the marmalade particularly pleased her, not only because it was so good but because it reminded her of Palestine. She continued that she had summed up and weighed the events of her life, and upon looking back over her twenty-three years decided they had been very colorful and eventful, her childhood happy and beautiful. Her accounting with life at such a tender age was like a dagger in my heart.

During the exercise period in the yard I began noticing children at Hannah's left and right, grabbing her arms, clinging to her. Two in particular struck me: a Polish boy and girl. One was eight, the other six, and they had been wandering for years with their mother from camp to camp, prison to prison. They immediately sensed a friend in Hannah and would not leave her side. Sometimes they even played tag, and the guards would "benevolently" look the other way. To please these children, Hannah began making dolls, concocting them ingeniously from bits and pieces of string, paper, rags, crayons. Eventually I heard, via the grapevine, that she had been placed in the communal cell where the children were, though I never did learn why. At once she began teaching them to read and write, played with them, told them stories. She thought of things to occupy the adults too, and entertained them with anecdotes and songs about Palestine. She was soon back in solitary confinement, but the manufacturing of dolls continued, and our "window correspondence" flourished once again.

Of the three matrons, each of whom worked eight-hour shifts, the most dreaded and implacable was Marietta. She was so unrelentingly cruel to the prisoners that many sacrificed the longed-for daily ten-minute walk if she was on yard duty. She used to stand in the center of the yard, bullwhip in hand like an animal trainer in the circus, directing the prisoners, "Faster, slower, still faster, on the run!" Often she made them run in circles. On one of the rare occasions Hannah and I met in the yard, Marietta was the matron on duty, and Hannah related an incident she had had with the woman. One morning she was so completely absorbed in our "window correspondence" that she failed to hear approaching footsteps. Suddenly the door burst open, and Marietta, who had already seen her in the act of "writing" through the peephole, stormed in, completely beside herself. She began shouting at the top of her strong voice, demanding an explanation from Hannah, who, she said, knew only too well that signaling, or communicating in any fashion through the window, was strictly forbidden. She demanded the name of the person or persons with whom Hannah was attempting to make contact, and Hannah, shouting from her perch in equally energetic tones, answered that she was trying to "talk" to her mother, whom she had not seen in five years.

Marietta left without another word, and from then on, whenever she came on duty, she would immediately take a chair into Hannah's cell. This same Marietta, learning that the female British officer did not receive any parcels, assembled a package with an exceptionally fine assortment of delicacies pilfered from prisoners' parcels and sent it to her. The materials Hannah needed to make her dolls were supplied by the generally feared matrons. One day I received some paper dolls: a boy and girl walking hand in hand. I was enchanted. My cell-mates were equally delighted, the monotony of prison life being such that everything and anything outside the deadly routine aroused comment and admiration. I sent Hannah a note thanking her for the dolls and added, "Though I have always dreamed of the day you would present me with grandchildren, for the time being these substitutes will do."

Gradually more and more of her dolls turned up, and the more she made the more ingenious, varied, and colorful they became. She sent them not only to the prisoners but also to the matrons, who cherished them equally. She made Biedermeier dolls, Rococo dolls, ballet dancer dolls, Carmens, Madame Butterfly dolls, Toscas, and so on. But most popular were her Palestine dolls, likenesses of the boy and girl kibbutzniks, shouldering picks and shovels. She told me once, "I'm glad my time here isn't entirely wasted. I've converted a good many people to Zionism." At the same time she said she could not understand that no sign or word had reached her from the outside. She was sure "they" were unaware she was in prison.

The next parcel-day I slipped a note into the empty suitcase in which Margit had packed clean clothes and toilet articles, and which she would pick up the next day. I thanked her for her efforts on my behalf and asked her to send two parcels henceforth, since I shared everything with Hannah, and one was not quite enough for both of us. The suitcase passed inspection and reached Margit. She immediately sent the note to my sister, who generally contributed to the parcels and helped assemble them. My sister, secure in the belief that Hannah was in Palestine, was shattered to think that I had lost my reason and imagined my daughter was in the same prison as I. Not for an instant did it occur to her there could possibly be any truth in my note—until the following day, when quite by chance she heard the same thing from an entirely different source. For this was already the first week in August, and—with the occasional release of prisoners—bits of news had begun to filter out of the prison.

The next time we met in the yard, I questioned Hannah about the mission for which she had volunteered. "I can't tell you because it's a military secret," she said. "But the war will soon be over, and then you'll know everything. However, even if I could, I wouldn't tell you, since it's difficult enough to maintain silence during interrogations anyway, and the less you know the better off you are. In fact, it's best if you know absolutely nothing."

"Even if you don't tell me," I replied, "I'm sure your enthusiasm for the British didn't prompt you to volunteer in the army. There must be some sort of Jewish affair behind all this."

Pressing my hand, she said, "If that's the way you feel ... you're on the right track."

"The only question is whether it's worth risking your life for your boundless fanaticism."

She answered softly but categorically: "Look, Mother, it's worth it to me." She added, "But you can rest assured, I've done absolutely nothing that can in any way be injurious to the interests of Hungary. On the contrary. And remember, what's considered a crime today will probably be considered a virtue in the near future, justified by coming events."

At another meeting she told me that during her first interrogation she actually fell into a trap. When they were unable to force an explanation from her concerning the earphones, they said, "It doesn't matter; we know enough already. One of the boys has confessed everything, and he'll be executed tomorrow." She took the bait. "He had absolutely nothing to do with the matter. The radio is mine." Subsequently they tortured her in an effort to make her divulge the code. Once during a "window conversation" she asked whether I would like to learn Hebrew—pointing out that I would never have a better opportunity, considering all the time on my hands. Though I was not exactly in the mood to study anything, I knew that if I agreed she would be pleased. From then on, excellently organized and prepared lessons arrived daily.

As a widow I had long since stopped observing my wedding anniversary. But during the first week of that sad August in prison, Hannah remembered my silver anniversary in a most touching manner. She covered an empty talcum powder tin with silver foil, attached white buds made of paper onto twenty-five blades of straw pulled from her mattress, and fitted these into the holes in the top of the can, which then looked like a delightful little bouquet of white roses. She glued a lace doily, also made of tissue paper, to the bottom of the can. Accompanying the "flowers" was an exquisite little paper doll bride with a long veil, carrying a minute bouquet of tissue paper roses. (For some reason one of the few things one could purchase in prison was tissue paper.) The gift was surpassed by a delightful accompanying poem, which, unfortunately, I destroyed, along with all communication from Hannah, since there was the constant danger of being searched and thus of implicating her in further difficulties.

Meanwhile, Hannah's manifold accomplishments reached their zenith. Her window signals were no longer directed only to me. They served as a daily news report and were watched for avidly by every prisoner whose window faced the yard. I was distressed by her courage and recklessness, afraid that her already precarious situation would be aggravated if her foolhardy actions came to the attention of the commandant. But my warnings had no effect upon her.

One morning she placed her middle and index fingers horizontally on her lip, then drew her hand, palm down, across her throat as if cutting it. She repeated this pantomime several times. Everyone understood she was referring to Hitler. That afternoon, during exercise time, word was passed that there had been an attempt on Hitler's life. How did she get her information? Those known as free prisoners—Hungarian political prisoners allowed special privileges—sent her newspapers, books, scraps of news. But she also heard a great deal on her almost daily trips to the Hill in the police van, and in the Hill waiting room. Many of my cellmates had occasion to talk to her under these circumstances, and they were greatly impressed by the special treatment extended her by the Germans. She was served a good lunch—which, they told me, she invariably shared—and often she was given newspapers. The guards, mainly Serbs from southern Hungary, were not too strict with her. She gained their sympathy by talking to them in their own language, which she had picked up during her stay with the partisans. One evening, four new prisoners were brought to our overcrowded cell. Two of them were hardly more than children, who had attempted to escape and been caught at the frontier. They had already been taken to Schwab Hill for questioning and were eager to share their experiences with us. One of them asked, "Do any of you know a charming and knowledgeable young woman prisoner who greets new prisoners and gives them advice, encourages them, tells them how to answer questions, and seems to have a great deal of information about everything?" One of my cellmates laughed. "That's Hannah ... Catherine's daughter. She's not afraid of anything or anyone, and knows everything." One of the young girls related that she had spent a couple of hours with Hannah at the Gestapo main headquarters, where she had been taken that day by an SS guard. Hannah asked him in German, "If it depended upon you, what sort of punishment would you give me?" And he had answered, "If it was up to me, I wouldn't punish you at all because I've never known a woman as brave as you."

When I repeated some of these things I had heard to Hannah she laughed. "Yes, it's true. The Germans haven't tortured me the way the Hungarians have, or used any truly drastic measures. They're trying to achieve their ends by psychological means." Seifert was her interrogator as well as mine. She told me she had kept her knowledge of German from him and always asked for an interpreter. She insisted upon this, since it gave her time to formulate her answers. She told me that on several occasions, after long interrogations, the Nazis had offered her cigarettes or coffee and asked her to tell them about Palestine. Lately, after protracted interrogations, they would say, "Enough for today. Now tell us about Palestine."

By mid-August the atmosphere seemed more relaxed, discipline less severe. Hannah was not summoned as frequently for interrogation, and then suddenly the questions stopped entirely. The stepped-up bombings and victories of the Allies and the rapid advance of the Russians increased our confidence that the end of the war was near. Everyone was hopeful that we would be transferred to Kistarcsa, the Hungarian internment camp, where, it was said, discipline was less rigid and the treatment in general incomparably better. Rumor spread that prisoners under Hungarian jurisdiction were not being deported, whereas German deportations continued without pause. By the end of August, conditions had improved considerably. The cell was no longer crowded; now and then I even had a bed entirely to myself. One exceptionally quiet and beautiful night I found it impossible to sleep, and I had the distinct feeling Hannah was not sleeping either. I crept to the window, fearful I would wake someone in the still night. The moon was shining so brightly it was almost like daylight, and I clearly saw Hannah silhouetted against the half-opened window, wearing her light blue dressing gown, her hair softly framing her lovely face. She was entirely lost in thought, and the moon appeared to form a soft halo around her head. It seemed to me her soul was mirrored in her face at that instant. Overwhelmed by infinite sadness, I returned to my bed, fell upon it, and buried my head in my arms to stifle my sobs. I was crying for my child, for her youth, for her cruel predicament and probably hopeless fate. Throughout her interrogations they had promised that once the questioning was over we would be permitted to meet. But when the time came the promise was, of course, forgotten. She repeatedly asked the prison commandant, with whom she often carried on heated political discussions, to move her, but he said he had not been authorized to do so and could not on his own initiative. When Hannah insisted with increasing vehemence, he capitulated. "All right, I'll take the chance. But it will be just between us."

At the beginning of September, Hannah was placed in a cell next to mine. We were able to take our daily walk in the same group, sometimes even to walk together, and thus managed, at times, brief whispered conversations. The water tap for the floor was directly opposite my cell door, and three times a day a prisoner from each cell was designated to carry in the water allotment. Naturally, everyone competed for this assignment, since it was one of the few opportunities to leave the hated confinement of the cell. The door of my cell opened directly onto the tap. Knowing this, Hannah's cellmates self-sacrificingly delegated her to be the sole water carrier. In this way I was able to look at her frequently, and she would signal to me. There were even times when a matron would call me into the corridor under some pretext when Hannah was at the tap, thus giving me an opportunity to embrace her, to hold her in my arms.

A mood of optimism reigned. Food, always a favorite topic in prison, now became the primary topic. Recipes for gourmet dishes were discussed and exchanged. One of the prisoners, the wife of a bank president, invited us all to a sumptuous supper in the near future, positive we would soon be freed. One Polish prisoner, originally from Cracow, who had been roaming from country to country for years, punctured our lovely daydreams by saying, "What folly! Most of us will probably end up in Auschwitz."

Auschwitz? What was that? It was the first time I had ever heard about the Nazi extermination camps. But soon afterwards a young Polish girl came to our cell and confirmed what the woman had said, adding that Auschwitz was not the only extermination center, but the largest of many. Nevertheless, we felt a definite change for the better, an improvement in conditions all along the line. The behavior of the matrons became more humane, and a few prisoners were even liberated, one of my cellmates among them. Of course the ransoms demanded—and paid—for freedom were vast. We also heard that the Hungarian government would no longer tolerate citizens being transported beyond the country's border and that our prison was surrounded by police to protect us from deportations. Then, during the night of September 10–11, all the lights were suddenly turned on, and moaning, weeping, and screams slashed the stillness of the early morning. We listened in terror and learned that most of the Polish prisoners were being rounded up for deportation. I had heard of the night roundups but had never before witnessed one. Our door was opened by a soldier, who read off the name of the unfortunate woman from Cracow. He left the door open, and we could see the group of victims in the corridor, wailing and sobbing.

At that very moment there was a violent bombing raid, and the lights went out as suddenly as they had been turned on. As we crouched in fear we were at least hopeful the attack would disrupt the evil project of the Nazis. It did not. It merely delayed it a half hour. I was told that Hannah fell on the bed and sobbed when they took several of her cellmates. Those who remained were surprised, considering her usual moral strength and courage. But she pulled herself together, and soon she was again the one to instill hope in others. The following morning, September 11, a young prisoner working in the corridor called me to the door and told me that Hannah had just been taken away, adding, "But don't worry about her. Wherever they've taken her, it can't be much worse than this."

Small consolation. That afternoon in the yard her cellmates confirmed the sickening news. I was destroyed, entirely without hope, my world at an end. They attempted to comfort me with stories of her bravery and goodness. They told me that before knowing her they had been despondent and had tried to kill the unending hours one way or another. She had brought spirit and hope to them; planned activities; taught them songs, games, dances; told them endless stories about Palestine; gave them Hebrew lessons. And proselytizing as always, she converted many to Zionism by tirelessly detailing the life on the settlements, the history of the Land, its promise for the future.

Rumors multiplied. Word spread that we were to be transferred to a better place. On September 12 they actually did take several from our cell. Two days after Hannah left, my name was read from a list, along with those of many of the other prisoners in my cell. That left only three behind. A tremendous crowd was already assembled in the corridor. The roll was called, and then personal belongings that had been taken from us were returned—excepting money and valuables. I saw the civilian who had been in the office when I had arrived, and managed to ask in a whisper where they had taken Hannah. He said he had no idea but imagined it would be a better place. We were transported in huge vans to the internment camp of Kistarcsa, on the outskirts of the city. There, an enormous crowd awaited us, and we gazed at one another, our eyes seeking familiar faces—sisters, brothers, children, friends. Some families were reunited, erstwhile prisonmates recognized one another, old friends embraced. But there were many bitter disappointments.

After the rigid discipline of the Gestapo prison, the Hungarian camp was like a summer resort, the atmosphere relatively relaxed. We were allowed to walk about the huge fenced-in grounds without restraint, to write as many letters as we liked, and to receive unlimited packages. In exceptional cases we were even allowed to receive visitors. I was tormented by worry about Hannah and wrote to Margit, asking her to visit me. In a day or so I was called to the office and found Margit there, accompanied by her friend Hilda Gobby, also a well-known actress. A prison official was with them. I happily threw my arms around her, but she failed to respond. Standing stiff as a ramrod, her voice frigid, she said, "Madame, I urgently need your signature on this contract for the flat. I've even brought a deposit along so we can settle the matter at once." Of course I understood immediately that she had used the contract as a pretext to gain admission. We could barely contain our laughter. However, at that time the political climate was such that the official supposedly watching us turned the other way, busied himself with paperwork, and gave us an opportunity to talk freely and at length. I begged Margit to make every attempt to trace Hannah's whereabouts.

Going down the stairs, Margit was surrounded by a crowd. There were many in the camp from the world of the theatre, and news of her visit had spread like wildfire. They asked for news of friends and relatives they thought she might know, and begged her to take messages. The general mood was, on the whole, remarkably good. Internees were filled with confidence, and there was even a special dinner served on Rosh Hashanah, brought to the camp by the various Jewish organizations. I was in constant touch with my sister, and in one of her letters she wrote that various countries, among them Switzerland, were issuing safe-conduct papers to Jews. She said she was making every possible effort to obtain one for me, which would mean my release. But still no news of Hannah.

Toward the end of September—on Yom Kippur, to be exact—everyone was suddenly released. Thanks to an order from the minister of the interior, the Kistarcsa internment camp was to be closed. It was late afternoon before the roll call was exhausted and the last prisoner released. I made my way to my sister's, who then lived in one of the yellow star–designated houses in Alkotmány Street. She could hardly believe her eyes when she saw me, and I, for my part, was shocked by my sister's appearance. Worry and constant running from place to place in futile attempts to find Hannah and to effect my release had changed her into a prematurely aged, careworn matron. The important news was that Hannah had sent word. The previous day a young Hungarian lawyer named Nánay had called on her at Conti Street Prison, offering to defend her if her case came to trial. Hannah asked him to contact her family through Margit, whose address was the only one she knew, and discuss her case with them. She said it was up to them to decide about her defense.

The next day my brother-in-law, also a lawyer, and I called on Dr. Nánay. The young lawyer informed us that there were others involved with Hannah, also parachutists. They had empowered him to act on their behalf, he said, and he was preparing their defense. He produced an authorization signed by them. However, I wanted to consult our friend and family counselor, Dr. Palágyi, before making a decision, and above all to talk to Hannah and ask her what she wanted me to do. I explained this to Dr. Nánay, and he promised he would procure a visitor's pass for me within the next day or so—but only if I agreed to discard the yellow star sewn on my coat.

Then I went to visit my home, and Margit gave me an envelope that, she said, had been brought to her dressing room in the theatre the previous evening by two young men. There was a considerable sum of money in it, and Margit said the men had asked her to see that Hannah lacked for nothing in prison. Someone named Geri sent the money, and they asked that regards from him be given to Hannah. Of course at the time I had no idea who the mysterious Geri was, but later I discovered he was Reuven Dafne, her parachutist comrade who had been with her in Yugoslavia among the partisans. A day or so later, Dr. Nánay came and took me to Conti Street Prison, where I was to be allowed ten minutes with Hannah. He left me there, and I waited in a tiny room until she appeared, flanked by two guards. She looked remarkably well. Naturally, our conversation was circumscribed, but at least we could embrace, and she opened the package I brought. The war was already in its fifth year, and there were serious food shortages; but when friends and relatives heard I was going to visit Hannah, they had hurriedly brought whatever they could, including items of clothing and other odds and ends they thought might please her. I had unearthed a sewing set she had received as a child, and included it in the parcel. As an experienced ex-prisoner I knew the importance of such a thing. Everything delighted her, but this pleased her above all. It brought tears to her eyes, and she asked, "Does this thing still exist? Was there ever such a time ... a time of childhood and carefree happiness?"

I asked what she needed or wanted. She quickly replied, "Books ... good books ... as many as you can send. Reading is allowed here. But I warn you, you won't get them back because they're confiscated for the prison library. But more than anything else, I'd like a Bible. A Hebrew Bible."

Hearing this, one of the guards said, "How is it that Hannah is Jewish and you, her mother, Gentile?"

"Not at all," I said. "I'm Jewish, too."

"Then where is your yellow star?"

I knew that a recent government regulation granted exemption from the wearing of the yellow star to Jews responsible for cultural achievements, or those who merited special consideration for enhancing Hungary's prestige. In view of my late husband's achievements I had been recommended for such exemption. The application had received the enthusiastic endorsement of various theatres as

well as of the *Pesti Hirlap*, the newspaper with which my husband
had been associated. So I replied, "I am exempt from wearing the
yellow star in view of the literary activities of my late husband." The
guards believed me, and Hannah smiled proudly.

One of the guards said, "But of course! I remember Mr. Senesh.
In fact I knew him well. I was a waiter in the café where he often
used to go."

I gave Hannah the greetings from Geri. Her eyes sparkled, and she
beamed. Then I asked again what she needed or would like other
than the books. It was the beginning of October, and the weather
was turning cold.

"If possible, I'd like some warmer clothes. It's cold in the cell."
Otherwise, she said, she was well. She was not in solitary confinement. On the contrary, everyone in her cell was young, spirited, and
optimistic. (Actually, during all the months she was imprisoned, I
never heard her complain about anything.) Finally, she told me the
most important thing: "I'm going to be tried soon. I need a lawyer
to defend me. Decide on someone as soon as possible." The ten minutes were up.

Friends and relatives heard that I had been released. I was inun-
dated with advice on how to rescue Hannah. The majority insisted
that I must contact the Zionist Organization and ask for legal assistance. After calling on Dr. Nánay, I went to the head office of the
Zionist Organization at Glass House, in Vadász Street, and was directed
to a young man who assured me everything possible was being done
to obtain the release of the imprisoned parachutists. When I gave
him details of the case, he insisted he was completely informed about
everything. But in the course of our relatively brief conversation it
transpired that he didn't even know Hannah had already been in the
Conti Street Prison for nearly three weeks. He thought she was in
the Margit Boulevard Prison, along with her comrades. He promised
again to do everything in his power for all of them.

I asked Dr. Palágyi, who had never heard of Dr. Nánay, to examine the list of available defense lawyers with the utmost care and to
choose the one he thought the very best. (Jewish lawyers, of course,
were not permitted to practice.) Dr. Palágyi's first choice handled

only civil cases, and thus declined. Finally he chose Dr. Szelecsényi, who, he said, had recently won a string of complicated cases. However, before I entrusted him with Hannah's defense, I was advised by several friends that instead of discussing the matter with nondescript office clerks at the Zionist Organization, I should contact influential officials at the very top. All my attempts to do so ended in an absolute fiasco. It is pointless to detail the events that ensued in the following weeks, nor can I describe the tension, disappointments, and disillusionment. On October 12, when I was definitely convinced it was useless to wait for the Zionist Organization to do anything, I called upon Dr. Szelecsényi, accompanied by Dr. Palágyi, and entrusted him with the defense of my daughter. He promised that he would see her in prison the next day and would make every effort to obtain a pass for me to visit her.

Meanwhile, I tried in vain to find a Hebrew Bible. All bookshops dealing in Jewish or Hebrew literature had been closed months before. I even called at the home of the former proprietor of the largest shop of this kind in Budapest, but he had fled the country. In the well-known shop dealing in religious books in Deák Square, I was received with surprise: they had the Bible in all languages, but certainly not in Hebrew. Friends who had a Hebrew Bible were, on the other hand, reluctant to part with it for fear they would never get it back. To my everlasting sorrow, I was unable to fulfill Hannah's last wish.

A few years later, one of her former cellmates related how Hannah had won their hearts in the very short time they were together. She told them she was a Zionist, and being Communists they did not know exactly what "Zionist" meant. Thus, they were suspicious and kept away from her at first. But they soon realized she was helpful to all of them and, though not a Communist herself, shared with them or gave them whatever she had. She taught the illiterates to read and write, and gave interesting lectures on the labor movement and the Histadrut institutions in Palestine. Soon the barrier between them was torn down, and they all felt her warmth and kind-heartedness.

During those days I received a long, censored letter from her detailing her activities, praising her cellmates, and assuring me she kept herself busy and that she was well. Of course, she said, all this feverish activity served to help her forget reality.

Dr. Szelecsényi could not go to the prison to see her on October 13 because of a massive air raid. So it was Saturday, the 14th, before he was able to see her. That afternoon I went to his office, and he told me he had talked to her for a considerable time, since there had been another large air raid and he had been trapped in the prison. He did not go into detail but said only that he doubted whether one man in a thousand would have undertaken and accomplished the things Hannah had. He also said that if her case went to trial she would definitely be convicted, and he had no idea what the sentence would be: five years, two years, perhaps even seven. But he said that the length of the sentence was of absolutely no importance, since at the end of the war political prisoners would be released immediately. "And I don't need to tell you how the war stands now," he added. "There is absolutely no possibility of a death sentence. I'm not saying this just to calm your fears, but because that is my sincere conviction."

He promised he would notify me immediately when the trial date was set so I could be present. In fact, he insisted I should be in the corridor during the session, and felt sure I would be able to talk to Hannah during the recess. Captain Simon, the judge advocate, had refused me a visitor's pass to see her in prison until after the trial.

But on the following day, October 15, the destiny of what remained of Hungarian Jewry was sealed. Szálasi came into power, and whatever hardship or atrocities the Jews had hitherto endured were as nothing compared to the atrocities and bloodbath that ensued under the rule of the bestial Hungarian Nazis, the Arrow-Crossers. Jews were permitted to leave their houses for only two hours a day—on certain days. House superintendents who had, until then, looked the other way if Jewish tenants ventured out without the yellow star, now insisted the brand must always be worn—which meant we did not dare to venture out on the unspecified days. This prevented me from calling upon Szelecsényi again. My sister and her husband, both under Swedish protection and thus exempt from wearing the yellow star, maintained contact with him. Through them I was told the trial had been set for October 28.

I telephoned the lawyer from the home of a Gentile family. To my desperate question as to what would happen in view of the changed political situation, he said, "It is possible that the sentence will be ten or twenty years, maybe even life. However, this does not essentially change matters." He again reminded me that whatever the sentence, it would be meaningless in view of the military situation, and again asked me to be present on the day of the trial, since there was a possibility I would be permitted to see Hannah during the recess. On October 28, I went to Margit Boulevard Prison and was appalled by the mob milling about. I waited in the antechamber of the courtroom bearing the sign "Hannah Senesh and Accomplices." I was not allowed inside the courtroom.

At eleven o'clock, when the judges retired to deliberate, the doors were flung open and I glimpsed Hannah amidst the group streaming out. She had no idea I would be there. Rushing over, she threw her arms around me. The guard separated us and said he could permit us to talk only after sentence had been passed. I was deathly pale, but she was flushed, excited, her eyes brilliant, her smile self-confident. They were soon recalled but after a few tense moments appeared again. Hannah told me that judgment had been postponed for eight days, which meant until the following Saturday, November 4.

This unexpected turn of events was enormously depressing, and I asked Szelecsényi, who was standing nearby, what it signified. He said the delay had absolutely no significance, and although such a postponement was rare, it had been known to happen.

Hannah said, "Dr. Szelecsényi's defense was brilliant, Mother. Do thank him."

The lawyer was flattered and pleased by the compliment. (He later told my sister that he had been vehemently attacked by members of the court for accepting the defense of a "Jew girl.") He rushed away to another trial after advising us to make the most of the time we had left together. I could not hide my anxiety and depression. Hannah tried to reassure me by saying that in her case the delay made no difference, since she would not be released from prison anyway while the war continued. "But I'm astonished that you walk about the streets so freely under existing conditions," she chided.

"Why don't you disappear? What about all your Gentile friends? Can't they hide you?"

When I said I wanted her case to be settled before I thought of hiding, she said, "I'll muddle through this somehow, believe me. But I won't have a moment's peace as long as you're so careless."

The guard (the ex-waiter) warned us that our time was up but reminded me that now the trial was over, there was nothing to prevent me from visiting my daughter in Conti Street Prison. He said I could obtain a visitor's pass without any trouble at the prison office, so I promised to visit her on Monday, October 30. We walked down the stairs together, and the guard said he would run ahead to see if the prison car had arrived—to which Hannah commented that she would much rather have gone by tram and seen the busy life in the city's streets. I watched her walk away until she disappeared from view, lost in the mob.

On October 30 and 31, there were such intense air raids that I couldn't leave the house. On November 1, I presented myself at the office, only to be told that since it was a holiday—All Saints' Day—visitors were not allowed. On November 2, I tried again but was told that since sentence had not been passed it would be necessary to obtain a pass from Captain Simon, the judge advocate, whose office was at the Hadik Barracks. It was impossible to go there that same day, so it was not until November 3 that I applied for a pass at the office of Captain Simon. But there I was given to understand that Captain Simon was out of town and could not be reached until Tuesday, November 7. When I explained why I had come, and asked who was replacing Captain Simon during his absence, they told me no one was authorized to issue a visitor's pass while Captain Simon was away.

In the meantime—and before the eight days had expired—I wrote to Dr. Szelecsényi and asked why he had not notified me about the date of sentence. He answered that the date had been postponed once again because a new judge advocate had been appointed to handle the case. He promised he would let me know without an instant's delay when he was notified. On November 7, the eleventh day after the trial, I called again at the office of Captain Simon in the

Hadik Barracks, only to find total confusion. One crammed moving van after another trundled out. The doorman told me it was pointless entering the building because as far as he knew everyone had already gone. Certainly, the roar of the Russian guns was increasing even as we talked; the mass flight of the Fascists to the west had begun. But despite the increased bombardment and the porter's certainty that Captain Simon was already gone, I insisted upon going to his office on the chance that he might still be there. After a great deal of persuasion, the porter agreed to let me enter the building and try the captain's office.

Everything had indeed been packed, but I found two female clerks in hats and coats, and a young officer. All were on the point of leaving. The officer was the one I had talked to on my last visit, when Captain Simon was out of town. I explained once again that I still desperately wanted the visitor's permit. The officer answered that Simon had been transferred the previous day to Margit Boulevard Military Prison, and he gave me the number of the captain's office there. Then, glancing at his watch, he added, "You had better hurry." I understood this last to mean that the captain would soon be leaving his office and that if I wanted to catch him I should move fast. I reached Margit Boulevard at about ten-thirty. It was quiet and comparatively deserted. From the sentry at the entrance to the captain's office, I did not pass a soul, and I had the impression everyone had fled the building. After wandering up and down the corridors of the seemingly deserted building, I found the right office. It was empty, but a briefcase on one of the desks, with a pair of gloves resting on it, indicated that its owner was still in the building. I waited in the corridor. A clerk appeared, who confirmed that Captain Simon was still there. At eleven forty-five he returned to his office. I followed him in, introduced myself, and asked for a visitor's pass.

"The case no longer has anything to do with me," he answered, apparently ill at ease.

"Since when?" I asked.

"Since yesterday," he answered.

"Then who is in charge of the case?"

"I don't know."

"Who is authorized to grant me a visitor's permit?"

"I don't know."

"Shall I go to the Conti Street Prison and ask the warden for one?"

"You can. Go there. Try."

His brusque, summary answers released all my bitterness. "Captain, at least be helpful enough to direct me to the proper authorities, and tell me what I must do in order to see my daughter. As it is, I can't understand why it's so difficult for me to obtain a pass when relatives of other prisoners have been permitted frequent visiting rights. I have been granted permission to see my daughter only once, and then only for minutes."

"Really?" he remarked, almost in wonder. "I didn't grant you permission to see her even once?"

"And how is it possible that there still has not been a date set for sentencing? The eight-day postponement has long since expired." He did not answer, so I continued. "Or has sentence been passed?"

"Even if it has been, I'm not in a position to tell you what it entails."

"What do you mean? You don't mean to tell me it would be possible to keep such information from me?" Since he did not reply, I repeated, "Has sentence been passed?"

Captain Simon then went to his desk, sat down, and pointed to the chair opposite. "Sit down." After another embarrassing silence he continued, "Are you a Jew? Or was only your husband one?"

"He was, and I am. We're all Jews," I answered.

"I don't see the yellow star."

I uncovered the star, which had inadvertently been hidden by my large bag.

Finally he came to the point. "Are you familiar with your daughter's case?"

"Yes. The lawyer has briefed me."

Ignoring this answer, he went on and summarized the case. "Your daughter, after renouncing her Hungarian citizenship, joined the British Armed Forces and was a radio officer in the Parachute Corps. Last spring she flew from Cairo, via Italy, to Yugoslavia, where she was dropped, and spent a considerable length of time with the partisans. From Yugoslavia she made her way to Hungary, supposedly for the purpose of rescuing Jews and British prisoners of war. In other words, she is guilty of major crimes against the interests of Hungary...."

"That isn't true," I interjected. "I'm positive that isn't true because once, when we met in the Gestapo prison yard, I questioned her about her mission. She said she could not answer my questions because she was bound by military secrecy; but she assured me she had positively not undertaken, nor committed, any act that could possibly be detrimental to the welfare of Hungary. On the contrary!"

"But Hungary is under martial law, and your daughter was found with a radio transmitter. Consequently the Military Tribunal found her guilty of treason and demanded the supreme penalty. And this ... penalty ... has already been ... carried out."

I looked at him, petrified. The world went black. Suddenly I remembered Szelecsényi's letter. Perhaps this man was merely deriving some form of brutal pleasure from torturing me. I clung to this thought as a last straw and finally said, "No, no. That's impossible. It can't be. Why, only this morning I received a letter from the lawyer telling me sentence had not yet been passed, and that he would let me know when the day was fixed for sentencing. Certainly the lawyer would have been informed if anything had happened."

"Yes, of course," Captain Simon said. "He knows, but he probably wants to spare you."

"Spare me? What sense would that make? How long do you suppose I would be spared? No. The lawyer must have told me the truth."

"What's the name of the lawyer?"

"Dr. Andre Szelecsényi. But I have his letter with me." I fumbled for it in my handbag, then handed it to him.

He glanced at the letter, made a note of the lawyer's name and telephone number, and said, "All right, we'll inform him by phone."

I knew there was no hope left. "And this is the way it happens? Such things exist? They can really happen?" I stammered. "And I wasn't even allowed to see her, to talk to her."

"She didn't want to see you. She wanted to spare you the shock." (Later he told Dr. Szelecsényi just the opposite. Hannah did indeed ask to see me. It was her last request, but they "dissuaded" her.) After a moment's silence, he continued, "But you'll be given the farewell letters. She wrote several." After yet another terrible silence he said, "I must pay tribute to your daughter's exceptional courage and strength of character, both of which she manifested until the very last moment. She was truly proud of being a Jew." He stated that with undisguised, if puzzled, admiration.

I replied, "I don't know the military laws and whether my daughter has transgressed them, and if she did, what that act was...."

"Her offense was exceedingly grave," he interrupted.

"But that she stands innocent before man and God," I went on, "I don't doubt at all. Because anyone so gifted, so endowed with talent, could only have volunteered for a great and noble cause."

"True, she was an exceptional human being. But it is just such people who volunteer for unusual assignments. Pity she chose the wrong path. Accept what has happened," he continued. "This war has claimed so many lives, such horrible sacrifices; consider her one of them."

I asked for the farewell letters. He said I could pick them up any morning at Conti Street Prison.

As I staggered down the stairs, unseeing, it suddenly struck me that Simon had just come from the execution. This was later verified.

Shortly after my departure, Dr. Szelecsényi passed by Margit Boulevard Prison and saw a hearse pull out.

"What's that?" he asked the sentry. "Have there been any recent executions?"

"Yes. They executed the British woman officer," the sentry replied.

Dr. Szelecsényi rushed upstairs to Captain Simon and accused him of murder, stating that the "judicial murder" had been an unlawful execution carried out without final sentence having been passed. When, after the war, Captain Simon was brought to trial, the fact of illegal execution was actually established. A few days later, my sister and I went to Conti Street Prison and asked for the letters. They were surprised at our request and said they must be at Margit Boulevard Prison. And they actually were—in the possession of

Captain Simon. Szelecsényi, who was deeply disturbed by the series of illegal events, asked for the letters. Simon read them to him but refused to part with them. According to the lawyer, Simon took the letters, along with the documents relating to the case, when he fled the country.

At Conti Street Prison I was given a few of Hannah's personal effects. In the pockets of the dresses I found two scraps of paper. On one was a poem she must have written in her cell in Hadik Barracks after our last meeting, and a few undated lines of farewell:

> Dearest Mother:
>
> I don't know what to say—only this: a million thanks, and forgive me, if you can.
>
> You know so well why words aren't necessary.
>
> With love forever,
>
> Your daughter

Catherine Senesh

Catherine Senesh with Prime Minister Golda Meir
at the Roman Theater in Caesarea celebrating
the twenty-fifth anniversary of
Kibbutz Sdot Yam in 1965.

SELECTED POEMS

Mother

If the world offered a reward,
A laurel for patience and love,
One person alone would be worthy:
Mother.

Let there be thanks in your hearts
And on your lips a prayer,
Whenever you hear that most beautiful word:
Mother.

Budapest, 1933 (aged 12)

Translated from the Hungarian by Peter Hay

Now

Now—now I'd like to say something,
Something more than mere words,
More dappled than color,
More musical than rhythm or rhyme,
Something a million people haven't already said or
heard.

Just something.
All about the land is silent, listening,
The forest gazing at me, expectant.
The sky watches me with a curious eye.
Everything is silent. And so am I.

Tatra, Biela Voda, 1938

Translated from the Hungarian by Peter Hay

Leaves

First it was green,
Then it turned yellow.
Soon its face changed to wine-red.
Tomorrow it will hide in a monk's robe,
And its next color will spell death.

                    Tatra, Biela Voda, 1938

Translated from the Hungarian by Marta Cohn

Harvest

Our people are working the black soil,
Their arms reap the gold sheaves,
And now when the last ear its stalk leaves
Our faces glitter as with gilded oil.

From where comes the new light and voice,
From where the resounding song at hand?
From where the fighting spirit and new faith?
From you, fertile Emek, from you, my land.

                    Nahalal, 1940

Translated from the Hungarian by Peter Hay

To My Mother[1]

From where have you learned to wipe the tears,
To quietly bear the pain,
To hide in your heart the cry, the hurt,
The suffering and the complaint?

Hear the wind!
Its open maw
Roars through hill and dale.
See the ocean ...
The giant rocks,
In anger and wrath it flails.

Nature all arush, agush
Breaks out of each form and fence.
From where is this quiet in your hearts,
From where have you learned strength?

Nahalal, 1940

Translated from the Hebrew by Ruth Finer Mintz

To a Good Friend

I wounded another not knowing
Both ends of an arrow mar.
I too was hurt in the battle
And shall bear a scar.

Nahalal, 1941

Translated from the Hebrew by Ziva Shapiro

For the Brothers[2]

Should we break,
Then take the burden
Heavy and great
Upon you.

Build upon sand
Under the blue
Sky ... everything
Anew.

And know, costly
The road to the just
And the true.

Nahalal, 1941

Translated from the Hebrew by Ruth Finer Mintz

To Die ...

To die ... so young to die ... no, no, not I.
I love the warm sunny skies,
Light, songs, shining eyes.
I want no war, no battle cry—
No, no ... Not I.

But if it must be that I live today
With blood and death on every hand,
Praised be He for the grace, I'll say
To live, if I should die this day ...
Upon your soil, my home, my land.

Nahalal, 1941

Translated from the Hebrew by Dorothy H. Rochmis

To Caesarea

Hush, cease all sound.
Across the sea is the sand,
The shore known and near,
The shore golden, dear,
Home, the Homeland.

With step twisting and light
Among strangers we move,
Word and song hushed,
Toward the future-past
Caesarea ...

But reaching the city of ruins
Soft a few words we intone.
We return. We are here.
Soft answers the silence of stone,
We awaited you two thousand years.

Sdot Yam, Caesarea, 1941
Translated from the Hebrew by Ruth Finer Mintz

Kibbutz Ginosar[3]

In the black fields on a dark night
Candles kindled, scattering light
in the furrows' festive joy.

In the dark night on white fields
Bonfires flared, flames spread ...
Worlds were destroyed.

In the black fields,
The future's sparkling song,
The tractor sang.

In the white fields
There groaned
A dying man.

Sdot Yam, Caesarea, 1941
Translated from the Hebrew by Ruth Finer Mintz

To Mothers in the Diaspora

A day, two days, a week, a month,
One year, ten years ... to wait
For a line, a word, no matter how late.

Through endless plight
To gather and to store
The terror of the night.

Concealing in the dread
Vast seas of blood
A tear.

Then what word can we say?
Only a look, a word today or any day:
Mother! Mother!

Sdot Yam, 1942

Translated from the Hebrew by I. M. Lask

If Only You Had Come[4]

If only you had come suddenly toward me on the street
hands in your pockets and a smile on your face
the rhythm of your stride, a familiar pace—
I would have stopped, amazed and overwhelmed
at the wonderful sight, precious and profound.

As the image of you bursts forth to the depths
all traces of doubt within me will flee,
I will fling my arms toward you, hold you near to me
both laughing and weeping: if only it could be!

Sdot Yam, 1942

Translated from the Hebrew by Rochelle Mass

Loneliness

Could I meet one who understood all ...
Without word, without search,
Confession or lie,
Without asking why.

I would spread before him, like a white cloth,
The heart and the soul ...
The filth and the gold.
Perceptive, he would understand.

And after I had plundered the heart,
When all had been emptied and given away,
I would feel neither anguish nor pain,
But would know how rich I became.

Sdot Yam, Caesarea, 1942

Translated from the Hebrew by Ruth Finer Mintz

A Glance

How far, far have the people lagged,
Infinitely far have the seas receded.
How distant now the gay and dancing times,
How languid the once proud songs and rhymes,
How distant ... How languid ...

Sdot Yam, Caesarea, 1942

Translated from the Hungarian by Peter Hay

Walk to Caesarea

God—may there be no end
to sea, to sand,
water's splash,
lightning's flash,
the prayer of man

Caesarea, 1942

Translated from the Hebrew by Ziva Shapiro

Seed

Seed falls, the golden grain takes root,
Not on the rock, not on the paved road.
Gather it in, black dust,
And blanket it against the heat and frost.
This speck of life enclosed within a husk.
Seed of infinity, this tiny little grain,
Pressed underneath the dust and waiting for a sign,
For mark of Spring, for ray of light, for sun,
For day.

1942

Translated from the Hebrew by I. M. Lask

At the Crossroads

A voice called. I went.
I went, for it called.
I went, lest I fall.

At the crossroads
I blocked both ears with white frost
And cried
For what I had lost.

Caesarea, 1942

Translated from the Hebrew by Ziva Shapiro

You Are Not Alone

You are not alone, for the sea is yours—
In soft flowing whispers, it will ask you
of your dreams, your hopes for the future too.

They've waited, they all waited for your coming—
the waves and the sea, the rocks, the shore and the sand.
you'll appear on a dark, gloomy night, they understand.

While thousands of heavenly eyes high in the air
understand the comradeship of that pair
who steal endless water—and weep.

Caesarea, 1943

Translated from the Hebrew by Rochelle Mass

We Gather Flowers

We gathered flowers in the fields and mountains,
We breathed the fresh winds of spring,
We were drenched with the warmth of the sun's rays
In our Homeland, in our beloved home.

We go out to our brothers in exile,
To the suffering of winter, to frost in the night.
Our hearts will bring tidings of springtime,
Our lips sing the song of light.

1944

Translated from the Hebrew by Dorothy Bar-Adon

Blessed Is the Match

Blessed is the match consumed
        in kindling flame.
Blessed is the flame that burns
        in the secret fastness of the heart.
Blessed is the heart with strength to stop
        its beating for honor's sake.
Blessed is the match consumed
        in kindling flame.

                                        Sardice, Yugoslavia, May 2, 1944
Translated from the Hebrew by Marie Syrkin

One—Two—Three[5]

One—two—three …
        eight feet long,
Two strides across, the rest is dark …
Life hangs over me like a question mark.

One—two—three …
        maybe another week,
Or next month may still find me here,
But death, I feel, is very near.

I could have been
        twenty-three next July;
I gambled on what mattered most,
The dice were cast. I lost.

                                        Budapest, 1944

Translated from the Hungarian by Peter Hay

Hannah Senesh lies in state in Haifa.
Her body was brought to Israel in 1951, where she was buried
with full military honors.

AFTERWORD

My film *Blessed Is the Match: The Life and Death of Hannah Senesh* is the first feature-length documentary about Hannah Senesh. Having the opportunity to tell Hannah's story is a lifelong dream come true. It's both an honor and a tremendous responsibility. Despite Hannah's status in Israel as a national heroine, her story remains a little-known part of history to the rest of the world. I hope that my film, along with this paperback edition of her diary, will help to change that.

I first read Hannah's diary in junior high school and was captivated by her courage and touched by her vulnerability. Later, as a history student in college, I wrote my senior thesis on the Nazi SS, and Hannah's story continued to inspire me. Why? Because she fought back. In the face of monolithic evil, she chose action as her weapon, joining a noble, against-all-odds mission and, in the end, dying for what she believed.

For the past twenty years, as I've worked as a documentary filmmaker, my interest in Hannah has persisted. My fascination with her story, however, has come to include her mother, Catherine's, experience as well. This is not just because I've grown from a student Hannah's age to a mother closer to Catherine's age (though, admittedly, that could be part of it), but, in many ways, Catherine is a figure I am better able to understand. Hannah is a modern-day Joan of Arc, the type of heroine who comes along once in a century— bold, brilliant, and uncommonly courageous. Catherine, on the other hand, is someone who is universally relatable. As a worried mother, she watched Hannah drift away, pursue her own path, and then make the ultimate sacrifice.

In 2005, my producing partner, Lisa Thomas, and I initiated talks with Eitan Senesh, Hannah's nephew and the official keeper of her legacy in Israel, in regard to making a documentary about Hannah.

After traveling to Israel to meet Eitan and his brother David in person, they granted us the rights to Hannah's life story and unprecedented access to the Senesh family archive. In this rich archive are hundreds of unpublished letters and nearly 1,300 never-before-seen photos of remarkable quality, more than half taken by Hannah herself. (Hannah, I discovered, meticulously recorded her life not only in words, but also in pictures!)

Working with writer Sophie Sartain, we made the decision to tell Hannah's story as a mother-daughter love story. From that point, it followed naturally to use Catherine Senesh's raw and revelatory memoirs (included in this volume) as the narrative voice of the film and the most appropriate vehicle to help tell Hannah's story. Of course, Hannah's voice also runs throughout the film, not only through her diary and poems, but also in many never-before-translated or published letters to her mother and brother, Gyuri.

We shot most of the film in Hungary, Israel, and the Czech Republic. Our interview subjects included world-renowned scholars, such as Michael Berenbaum and Sir Martin Gilbert, and survivors, witnesses, and friends of Hannah's from Budapest and Palestine. We learned about Hannah as a real girl from childhood friends, classmates at the Girl's Agricultural School at Nahalal, pioneering members of Kibbutz Sdot Yam, and even from former Israeli Prime Minister Shimon Peres, who met Hannah when they were both in their twenties. We gained new insight into the daring parachutists' mission from the two surviving parachutists at the time, Surika Braverman and Reuven Dafne. Shortly before his death, Dafne relayed the story of Hannah handing him the poem, "Blessed Is the Match,"—also in his essay in this book—just before she crossed the border into Hungary. Perhaps the most chilling interviews were conducted with four women who were in the same Gestapo and Hungarian prisons as Catherine and Hannah Senesh in 1944. Finally, interviews with Hannah's nephews, David and Eitan Senesh, illuminated the family dynamics after Hannah's death: how their father, Gyuri, often lived in the shadow of his martyred sister, and how their grandmother, Catherine, embraced life in the new state of Israel, but never fully recovered from Hannah's death. In fact, they revealed, Catherine made preserving Hannah's legacy her own life's mission, until she died in her 90s.

Making *Blessed Is the Match* has been a long and complex journey. We hope our film not only does justice to Hannah's life—to her character, her creativity, and her courage—but that it also tells a moving, multilayered, mother–daughter story. In so doing, we hope to honor the legacies of both Hannah and Catherine Senesh for years to come. For more information on *Blessed Is the Match*, please visit www.blessedisthematch.com.

Roberta Grossman
Director, *Blessed Is the Match*

READER'S GUIDE

1. Why did Hannah return to Hungary?

She has been called a Zionist Joan of Arc; the implication is that she was driven by a faith in Israel's destiny that was so absolute and unyielding that it might have been imbued by divine revelation. Yet in Hannah Senesh's diary entry of January 8, 1943, when she first conceived her plan of returning to Hungary, and in many of the entries that follow, she writes of her intense loneliness, of her boredom and restlessness, of her guilt about leaving her mother behind when she emigrated to Israel and of her desire to secure her mother's safety.

What do you think impelled Hannah more, the personal or the universal? Does it matter?

2. Why did Hannah choose martyrdom?

Senator John McCain, who as a young man was imprisoned and tortured as a prisoner of war in Vietnam, has wrestled with this very question. "It seems [Hannah] had a chance to survive," he wrote in his book *Why Courage Matters*. "Neither her mission nor the people she had come to rescue would have been any the worse for it. She was not asked, at least not in advance of requesting clemency, to betray a confidence or inform on her comrades. Did she really need to accept martyrdom for her cause?" McCain contrasts Hannah's sacrifice with that of a soldier who spontaneously throws himself on a grenade to save his comrades, or to a religious martyr, who dies for "the sake of something encompassing but also surpassing human suffering," concluding finally that she might have chosen to die for the sake of her "dignity and sense of honor."

> *Blessed is the heart with strength to stop*
> *its beating for honor's sake.*
> —Hannah Senesh

"I don't think Hannah wanted to die for the sake of having her memory exalted in history or to prove herself equal to a romantic image she
conceived for herself," Senator McCain writes. "Her heroism wasn't a
fashion. She made a choice to be heroic, but to be heroic in order to
be true. Her purpose wasn't to die. She died for her life's purpose."

What do you think Hannah's "life's purpose" was?

3. How was Hannah a hero?

On April 12, 1941, more than three years before she died, Hannah
presaged her own fate: "Sometimes I feel I am an emissary who
has been entrusted with a mission," she wrote. "What this mission
is—is not clear to me. (After all, everyone has a mission in life.) I
feel I have a duty toward others, as if I were obligated to them. At
times this appears to be all sheer nonsense, and I wonder why all
this individual effort … and why particularly me?"

**Was Hannah's mission ultimately fulfilled by her murder, as
a match's purpose is by its own immolation?**

**Much has been made of the courageous way that Hannah
died, but in fact the sole witnesses to her last moments
were her executioners. Her diary and her poems bear elo-
quent witness to the values that informed the entirety of
her short life, and provide ample grounds for the
contention that she would have been heroic even if she
hadn't returned to Hungary. Do you agree?**

4. What mattered most to Hannah?

On April 23, 1941, when the Nazis overran Yugoslavia, Hannah
contemplated the horrible possibility that Palestine, too, would
suffer the same fate. She expresses her hope that her people would
face such a catastrophe with honor. But then she asks, "What is a
heroic death? To consecrate God's name? Is it possible to consecrate God's name in a manner divorced from life itself? Is there
anything more holy than life itself?"

In her final poem, composed literally moments before her
death, she wrote:

I gambled on what mattered most,
The dice were cast, I lost.

Though she had been prepared to die, do you think she expected to?

5. **What might Hannah have to say about the "Palestinian question"?**

On March 6, 1940, writing in her diary of the imminent likelihood of an uprising against the British rulers of Palestine, eighteen-year-old Hannah declared, "I don't know what it is within me—love for the land and the people, or horror of all wars, or perhaps a point of view that belongs in another world—but I still condemn any step that leads to hopeless, unnecessary bloodshed."

She goes on to write, "As far as I'm concerned, I think they ought to build with greatly renewed energy within the designated areas, and then, when the existing lands are irrevocably in our hands, and if the British political situation does not change meanwhile—then if we still must fight, we can do so with guns."

If Hannah had lived, she would be in her 80s. What do you think she would make of the situation in Israel today?

6. **What were Hannah's "spiritual necessities"?**

On September 18, 1936, when the precocious Hannah Senesh was all of fifteen years old, she wrote, "I am not quite clear just how I stand: synagogue, religion, the question of God. About the last and most difficult question I am the least disturbed. I believe in God—even if I can't express just how. Actually I'm relatively clear on the subject of religion, too, because Judaism fits in best with my way of thinking. But the trouble with the synagogue is that I don't find it at all important, and I don't feel it to be a spiritual necessity; I can pray equally well at home." Four years later, on November 2, 1940, she wrote, "I was never able to pray in the usual manner, by rote, and even now neither can nor want to. But the dialogue man holds with his Creator ... is what I, too, have found. I see the sincere, inner link, even if it comes through struggle within myself and through some doubt."

What do you think she had found in her spiritual life?

After her body was moved to Israel,
a figurative tombstone remained at Hannah's grave at the
Jewish Cemetery of Budapest.

Historical Note

When asked why he didn't include Joan of Arc in his landmark history *The Waning of the Middle Ages*, Johan Huizinga is said to have replied, "Because I didn't want my story to have a heroine." The great Dutch historian had no objection to women per se; rather, he feared that such a charismatic character would overshadow the relatively impersonal processes that were his book's principal focus. But just as it is impossible to fully understand the Middle Ages without knowing about the men and women who lived through them, no history of the Holocaust can be written in isolation from the people who experienced it. A special chapter must be devoted to the heroes and heroines who resisted the Nazis and their henchmen, and an even more unique one to those Jews who managed to escape occupied Europe but returned to assist their persecuted brethren. One of those was Hannah Senesh.

Hannah Senesh was born in Budapest on July 17, 1921, to a wealthy, distinguished, and acculturated Hungarian Jewish family. Her father, Bela Senesh, who died when she was a child, had been a well-known writer and dramatist, and her mother, Catherine, an elegant homemaker. Senesh was educated in Hungarian schools, but the anti-Semitism she experienced during her high school years forcibly reminded her of her Jewish origins. She joined a Zionist youth movement and learned Hebrew; when she graduated from high school in 1939, she emigrated to Palestine. After completing a two-year course at the girls' agricultural school in Nahalal, Senesh joined the Sdot Yam Kibbutz at Caesarea, where she worked in the kitchen and the laundry.

In 1943, officials from the Jewish Agency for Palestine approached Senesh with a proposal: to join a clandestine military project to aid European Jews. She accepted immediately. Having joined the Palmach (the pre-state fighting forces) she began training for her secret mission. Initially, she and several dozen other volunteers trained as wireless operators and paratroopers, as they were to be dropped into Europe to aid the Allied forces. Having been inducted into the British army, ostensibly she was to help downed Allied pilots find their way back to safety across the lines. Her Jewish mission was in fact a secondary one, to which the British secret services had agreed once the paratroopers had completed their British mission.

Senesh's mission commenced in mid-March 1944, when she and several other Palestinian-Jewish volunteers were dropped into Yugoslavia. The Nazi invasion of Hungary had temporarily sealed its borders; Hannah and her comrades fought with the partisans in Yugoslavia until June 4, when she was the first of the group to cross into Hungary. Captured within hours, she was tortured by Hungarian authorities, who hoped she would reveal Allied wireless codes. Within days, her co-parachutists were also captured. Only one of them—Yoel Palgi—would survive the war.

When her captors realized that Senesh could not be broken, they arrested her mother. Catherine Senesh had not laid eyes on her daughter in five years; she had no idea that she had even left Palestine, never mind that she was in Budapest. Initially shocked to see her—now a haggard young woman with bruised eyes and a miss-ing front tooth—Catherine rapidly regained her composure, and she comported herself throughout their meeting with incredible dignity and self-restraint. For three months the two women were incarcer-ated in the same prison but were unable to catch more than short glimpses of each other. Following her sudden release in September 1944, Catherine Senesh spent most of her waking hours seeking legal assistance for Hannah, who—a Hungarian national—was to be tried as a spy. In November 1944, in spite of the fact that her mother had found a lawyer, Hannah eloquently pleaded her own cause before a tribunal, warning her judges that their own fates would soon hang in the balance too, as the war was nearing its end. She was found guilty and sentenced to death.

On the morning of November 7, Colonel Simon, the officer in charge of her case, presented Senesh with two choices: to beg for a pardon, or stand before a firing squad. Refusing to the end to acknowledge her captors' authority, the twenty-three-year-old penned short farewell notes to her mother and her comrades. Then she was led out to a snow-covered Budapest courtyard, where she refused a blindfold in order to face her murderers at the moment of her death. Her body was buried by unknown persons in the Jewish graveyard in Budapest.

Shortly afterwards, Catherine Senesh was sent on the infamous Budapest "Death March." She escaped and hid in the Hungarian capital until its liberation by Soviet forces in 1945, when she joined her surviving child, Gyuri, in Palestine. In 1946, the kibbutz movement to which Hannah Senesh had belonged—HaKibbutz HaMeuchad—published a book containing parts of her diary, poetry, and plays. There have been fifteen subsequent Hebrew language editions since then; the first English edition was published in 1971. This new edition contains additional material that has never before been published in English, allowing readers throughout the world to learn more about the life and thoughts of this unique and talented young woman.

Senesh's biography, as tragically short and truncated as it is, contains several major themes of modern Jewish life: initially assimilation, then Jewish nationalism, and finally Zionist sacrifice. The Senesh family's experiences as they attempted to acculturate into their non-Jewish surroundings were shared by hundreds of thousands—possibly millions—of Jews during the twentieth century. So was Hannah's response to the rise of anti-Semitism: interest in a Jewish national movement that would remove Jews from their position of powerlessness. The fate she met as a result of her efforts to help her fellow Jews propelled her not only into the Zionist pantheon but into the forefront of Jewish heroism of the modern era. Hannah Senesh's heroic odyssey came to an end in 1950, when her remains were returned to Israel and reburied in the "Parachutists section" of the military cemetery on Mt. Herzl in Jerusalem.

Professor Judith Tydor Baumel
Chair, Interdisciplinary Graduate Program in Contemporary Jewry,
Bar-Ilan University, Ramat-Gan, Israel

NOTES

Memories of Hannah's Childhood

1. Bela Senesh wrote a popular humorous column in the Sunday magazine section of *Pesti Hirlap*, a paper with a circulation of one-hundred thousand.

The Diary

1. Hungarian children customarily call all adults, including teachers, uncle and aunt.
2. In Orthodox synagogues men sit downstairs, women in the balcony.
3. Approximately £2.50 or $4.70.
4. In the spring of 1919, a small "national army" was raised under the command of Admiral Miklos Horthy, one-time commander-in-chief of the Austro-Hungarian Imperial and Royal Adriatic Fleet, to counteract the Communist-inspired uprising of Bela Kun. In November of that year, with the blessing of the Allies, Horthy was elected regent of Hungary. He remained the head of the government until October 16, 1944, when he was forced to resign by the Nazis.
5. Her maternal grandmother.
6. Her cousin, who was killed at Auschwitz.
7. Imré Madách's *The Tragedy of Man* (1862) is a verse drama about Adam's dream about the future of mankind.
8. Mihály Munkácsy (Michael von Munkácsy), 1844–1900.
9. Alajos Stróbl, 1856–1926.
10. Loosely translated: "What others gain in battle, Austria gains in wedlock!" It refers to the fact that all the Habsburgs married for political expediency rather than for love.
11. Maximilian Bircher-Benner (1867–1939): Swiss doctor and nutritionist best known as the inventor of muesli cereal.
12. Bronislav Hubermann (1882–1947): violinist, founder of Palestine Symphony Orchestra.

13. A schoolteacher, also referred to as "Mama Kiss."

14. Hannah is staying with cousins who are studying in Italy.

15. Undoubtedly the Certosa di Pavia, also known as the Carthusian Monastery.

16. Probably Santa Maria delle Grazie, where the *Last Supper* is hung in the adjacent Dominican Convent of Cenacolo Vinciano.

17. Santa Maria Gloriosa dei Frari.

18. Old Hungarian superstition: too much salt indicates the cook is passionately in love.

19. A cousin.

20. On March 11, 1938, as a result of the Austrian Anschluss, anti-Semitism increased in Hungary, and a debate on the "Jewish Question" was opened in the Hungarian Parliament. This resulted in the "Jewish Bill," which became the first "Jewish Law" and reduced the ratio of Jewish representation in the economic field to twenty percent. It was also stated that "the expansion of the Jews is as detrimental to the nation as it is dangerous; we must take steps to defend ourselves against their propagation. Their relegation to the background is a national duty."

21. Hungarian Nazis.

22. A novel by Baron Joseph Eötvös, once compulsory reading in all Hungarian schools.

23. Translated from the Hungarian by Peter Hay.

24. The foremost Hungarian literary magazine of that era.

25. The Godesberg memorandum to Czechoslovakia.

26. Following the Munich Agreement, Hungary was awarded 7,500 square miles of the Czechoslovak Highlands, with a population of 500,000 Hungarians and 272,000 Slovaks. This was originally part of Hungary and was lost in World War I.

27. Four to five percent of the land was in Jewish hands when the law of 1939 authorized the government to order the sale of Jewish agricultural properties.

28. Jewish National Fund.

29. See note 20. The second Jewish Law was announced in 1939. The number of Jews in intellectual life was to be reduced to six percent in commerce, and in industry to twelve percent. A Jew could no longer be a member of Parliament, or a judge, teacher, lawyer, etc. On February 3, 1939, a bomb was thrown into the largest synagogue in Budapest during the Friday evening service. Many were injured, some fatally.

30. Nachum Sokolov (1861–1936): Zionist leader and Hebrew journalist; president of the World Zionist Organization and Jewish Agency, 1931–1935.
31. Theodor Herzl (1860–1904): founder of modern Zionism; devoted his life to the creation of a Jewish state.
32. A reference to the London Conference, which was to be followed by the British White Paper of 1939, restricting Jewish immigration to Palestine. Until 1948, Britain was the Mandatory Power in Palestine.
33. The Jewish community in Palestine.
34. Summa cum laude.
35. Up to this point, the diary was kept in Hungarian. From here on she alternated between Hungarian and Hebrew.
36. The immigration of Jews to Palestine.
37. The Land (Palestine).
38. The Valley of Jezreel, usually called Emek, which in Hebrew means "valley."
39. A Jew born in Palestine.
40. A family friend.
41. Friday night gathering of friends for social or discussion purposes.
42. The poem is "Harvest" (see page 298 for complete text).
43. From a poem by Imre Madách.
44. Yam Kinneret (the Sea of Galilee).
45. A *moshav* is an agricultural village whose inhabitants possess individual homes and smallholdings but cooperate in the purchase of equipment, the marketing of produce, etc.
46. This is her first poem in Hebrew. It is translated by Peter Hay.
47. Josef Kastein (1890–1946).
48. Shneur Zalman Shazar (1889–1974): scholar, newspaper editor, historian, third president of the State of Israel.
49. Socialist Youth Movement. All the others mentioned are also youth organizations.
50. She ends her third notebook here.
51. An extreme Zionist Party, founded in 1925 by Vladimir Jabotinsky, which opposed the "moderation" of official Zionist policy.
52. Called *The Violin*, it is based on kibbutz life and is popular with the youth in the kibbutzim.
53 Ilonka Krausz, friend of Artúr Thieben.
54. Abel Pann (1883–1963).
55. An ancient Roman port, twenty-two miles south of Haifa.

56. Workers' Union.
57. The striking fist of the Haganah, the clandestine Jewish self-defense force in Palestine.

The Letters

1. Her cousin.
2. Women's International Zionist Organization.
3. Mihály Fekete, professor of mathematics at the University of Jerusalem, a family friend from Budapest.
4. Her father's birthday.
5. The orthodox segment.
6. Hagar was her code name during the mission.

The Mission

1. Sereni parachuted into German-occupied northern Italy a few weeks later, was captured, and was murdered in Dachau on November 18, 1944, about ten days after Hannah's execution.
2. Peretz Goldstein of Kibbutz Ma'agan. He volunteered for the mission to Hungary and was one of the thirty-two parachutists. He was caught by the Gestapo and sent to Oranienburg, in Germany, where he died.
3. As it turned out, Hungary did not surrender to the Allies; there was again a Fascist takeover. The Nazis returned to power—including Adolf Eichmann, who had fled. On October 17, 1944, directly after the new (Szálasy) government took power, Eichmann resumed the deportation, and on the 20th the "big march" began, when the first of 50,000 Jews were herded on foot from Budapest, allegedly to work in Germany but actually to their deaths. Thousands died from hunger and exhaustion during the march, or were shot to death for "not marching fast enough."
4. Death's Head units (Totenkopf SS) carried out the acts of atrocity in concentration camps.

Selected Poems

1. This poem and most of the following poems were written in Hebrew.
2. Written a few days prior to Russia's entry into World War II.

3. This poem was written to celebrate the winter plowing of 500 *dunams* of land at Kibbutz Ginosar. That December in Russia the winter war was ravaging the snowbound fields.
4. Written to her brother.
5. Her last poem, written in prison.

Congregation Resources

Empowered Judaism: What Independent Minyanim Can Teach Us about Building Vibrant Jewish Communities
By Rabbi Elie Kaunfer; Foreword by Prof. Jonathan D. Sarna
Examines the independent minyan movement and what lessons these grassroots communities can provide. 6 x 9, 224 pp, Quality PB, 978-1-58023-412-2 **$18.99**

Spiritual Boredom: Rediscovering the Wonder of Judaism *By Dr. Erica Brown*
Breaks through the surface of spiritual boredom to find the reservoir of meaning within. 6 x 9, 208 pp, HC, 978-1-58023-405-4 **$21.99**

Building a Successful Volunteer Culture
Finding Meaning in Service in the Jewish Community
By Rabbi Charles Simon; Foreword by Shelley Lindauer; Preface by Dr. Ron Wolfson
Shows you how to develop and maintain the volunteers who are essential to the vitality of your organization and community. 6 x 9, 192 pp, Quality PB, 978-1-58023-408-5 **$16.99**

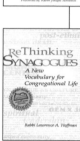

The Case for Jewish Peoplehood: Can We Be One?
By Dr. Erica Brown and Dr. Misha Galperin; Foreword by Rabbi Joseph Telushkin
6 x 9, 224 pp, HC, 978-1-58023-401-6 **$21.99**

Inspired Jewish Leadership: Practical Approaches to Building Strong Communities
By Dr. Erica Brown 6 x 9, 256 pp, HC, 978-1-58023-361-3 **$24.99**

Jewish Pastoral Care, 2nd Edition: A Practical Handbook from Traditional & Contemporary Sources *Edited by Rabbi Dayle A. Friedman, MSW, MAJCS, BCC*
6 x 9, 528 pp, Quality PB, 978-1-58023-427-6 **$30.00**

Rethinking Synagogues: A New Vocabulary for Congregational Life
By Rabbi Lawrence A. Hoffman 6 x 9, 240 pp, Quality PB, 978-1-58023-248-7 **$19.99**

The Spirituality of Welcoming: How to Transform Your Congregation into a Sacred Community *By Dr. Ron Wolfson* 6 x 9, 224 pp, Quality PB, 978-1-58023-244-9 **$19.99**

Children's Books

What You Will See Inside a Synagogue
By Rabbi Lawrence A. Hoffman, PhD, and Dr. Ron Wolfson; Full-color photos by Bill Aron
A colorful, fun-to-read introduction that explains the ways and whys of Jewish worship and religious life. 8½ x 10½, 32 pp, Full-color photos, Quality PB, 978-1-59473-256-0 **$8.99**
For ages 6 & up (A book from SkyLight Paths, Jewish Lights' sister imprint)

Because Nothing Looks Like God
By Lawrence Kushner and Karen Kushner Introduces children to the possibilities of spiritual life. 11 x 8½, 32 pp, Full-color illus., HC, 978-1-58023-092-6 **$17.99** *For ages 4 & up*
Board Book Companions to *Because Nothing Looks Like God*
5 x 5, 24 pp, Full-color illus., SkyLight Paths Board Books *For ages 0–4*

   What Does God Look Like? 978-1-893361-23-2 **$7.99**

   How Does God Make Things Happen? 978-1-893361-24-9 **$7.95**

   Where Is God? 978-1-893361-17-1 **$7.99**

The Book of Miracles: A Young Person's Guide to Jewish Spiritual Awareness
Written and illus. by Lawrence Kushner
6 x 9, 96 pp, 2-color illus., HC, 978-1-879045-78-1 **$16.95** *For ages 9 & up*

In God's Hands
By Lawrence Kushner and Gary Schmidt 9 x 12, 32 pp, HC, 978-1-58023-224-1 **$16.99**

In Our Image: God's First Creatures *By Nancy Sohn Swartz*
9 x 12, 32 pp, Full-color illus., HC, 978-1-879045-99-6 **$16.95** *For ages 4 & up*

Also Available as a Board Book: **How Did the Animals Help God?**
5 x 5, 24 pp, Full-color illus., Board Book, 978-1-59473-044-3 **$7.99** *For ages 0–4*
(A book from SkyLight Paths, Jewish Lights' sister imprint)

The Kids' Fun Book of Jewish Time
By Emily Sper 9 x 7½, 24 pp, Full-color illus., HC, 978-1-58023-311-8 **$16.99**

What Makes Someone a Jew? *By Lauren Seidman*
Reflects the changing face of American Judaism.
10 x 8½, 32 pp, Full-color photos, Quality PB, 978-1-58023-321-7 **$8.99** *For ages 3–6*

Theology/Philosophy/The Way Into... Series

The Way Into... series offers an accessible and highly usable "guided tour" of the Jewish faith, people, history and beliefs—in total, an introduction to Judaism that will enable you to understand and interact with the sacred texts of the Jewish tradition. Each volume is written by a leading contemporary scholar and teacher, and explores one key aspect of Judaism. The Way Into... series enables all readers to achieve a real sense of Jewish cultural literacy through guided study.

The Way Into Encountering God in Judaism
By Rabbi Neil Gillman, PhD
For everyone who wants to understand how Jews have encountered God throughout history and today.
6 x 9, 240 pp, Quality PB, 978-1-58023-199-2 **$18.99**; HC, 978-1-58023-025-4 **$21.95**
Also Available: **The Jewish Approach to God:** A Brief Introduction for Christians
By Rabbi Neil Gillman, PhD
5½ x 8½, 192 pp, Quality PB, 978-1-58023-190-9 **$16.95**

The Way Into Jewish Mystical Tradition
By Rabbi Lawrence Kushner
Allows readers to interact directly with the sacred mystical texts of the Jewish tradition. An accessible introduction to the concepts of Jewish mysticism, their religious and spiritual significance, and how they relate to life today.
6 x 9, 224 pp, Quality PB, 978-1-58023-200-5 **$18.99**; HC, 978-1-58023-029-2 **$21.95**

The Way Into Jewish Prayer
By Rabbi Lawrence A. Hoffman, PhD
Opens the door to 3,000 years of Jewish prayer, making available all anyone needs to feel at home in the Jewish way of communicating with God.
6 x 9, 208 pp, Quality PB, 978-1-58023-201-2 **$18.99**

Also Available: **The Way Into Jewish Prayer Teacher's Guide**
By Rabbi Jennifer Ossakow Goldsmith
8½ x 11, 42 pp, PB, 978-1-58023-345-3 **$8.99**
Download a free copy at www.jewishlights.com.

The Way Into Judaism and the Environment
By Jeremy Benstein, PhD
Explores the ways in which Judaism contributes to contemporary social-environmental issues, the extent to which Judaism is part of the problem and how it can be part of the solution.
6 x 9, 288 pp, Quality PB, 978-1-58023-368-2 **$18.99**; HC, 978-1-58023-268-5 **$24.99**

The Way Into *Tikkun Olam* (Repairing the World)
By Rabbi Elliot N. Dorff, PhD
An accessible introduction to the Jewish concept of the individual's responsibility to care for others and repair the world.
6 x 9, 304 pp, Quality PB, 978-1-58023-328-6 **$18.99**; 320 pp, HC, 978-1-58023-269-2 **$24.99**

The Way Into Torah
By Rabbi Norman J. Cohen, PhD
Helps guide in the exploration of the origins and development of Torah, explains why it should be studied and how to do it.
6 x 9, 176 pp, Quality PB, 978-1-58023-198-5 **$16.99**

The Way Into the Varieties of Jewishness
By Sylvia Barack Fishman, PhD
Explores the religious and historical understanding of what it has meant to be Jewish from ancient times to the present controversy over "Who is a Jew?"
6 x 9, 288 pp, Quality PB, 978-1-58023-367-5 **$18.99**; HC, 978-1-58023-030-8 **$24.99**

Theology/Philosophy

Jewish Theology in Our Time: A New Generation Explores the Foundations and Future of Jewish Belief *Edited by Rabbi Elliot J. Cosgrove, PhD*
A powerful and challenging examination of what Jews can believe—by a new generation's most dynamic and innovative thinkers.
6 x 9, 350 pp (est), HC, 978-1-58023-413-9 **$24.99**

Maimonides, Spinoza and Us: Toward an Intellectually Vibrant Judaism
By Rabbi Marc D. Angel, PhD A challenging look at two great Jewish philosophers, and what their thinking means to our understanding of God, truth, revelation and reason. 6 x 9, 224 pp, HC, 978-1-58023-411-5 **$24.99**

The Death of Death: Resurrection and Immortality in Jewish Thought
By Rabbi Neil Gillman, PhD 6 x 9, 336 pp, Quality PB, 978-1-58023-081-0 **$18.95**

Ethics of the Sages: Pirke Avot—Annotated & Explained
Translation & Annotation by Rabbi Rami Shapiro
5½ x 8½, 192 pp, Quality PB, 978-1-59473-207-2 **$16.99** *(A book from SkyLight Paths, Jewish Lights' sister imprint)*

Hasidic Tales: Annotated & Explained *Translation & Annotation by Rabbi Rami Shapiro*
5½ x 8½, 240 pp, Quality PB, 978-1-893361-86-7 **$16.95** *(A book from SkyLight Paths, Jewish Lights' sister imprint)*

A Heart of Many Rooms: Celebrating the Many Voices within Judaism
By Dr. David Hartman 6 x 9, 352 pp, Quality PB, 978-1-58023-156-5 **$19.95**

The Hebrew Prophets: Selections Annotated & Explained
Translation & Annotation by Rabbi Rami Shapiro; Foreword by Rabbi Zalman M. Schachter-Shalomi
5½ x 8½, 224 pp, Quality PB, 978-1-59473-037-5 **$16.99** *(A book from SkyLight Paths, Jewish Lights' sister imprint)*

A Jewish Understanding of the New Testament
By Rabbi Samuel Sandmel; Preface by Rabbi David Sandmel
5½ x 8½, 368 pp, Quality PB, 978-1-59473-048-1 **$19.99** *(A book from SkyLight Paths, Jewish Lights' sister imprint)*

Jews and Judaism in the 21st Century: Human Responsibility, the Presence of God and the Future of the Covenant *Edited by Rabbi Edward Feinstein; Foreword by Paula E. Hyman*
6 x 9, 192 pp, Quality PB, 978-1-58023-374-3 **$19.99**; HC, 978-1-58023-315-6 **$24.99**

Keeping Faith with the Psalms: Deepen Your Relationship with God Using the Book of Psalms *By Rabbi Daniel F. Polish, PhD* 6 x 9, 320 pp, Quality PB, 978-1-58023-300-2 **$18.99**

A Living Covenant: The Innovative Spirit in Traditional Judaism
By Dr. David Hartman 6 x 9, 368 pp, Quality PB, 978-1-58023-011-7 **$20.00**

Love and Terror in the God Encounter: The Theological Legacy of Rabbi Joseph B. Soloveitchik *By Dr. David Hartman* 6 x 9, 240 pp, Quality PB, 978-1-58023-176-3 **$19.95**

The Personhood of God: Biblical Theology, Human Faith and the Divine Image
By Dr. Yochanan Muffs; Foreword by Dr. David Hartman
6 x 9, 240 pp, Quality PB, 978-1-58023-338-5 **$18.99**; HC, 978-1-58023-265-4 **$24.99**

A Touch of the Sacred: A Theologian's Informal Guide to Jewish Belief
By Dr. Eugene B. Borowitz and Frances W. Schwartz
6 x 9, 256 pp, Quality PB, 978-1-58023-416-0 **$16.99**; HC, 978-1-58023-337-8 **$21.99**

Traces of God: Seeing God in Torah, History and Everyday Life *By Rabbi Neil Gillman, PhD*
6 x 9, 240 pp, Quality PB, 978-1-58023-369-9 **$16.99**; HC, 978-1-58023-249-4 **$21.99**

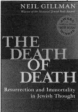

We Jews and Jesus: Exploring Theological Differences for Mutual Understanding
By Rabbi Samuel Sandmel; Preface by Rabbi David Sandmel
6 x 9, 192 pp, Quality PB, 978-1-59473-208-9 **$16.99** *(A book from SkyLight Paths, Jewish Lights' sister imprint)*

Your Word Is Fire: The Hasidic Masters on Contemplative Prayer
Edited and translated by Rabbi Arthur Green, PhD, and Barry W. Holtz
6 x 9, 160 pp, Quality PB, 978-1-879045-25-5 **$15.95**

I Am Jewish
Personal Reflections Inspired by the Last Words of Daniel Pearl
Almost 150 Jews—both famous and not—from all walks of life, from all around the world, write about many aspects of their Judaism.
Edited by Judea and Ruth Pearl 6 x 9, 304 pp, Deluxe PB w/ flaps, 978-1-58023-259-3 **$18.99**
Download a free copy of the *I Am Jewish Teacher's Guide* at www.jewishlights.com.

Hannah Senesh: Her Life and Diary, the First Complete Edition
By Hannah Senesh; Foreword by Marge Piercy; Preface by Eitan Senesh; Afterword by Roberta Grossman
6 x 9, 368 pp, b/w photos, Quality PB, 978-1-58023-342-2 **$19.99**

Spirituality/Prayer

Making Prayer Real: Leading Jewish Spiritual Voices on Why Prayer Is Difficult and What to Do about It *By Rabbi Mike Comins*
A no-holds-barred look at why so many find synagogue at best difficult, and at worst, meaningless and boring—and how to make it more satisfying.
6 x 9, 320 pp, Quality PB, 978-1-58023-417-7 **$18.99**

Witnesses to the One: The Spiritual History of the *Sh'ma*
By Rabbi Joseph B. Meszler; Foreword by Rabbi Elyse Goldstein
6 x 9, 176 pp, Quality PB, 978-1-58023-400-9 **$16.99**; HC, 978-1-58023-309-5 **$19.99**

My People's Prayer Book Series: Traditional Prayers, Modern Commentaries *Edited by Rabbi Lawrence A. Hoffman, PhD*
Provides diverse and exciting commentary to the traditional liturgy. Will help you find new wisdom in Jewish prayer, and bring liturgy into your life. Each book includes Hebrew text, modern translation and commentaries from all perspectives of the Jewish world.

Vol. 1—The *Sh'ma* and Its Blessings
  7 x 10, 168 pp, HC, 978-1-879045-79-8 **$24.99**
Vol. 2—The *Amidah* 7 x 10, 240 pp, HC, 978-1-879045-80-4 **$24.95**
Vol. 3—*P'sukei D'zimrah* (Morning Psalms)
  7 x 10, 240 pp, HC, 978-1-879045-81-1 **$24.95**
Vol. 4—*Seder K'riat Hatorah* (The Torah Service)
  7 x 10, 264 pp, HC, 978-1-879045-82-8 **$23.95**
Vol. 5—*Birkhot Hashachar* (Morning Blessings)
  7 x 10, 240 pp, HC, 978-1-879045-83-5 **$24.95**
Vol. 6—*Tachanun* and Concluding Prayers
  7 x 10, 240 pp, HC, 978-1-879045-84-2 **$24.95**
Vol. 7—Shabbat at Home 7 x 10, 240 pp, HC, 978-1-879045-85-9 **$24.95**
Vol. 8—*Kabbalat Shabbat* (Welcoming Shabbat in the Synagogue)
  7 x 10, 240 pp, HC, 978-1-58023-121-3 **$24.99**
Vol. 9—Welcoming the Night: *Minchah* and *Ma'ariv* (Afternoon and Evening Prayer) 7 x 10, 272 pp, HC, 978-1-58023-262-3 **$24.99**
Vol. 10—Shabbat Morning: *Shacharit* and *Musaf* (Morning and Additional Services) 7 x 10, 240 pp, HC, 978-1-58023-240-1 **$24.99**

Spirituality/Lawrence Kushner

The Book of Letters: A Mystical Hebrew Alphabet
Popular HC Edition, 6 x 9, 80 pp, 2-color text, 978-1-879045-00-2 **$24.95**
Collector's Limited Edition, 9 x 12, 80 pp, gold-foil-embossed pages, w/ limited-edition silkscreened print, 978-1-879045-04-0 **$349.00**

The Book of Miracles: A Young Person's Guide to Jewish Spiritual Awareness
6 x 9, 96 pp, 2-color illus., HC, 978-1-879045-78-1 **$16.95** *For ages 9–13*

The Book of Words: Talking Spiritual Life, Living Spiritual Talk
6 x 9, 160 pp, Quality PB, 978-1-58023-020-9 **$16.95**

Eyes Remade for Wonder: A Lawrence Kushner Reader *Introduction by Thomas Moore*
6 x 9, 240 pp, Quality PB, 978-1-58023-042-1 **$18.95**

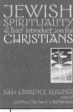

Filling Words with Light: Hasidic and Mystical Reflections on Jewish Prayer
By Rabbi Lawrence Kushner and Rabbi Nehemia Polen
5½ x 8½, 176 pp, Quality PB, 978-1-58023-238-8 **$16.99**; HC, 978-1-58023-216-6 **$21.99**

God Was in This Place & I, i Did Not Know: Finding Self, Spirituality and Ultimate Meaning 6 x 9, 192 pp, Quality PB, 978-1-879045-33-0 **$16.95**

Honey from the Rock: An Introduction to Jewish Mysticism
6 x 9, 176 pp, Quality PB, 978-1-58023-073-5 **$16.95**

Invisible Lines of Connection: Sacred Stories of the Ordinary
5½ x 8½, 160 pp, Quality PB, 978-1-879045-98-9 **$15.95**

Jewish Spirituality: A Brief Introduction for Christians
5½ x 8½, 112 pp, Quality PB, 978-1-58023-150-3 **$12.95**

The River of Light: Jewish Mystical Awareness
6 x 9, 192 pp, Quality PB, 978-1-58023-096-4 **$16.95**

The Way Into Jewish Mystical Tradition
6 x 9, 224 pp, Quality PB, 978-1-58023-200-5 **$18.99**; HC, 978-1-58023-029-2 **$21.95**

Spirituality

Repentance: The Meaning and Practice of *Teshuvah*
By Dr. Louis E. Newman; Foreword by Rabbi Harold M. Schulweis; Preface by Rabbi Karyn D. Kedar
Examines both the practical and philosophical dimensions of *teshuvah*, Judaism's core religious-moral teaching on repentance, and its value for us—Jews and non-Jews alike—today. 6 x 9, 256 pp, HC, 978-1-58023-426-9 **$24.99**

Tanya, the Masterpiece of Hasidic Wisdom
Selections Annotated & Explained
Translation & Annotation by Rabbi Rami Shapiro; Foreword by Rabbi Zalman M. Schachter-Shalomi
Brings the genius of the *Tanya* to anyone seeking to deepen their understanding of the soul and how it relates to and manifests the Divine Source.
5½ x 8½, 240 pp, Quality PB, 978-1-59473-275-1 **$16.99**
(A book from SkyLight Paths, Jewish Lights' sister imprint)

A Book of Life: Embracing Judaism as a Spiritual Practice
By Rabbi Michael Strassfeld 6 x 9, 544 pp, Quality PB, 978-1-58023-247-0 **$19.99**

Meaning and Mitzvah: Daily Practices for Reclaiming Judaism through Prayer, God, Torah, Hebrew, Mitzvot and Peoplehood *By Rabbi Goldie Milgram*
7 x 9, 336 pp, Quality PB, 978-1-58023-256-2 **$19.99**

The Soul of the Story: Meetings with Remarkable People
By Rabbi David Zeller 6 x 9, 288 pp, HC, 978-1-58023-272-2 **$21.99**

Aleph-Bet Yoga: Embodying the Hebrew Letters for Physical and Spiritual Well-Being
By Steven A. Rapp; Foreword by Tamar Frankiel, PhD, and Judy Greenfeld; Preface by Hart Lazer
7 x 10, 128 pp, b/w photos, Quality PB, Layflat binding, 978-1-58023-162-6 **$16.95**

Does the Soul Survive? A Jewish Journey to Belief in Afterlife, Past Lives & Living with Purpose *By Rabbi Elie Kaplan Spitz; Foreword by Brian L. Weiss, MD*
6 x 9, 288 pp, Quality PB, 978-1-58023-165-7 **$16.99**

First Steps to a New Jewish Spirit: Reb Zalman's Guide to Recapturing the Intimacy & Ecstasy in Your Relationship with God *By Rabbi Zalman M. Schachter-Shalomi with Donald Gropman* 6 x 9, 144 pp, Quality PB, 978-1-58023-182-4 **$16.95**

Foundations of Sephardic Spirituality: The Inner Life of Jews of the Ottoman Empire
By Rabbi Marc D. Angel, PhD 6 x 9, 224 pp, Quality PB, 978-1-58023-341-5 **$18.99**

God in Our Relationships: Spirituality between People from the Teachings of Martin Buber *By Rabbi Dennis S. Ross* 5½ x 8½, 160 pp, Quality PB, 978-1-58023-147-3 **$16.95**

Judaism, Physics and God: Searching for Sacred Metaphors in a Post-Einstein World
By Rabbi David W. Nelson 6 x 9, 352 pp, Quality PB, inc. reader's discussion guide,
978-1-58023-306-4 **$18.99**; HC, 352 pp, 978-1-58023-252-4 **$24.99**

The Jewish Lights Spirituality Handbook: A Guide to Understanding, Exploring & Living a Spiritual Life *Edited by Stuart M. Matlins*
What exactly is "Jewish" about spirituality? How do I make it a part of my life? Fifty of today's foremost spiritual leaders share their ideas and experience with us.
6 x 9, 456 pp, Quality PB, 978-1-58023-093-3 **$19.99**

Bringing the Psalms to Life: How to Understand and Use the Book of Psalms
By Rabbi Daniel F. Polish, PhD 6 x 9, 208 pp, Quality PB, 978-1-58023-157-2 **$16.95**

God & the Big Bang: Discovering Harmony between Science & Spirituality
By Dr. Daniel C. Matt 6 x 9, 216 pp, Quality PB, 978-1-879045-89-7 **$16.99**

Minding the Temple of the Soul: Balancing Body, Mind, and Spirit through Traditional Jewish Prayer, Movement, and Meditation *By Tamar Frankiel, PhD, and Judy Greenfeld*
7 x 10, 184 pp, illus., Quality PB, 978-1-879045-64-4 **$16.95**

One God Clapping: The Spiritual Path of a Zen Rabbi *By Alan Lew with Sherril Jaffe*
5½ x 8½, 336 pp, Quality PB, 978-1-58023-115-2 **$16.95**

There Is No Messiah ... and You're It: The Stunning Transformation of Judaism's Most Provocative Idea *By Rabbi Robert N. Levine, DD*
6 x 9, 192 pp, Quality PB, 978-1-58023-255-5 **$16.99**

These Are the Words: A Vocabulary of Jewish Spiritual Life
By Rabbi Arthur Green, PhD 6 x 9, 304 pp, Quality PB, 978-1-58023-107-7 **$18.95**

Meditation

Jewish Meditation Practices for Everyday Life
Awakening Your Heart, Connecting with God
By Rabbi Jeff Roth
Offers a fresh take on meditation that draws on life experience and living life with greater clarity as opposed to the traditional method of rigorous study.
6 x 9, 224 pp, Quality PB, 978-1-58023-397-2 **$18.99**

The Handbook of Jewish Meditation Practices
A Guide for Enriching the Sabbath and Other Days of Your Life
By Rabbi David A. Cooper Easy-to-learn meditation techniques.
6 x 9, 208 pp, Quality PB, 978-1-58023-102-2 **$16.95**

Discovering Jewish Meditation: Instruction & Guidance for Learning an Ancient Spiritual Practice By Nan Fink Gefen, PhD 6 x 9, 208 pp, Quality PB, 978-1-58023-067-4 **$16.95**

Meditation from the Heart of Judaism: Today's Teachers Share Their Practices, Techniques, and Faith Edited by Avram Davis
6 x 9, 256 pp, Quality PB, 978-1-58023-049-0 **$16.95**

Ritual/Sacred Practices

The Jewish Dream Book: The Key to Opening the Inner Meaning of Your Dreams By Vanessa L. Ochs, PhD, with Elizabeth Ochs; Illus. by Kristina Swarner
Instructions for how modern people can perform ancient Jewish dream practices and dream interpretations drawn from the Jewish wisdom tradition.
8 x 8, 128 pp, Full-color illus., Deluxe PB w/ flaps, 978-1-58023-132-9 **$16.95**

God in Your Body: Kabbalah, Mindfulness and Embodied Spiritual Practice
By Jay Michaelson
The first comprehensive treatment of the body in Jewish spiritual practice and an essential guide to the sacred.
6 x 9, 272 pp, Quality PB, 978-1-58023-304-0 **$18.99**

The Book of Jewish Sacred Practices: CLAL's Guide to Everyday &
Holiday Rituals & Blessings Edited by Rabbi Irwin Kula and Vanessa L. Ochs, PhD
6 x 9, 368 pp, Quality PB, 978-1-58023-152-7 **$18.95**

Jewish Ritual: A Brief Introduction for Christians
By Rabbi Kerry M. Olitzky and Rabbi Daniel Judson
5½ x 8½, 144 pp, Quality PB, 978-1-58023-210-4 **$14.99**

The Rituals & Practices of a Jewish Life: A Handbook for Personal Spiritual
Renewal Edited by Rabbi Kerry M. Olitzky and Rabbi Daniel Judson
6 x 9, 272 pp, illus., Quality PB, 978-1-58023-169-5 **$18.95**

The Sacred Art of Lovingkindness: Preparing to Practice
By Rabbi Rami Shapiro 5½ x 8½, 176 pp, Quality PB, 978-1-59473-151-8 **$16.99**
(A book from SkyLight Paths, Jewish Lights' sister imprint)

Science Fiction/Mystery & Detective Fiction

Criminal Kabbalah: An Intriguing Anthology of Jewish Mystery &
Detective Fiction Edited by Lawrence W. Raphael; Foreword by Laurie R. King
All-new stories from twelve of today's masters of mystery and detective fiction—sure to delight mystery buffs of all faith traditions.
6 x 9, 256 pp, Quality PB, 978-1-58023-109-1 **$16.95**

Mystery Midrash: An Anthology of Jewish Mystery & Detective Fiction
Edited by Lawrence W. Raphael; Preface by Joel Siegel
6 x 9, 304 pp, Quality PB, 978-1-58023-055-1 **$16.95**

Wandering Stars: An Anthology of Jewish Fantasy & Science Fiction
Edited by Jack Dann; Introduction by Isaac Asimov
6 x 9, 272 pp, Quality PB, 978-1-58023-005-6 **$18.99**

More Wandering Stars: An Anthology of Outstanding Stories of Jewish Fantasy and
Science Fiction Edited by Jack Dann; Introduction by Isaac Asimov
6 x 9, 192 pp, Quality PB, 978-1-58023-063-6 **$16.95**

Inspiration

The Seven Questions You're Asked in Heaven: Reviewing and Renewing Your Life on Earth *By Dr. Ron Wolfson*
An intriguing and entertaining resource for living a life that matters.
6 x 9, 176 pp, Quality PB, 978-1-58023-407-8 **$16.99**

Happiness and the Human Spirit: The Spirituality of Becoming the Best You Can Be *By Rabbi Abraham J. Twerski, MD*
Shows you that true happiness is attainable once you stop looking outside yourself for the source. 6 x 9, 176 pp, Quality PB, 978-1-58023-404-7 **$16.99**; HC, 978-1-58023-343-9 **$19.99**

Life's Daily Blessings: Inspiring Reflections on Gratitude and Joy for Every Day, Based on Jewish Wisdom *By Rabbi Kerry M. Olitzky* 4½ x 6½, 368 pp, Quality PB, 978-1-58023-396-5 **$16.99**

The Bridge to Forgiveness: Stories and Prayers for Finding God and Restoring Wholeness *By Rabbi Karyn D. Kedar*
Examines how forgiveness can be the bridge that connects us to wholeness and peace.
6 x 9, 176 pp, HC, 978-1-58023-324-8 **$19.99**

A Formula for Proper Living: Practical Lessons from Life and Torah
By Rabbi Abraham J. Twerski, MD
Gives you practical lessons for life that you can put to day-to-day use in dealing with yourself and others. 6 x 9, 144 pp, HC, 978-1-58023-402-3 **$19.99**

God's To-Do List: 103 Ways to Be an Angel and Do God's Work on Earth
By Dr. Ron Wolfson 6 x 9, 144 pp, Quality PB, 978-1-58023-301-9 **$16.99**

The Empty Chair: Finding Hope and Joy—Timeless Wisdom from a Hasidic Master, Rebbe Nachman of Breslov *Adapted by Moshe Mykoff and the Breslov Research Institute*
4 x 6, 128 pp, Deluxe PB w/ flaps, 978-1-879045-67-5 **$9.99**

The Gentle Weapon: Prayers for Everyday and Not-So-Everyday Moments— Timeless Wisdom from the Teachings of the Hasidic Master, Rebbe Nachman of Breslov *Adapted by Moshe Mykoff and S. C. Mizrahi, together with the Breslov Research Institute*
4 x 6, 144 pp, Deluxe PB w/ flaps, 978-1-58023-022-3 **$9.99**

God Whispers: Stories of the Soul, Lessons of the Heart *By Rabbi Karyn D. Kedar*
6 x 9, 176 pp, Quality PB, 978-1-58023-088-9 **$15.95**

Restful Reflections: Nighttime Inspiration to Calm the Soul, Based on Jewish Wisdom
By Rabbi Kerry M. Olitzky and Rabbi Lori Forman 4½ x 6½, 448 pp, Quality PB, 978-1-58023-091-9 **$15.95**

Sacred Intentions: Daily Inspiration to Strengthen the Spirit, Based on Jewish Wisdom
By Rabbi Kerry M. Olitzky and Rabbi Lori Forman 4½ x 6½, 448 pp, Quality PB, 978-1-58023-061-2 **$15.95**

Kabbalah/Mysticism

Seek My Face: A Jewish Mystical Theology *By Rabbi Arthur Green, PhD*
6 x 9, 304 pp, Quality PB, 978-1-58023-130-5 **$19.95**

Zohar: Annotated & Explained *Translation & Annotation by Daniel C. Matt; Foreword by Andrew Harvey* 5½ x 8½, 176 pp, Quality PB, 978-1-893361-51-5 **$15.99**
(A book from SkyLight Paths, Jewish Lights' sister imprint)

Ehyeh: A Kabbalah for Tomorrow
By Rabbi Arthur Green, PhD 6 x 9, 224 pp, Quality PB, 978-1-58023-213-5 **$16.99**

The Flame of the Heart: Prayers of a Chasidic Mystic
By Reb Noson of Breslov; Translated and adapted by David Sears, with the Breslov Research Institute
5 x 7¼, 160 pp, Quality PB, 978-1-58023-246-3 **$15.99**

The Gift of Kabbalah: Discovering the Secrets of Heaven, Renewing Your Life on Earth
By Tamar Frankiel, PhD 6 x 9, 256 pp, Quality PB, 978-1-58023-141-1 **$16.95**

Kabbalah: A Brief Introduction for Christians
By Tamar Frankiel, PhD 5½ x 8½, 208 pp, Quality PB, 978-1-58023-303-3 **$16.99**

The Lost Princess & Other Kabbalistic Tales of Rebbe Nachman of Breslov
The Seven Beggars & Other Kabbalistic Tales of Rebbe Nachman of Breslov
Translated by Rabbi Aryeh Kaplan; Preface by Rabbi Chaim Kramer
Lost Princess: 6 x 9, 400 pp, Quality PB, 978-1-58023-217-3 **$18.99**
Seven Beggars: 6 x 9, 192 pp, Quality PB, 978-1-58023-250-0 **$16.99**

See also *The Way Into Jewish Mystical Tradition* in The Way Into... Series.

Holidays/Holy Days

Who by Fire, Who by Water—Un'taneh Tokef
Edited by Rabbi Lawrence A. Hoffman, PhD

Examines the prayer's theology, authorship and poetry through a set of lively essays, all written in accessible language.
6 x 9, 272 pp, HC, 978-1-58023-424-5 **$24.99**

Rosh Hashanah Readings: Inspiration, Information and Contemplation
Yom Kippur Readings: Inspiration, Information and Contemplation
Edited by Rabbi Dov Peretz Elkins; Section Introductions from Arthur Green's These Are the Words

An extraordinary collection of readings, prayers and insights that will enable you to enter into the spirit of the High Holy Days in a personal and powerful way, permitting the meaning of the Jewish New Year to enter the heart.
Rosh Hashanah: 6 x 9, 400 pp, HC, 978-1-58023-239-5 **$24.99**
Yom Kippur: 6 x 9, 368 pp, HC, 978-1-58023-271-5 **$24.99**

Jewish Holidays: A Brief Introduction for Christians
By Rabbi Kerry M. Olitzky and Rabbi Daniel Judson
5½ x 8½, 176 pp, Quality PB, 978-1-58023-302-6 **$16.99**

Reclaiming Judaism as a Spiritual Practice: Holy Days and Shabbat
By Rabbi Goldie Milgram 7 x 9, 272 pp, Quality PB, 978-1-58023-205-0 **$19.99**

7th Heaven: Celebrating Shabbat with Rebbe Nachman of Breslov
By Moshe Mykoff with the Breslov Research Institute
5⅛ x 8¼, 224 pp, Deluxe PB w/ flaps, 978-1-58023-175-6 **$18.95**

Shabbat, 2nd Edition: The Family Guide to Preparing for and Celebrating the Sabbath By Dr. Ron Wolfson
7 x 9, 320 pp, illus., Quality PB, 978-1-58023-164-0 **$19.99**

Hanukkah, 2nd Edition: The Family Guide to Spiritual Celebration
By Dr. Ron Wolfson 7 x 9, 240 pp, illus., Quality PB, 978-1-58023-122-0 **$18.95**

The Jewish Family Fun Book, 2nd Edition: Holiday Projects, Everyday Activities, and Travel Ideas with Jewish Themes By Danielle Dardashti and Roni Sarig; Illus. by Avi Katz
6 x 9, 304 pp, 70+ b/w illus. & diagrams, Quality PB, 978-1-58023-333-0 **$18.99**

The Jewish Lights Book of Fun Classroom Activities: Simple and Seasonal Projects for Teachers and Students By Danielle Dardashti and Roni Sarig
6 x 9, 240 pp, Quality PB, 978-1-58023-206-7 **$19.99**

Passover

My People's Passover Haggadah
Traditional Texts, Modern Commentaries
Edited by Rabbi Lawrence A. Hoffman, PhD, and David Arnow, PhD

A diverse and exciting collection of commentaries on the traditional Passover Haggadah—in two volumes!
Vol. 1: 7 x 10, 304 pp, HC, 978-1-58023-354-5 **$24.99**
Vol. 2: 7 x 10, 320 pp, HC, 978-1-58023-346-0 **$24.99**

Leading the Passover Journey: The Seder's Meaning Revealed, the Haggadah's Story Retold By Rabbi Nathan Laufer
Uncovers the hidden meaning of the Seder's rituals and customs.
6 x 9, 224 pp, Quality PB, 978-1-58023-399-6 **$18.99**; HC, 978-1-58023-211-1 **$24.99**

The Women's Passover Companion: Women's Reflections on the Festival of Freedom
Edited by Rabbi Sharon Cohen Anisfeld, Tara Mohr and Catherine Spector; Foreword by Paula E. Hyman
6 x 9, 352 pp, Quality PB, 978-1-58023-231-9 **$19.99**

The Women's Seder Sourcebook: Rituals & Readings for Use at the Passover Seder
Edited by Rabbi Sharon Cohen Anisfeld, Tara Mohr and Catherine Spector; Foreword by Paula E. Hyman
6 x 9, 384 pp, Quality PB, 978-1-58023-232-6 **$19.99**

Creating Lively Passover Seders: A Sourcebook of Engaging Tales, Texts & Activities
By David Arnow, PhD 7 x 9, 416 pp, Quality PB, 978-1-58023-184-8 **$24.99**

Passover, 2nd Edition: The Family Guide to Spiritual Celebration
By Dr. Ron Wolfson with Joel Lurie Grishaver 7 x 9, 416 pp, Quality PB, 978-1-58023-174-9 **$19.95**

Life Cycle
Marriage/Parenting/Family/Aging

The New Jewish Baby Album: Creating and Celebrating the Beginning of a Spiritual Life—A Jewish Lights Companion
By the Editors at Jewish Lights; Foreword by Anita Diamant; Preface by Rabbi Sandy Eisenberg Sasso
A spiritual keepsake that will be treasured for generations. More than just a memory book, *shows you how—and why it's important*—to create a Jewish home and a Jewish life. 8 x 10, 64 pp, Deluxe Padded HC, Full-color illus., 978-1-58023-138-1 **$19.95**

The Jewish Pregnancy Book: A Resource for the Soul, Body & Mind during Pregnancy, Birth & the First Three Months
By Sandy Falk, MD, and Rabbi Daniel Judson, with Steven A. Rapp
Includes medical information, prayers and rituals for each stage of pregnancy, from a liberal Jewish perspective. 7 x 10, 208 pp, b/w photos, Quality PB, 978-1-58023-178-7 **$16.95**

Celebrating Your New Jewish Daughter: Creating Jewish Ways to Welcome Baby Girls into the Covenant—New and Traditional Ceremonies *By Debra Nussbaum Cohen; Foreword by Rabbi Sandy Eisenberg Sasso* 6 x 9, 272 pp, Quality PB, 978-1-58023-090-2 **$18.95**

The New Jewish Baby Book, 2nd Edition: Names, Ceremonies & Customs—A Guide for Today's Families *By Anita Diamant* 6 x 9, 336 pp, Quality PB, 978-1-58023-251-7 **$19.99**

Parenting as a Spiritual Journey: Deepening Ordinary and Extraordinary Events into Sacred Occasions *By Rabbi Nancy Fuchs-Kreimer*
6 x 9, 224 pp, Quality PB, 978-1-58023-016-2 **$16.95**

Parenting Jewish Teens: A Guide for the Perplexed
By Joanne Doades
Explores the questions and issues that shape the world in which today's Jewish teenagers live and offers constructive advice to parents.
6 x 9, 176 pp, Quality PB, 978-1-58023-305-7 **$16.99**

Judaism for Two: A Spiritual Guide for Strengthening and Celebrating Your Loving Relationship *By Rabbi Nancy Fuchs-Kreimer, PhD, and Rabbi Nancy H. Wiener, DMin; Foreword by Rabbi Elliot N. Dorff*
Addresses the ways Jewish teachings can enhance and strengthen committed relationships. 6 x 9, 224 pp, Quality PB, 978-1-58023-254-8 **$16.99**

The Creative Jewish Wedding Book, 2nd Edition: A Hands-On Guide to New & Old Traditions, Ceremonies & Celebrations *By Gabrielle Kaplan-Mayer*
9 x 9, 288 pp, b/w photos, Quality PB, 978-1-58023-398-9 **$19.99**

Divorce Is a Mitzvah: A Practical Guide to Finding Wholeness and Holiness When Your Marriage Dies *By Rabbi Perry Netter; Afterword by Rabbi Laura Geller*
6 x 9, 224 pp, Quality PB, 978-1-58023-172-5 **$16.95**

Embracing the Covenant: Converts to Judaism Talk About Why & How
By Rabbi Allan Berkowitz and Patti Moskovitz 6 x 9, 192 pp, Quality PB, 978-1-879045-50-7 **$16.95**

The Guide to Jewish Interfaith Family Life: An InterfaithFamily.com Handbook
Edited by Ronnie Friedland and Edmund Case
6 x 9, 384 pp, Quality PB, 978-1-58023-153-4 **$18.95**

A Heart of Wisdom: Making the Jewish Journey from Midlife through the Elder Years
Edited by Susan Berrin; Foreword by Harold Kushner
6 x 9, 384 pp, Quality PB, 978-1-58023-051-3 **$18.95**

Introducing My Faith and My Community: The Jewish Outreach Institute Guide for the Christian in a Jewish Interfaith Relationship
By Rabbi Kerry M. Olitzky 6 x 9, 176 pp, Quality PB, 978-1-58023-192-3 **$16.99**

Making a Successful Jewish Interfaith Marriage: The Jewish Outreach Institute Guide to Opportunities, Challenges and Resources *By Rabbi Kerry M. Olitzky with Joan Peterson Littman*
6 x 9, 176 pp, Quality PB, 978-1-58023-170-1 **$16.95**

So That Your Values Live On: Ethical Wills and How to Prepare Them
Edited by Jack Riemer and Nathaniel Stampfer
6 x 9, 272 pp, Quality PB, 978-1-879045-34-7 **$18.99**

Ecology/Environment

A Wild Faith: Jewish Ways into Wilderness, Wilderness Ways into Judaism
By Rabbi Mike Comins; Foreword by Nigel Savage 6 x 9, 240 pp, Quality PB, 978-1-58023-316-3 **$16.99**

Ecology & the Jewish Spirit: Where Nature & the Sacred Meet
Edited by Ellen Bernstein 6 x 9, 288 pp, Quality PB, 978-1-58023-082-7 **$18.99**

Torah of the Earth: Exploring 4,000 Years of Ecology in Jewish Thought
Vol. 1: Biblical Israel & Rabbinic Judaism; Vol. 2: Zionism & Eco-Judaism
Edited by Rabbi Arthur Waskow Vol. 1: 6 x 9, 272 pp, Quality PB, 978-1-58023-086-5 **$19.95**
Vol. 2: 6 x 9, 336 pp, Quality PB, 978-1-58023-087-2 **$19.95**

The Way Into Judaism and the Environment By Jeremy Benstein, PhD
6 x 9, 288 pp, Quality PB, 978-1-58023-368-2 **$18.99**; HC, 978-1-58023-268-5 **$24.99**

Graphic Novels/History

The Adventures of Rabbi Harvey: A Graphic Novel of Jewish Wisdom and Wit in the
Wild West By Steve Sheinkin 6 x 9, 144 pp, Full-color illus., Quality PB, 978-1-58023-310-1 **$16.99**

Rabbi Harvey Rides Again: A Graphic Novel of Jewish Folktales Let Loose in the
Wild West By Steve Sheinkin 6 x 9, 144 pp, Full-color illus., Quality PB, 978-1-58023-347-7 **$16.99**

Rabbi Harvey vs. the Wisdom Kid: A Graphic Novel of Dueling
Jewish Folktales in the Wild West By Steve Sheinkin
Rabbi Harvey's first book-length adventure—and toughest challenge.
6 x 9, 144 pp, Full-color illus., Quality PB, 978-1-58023-422-1 **$16.99**

The Story of the Jews: A 4,000-Year Adventure—A Graphic History Book
By Stan Mack 6 x 9, 288 pp, illus., Quality PB, 978-1-58023-155-8 **$16.99**

Grief/Healing

Facing Illness, Finding God: How Judaism Can Help You and Caregivers
Cope When Body or Spirit Fails By Rabbi Joseph B. Meszler
Helps you deal with the difficulties of disease when you are questioning where
God is when we get sick. 6 x 9, 208 pp, Quality PB, 978-1-58023-423-8 **$16.99**

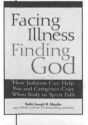

Midrash and Medicine: Healing Body and Soul in the Jewish Interpretive
Tradition Edited by Rabbi William Cutter, PhD
Explores how Midrash can help you see beyond the physical aspects of healing to
tune in to your spiritual source. 6 x 9, 240 pp (est), HC, 978-1-58023-428-3 **$24.99**

Healing from Despair: Choosing Wholeness in a Broken World
By Rabbi Elie Kaplan Spitz with Erica Shapiro Taylor; Foreword by Rabbi Abraham J. Twerski, MD
5½ x 8½, 208 pp, HC, 978-1-58023-360-6 **$21.99**

Healing and the Jewish Imagination: Spiritual and Practical Perspectives on
Judaism and Health Edited by Rabbi William Cutter, PhD
6 x 9, 240 pp, Quality PB, 978-1-58023-373-6 **$19.99**; HC, 978-1-58023-314-9 **$24.99**

Grief in Our Seasons: A Mourner's Kaddish Companion By Rabbi Kerry M. Olitzky
4½ x 6½, 448 pp, Quality PB, 978-1-879045-55-2 **$15.95**

Healing of Soul, Healing of Body: Spiritual Leaders Unfold the Strength & Solace
in Psalms Edited by Rabbi Simkha Y. Weintraub, CSW
6 x 9, 128 pp, 2-color illus. text, Quality PB, 978-1-879045-31-6 **$16.99**

Mourning & Mitzvah, 2nd Edition: A Guided Journal for Walking the Mourner's
Path through Grief to Healing By Anne Brener, LCSW
7½ x 9, 304 pp, Quality PB, 978-1-58023-113-8 **$19.99**

Tears of Sorrow, Seeds of Hope, 2nd Edition: A Jewish Spiritual Companion for
Infertility and Pregnancy Loss By Rabbi Nina Beth Cardin
6 x 9, 208 pp, Quality PB, 978-1-58023-233-3 **$18.99**

A Time to Mourn, a Time to Comfort, 2nd Edition: A Guide to Jewish
Bereavement By Dr. Ron Wolfson; Preface by Rabbi David J. Wolpe
7 x 9, 384 pp, Quality PB, 978-1-58023-253-1 **$19.99**

When a Grandparent Dies: A Kid's Own Remembering Workbook for Dealing
with Shiva and the Year Beyond By Nechama Liss-Levinson, PhD
8 x 10, 48 pp, 2-color text, HC, 978-1-879045-44-6 **$15.95** For ages 7–13

Social Justice

There Shall Be No Needy
Pursuing Social Justice through Jewish Law and Tradition
By Rabbi Jill Jacobs; Foreword by Rabbi Elliot N. Dorff, PhD; Preface by Simon Greer
Confronts the most pressing issues of twenty-first-century America from a deeply Jewish perspective.
6 x 9, 288 pp, Quality PB, 978-1-58023-425-2 **$16.99**; HC, 978-1-58023-394-1 **$21.99**
Also Available: **There Shall Be No Needy Teacher's Guide**
8½ x 11, 56 pp, PB, 978-1-58023-429-0 **$8.99**

Conscience: The Duty to Obey and the Duty to Disobey
By Rabbi Harold M. Schulweis
This clarion call to rethink our moral and political behavior examines the idea of conscience and the role conscience plays in our relationships to governments, law, ethics, religion, human nature, God—and to each other.
6 x 9, 160 pp, Quality PB, 978-1-58023-419-1 **$16.99**; HC, 978-1-58023-375-0 **$19.99**

Judaism and Justice: The Jewish Passion to Repair the World
By Rabbi Sidney Schwarz; Foreword by Ruth Messinger
Explores the relationship between Judaism, social justice and the Jewish identity of American Jews.
6 x 9, 352 pp, Quality PB, 978-1-58023-353-8 **$19.99**; HC, 978-1-58023-312-5 **$24.99**

Spiritual Activism: A Jewish Guide to Leadership and Repairing the World
By Rabbi Avraham Weiss; Foreword by Alan M. Dershowitz
6 x 9, 224 pp, Quality PB, 978-1-58023-418-4 **$16.99**; HC, 978-1-58023-355-2 **$24.99**

Righteous Indignation: A Jewish Call for Justice
Edited by Rabbi Or N. Rose, Jo Ellen Green Kaiser and Margie Klein; Foreword by Rabbi David Ellenson
Leading progressive Jewish activists explore meaningful intellectual and spiritual foundations for their social justice work.
6 x 9, 384 pp, Quality PB, 978-1-58023-414-6 **$19.99**; HC, 978-1-58023-336-1 **$24.99**

Spirituality/Women's Interest

New Jewish Feminism: Probing the Past, Forging the Future
Edited by Rabbi Elyse Goldstein; Foreword by Anita Diamant
Looks at the growth and accomplishments of Jewish feminism and what they mean for Jewish women today and tomorrow.
6 x 9, 480 pp, HC, 978-1-58023-359-0 **$24.99**

The Quotable Jewish Woman: Wisdom, Inspiration & Humor from the Mind & Heart
Edited by Elaine Bernstein Partnow 6 x 9, 496 pp, Quality PB, 978-1-58023-236-4 **$19.99**

The Divine Feminine in Biblical Wisdom Literature
Selections Annotated & Explained
Translated and Annotated by Rabbi Rami Shapiro
5½ x 8½, 240 pp, Quality PB, 978-1-59473-109-9 **$16.99**
(A book from SkyLight Paths, Jewish Lights' sister imprint)

The Women's Haftarah Commentary: New Insights from Women Rabbis on the 54 Weekly Haftarah Portions, the 5 Megillot & Special Shabbatot
Edited by Rabbi Elyse Goldstein Illuminates the historical significance of female portrayals in the Haftarah and the Five Megillot.
6 x 9, 560 pp, Quality PB, 978-1-58023-371-2 **$19.99**; HC, 978-1-58023-133-6 **$39.99**

The Women's Torah Commentary: New Insights from Women Rabbis on the 54 Weekly Torah Portions
Edited by Rabbi Elyse Goldstein
Over fifty women rabbis offer inspiring insights on the Torah, in a week-by-week format.
6 x 9, 496 pp, Quality PB, 978-1-58023-370-5 **$19.99**; HC, 978-1-58023-076-6 **$34.95**

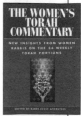

See Passover for *The Women's Passover Companion: Women's Reflections on the Festival of Freedom* and *The Women's Seder Sourcebook: Rituals & Readings for Use at the Passover Seder.*

About Jewish Lights

People of all faiths and backgrounds yearn for books that attract, engage, educate, and spiritually inspire.

Our principal goal is to stimulate thought and help all people learn about who the Jewish People are, where they come from, and what the future can be made to hold. While people of our diverse Jewish heritage are the primary audience, our books speak to people in the Christian world as well and will broaden their understanding of Judaism and the roots of their own faith.

We bring to you authors who are at the forefront of spiritual thought and experience. While each has something different to say, they all say it in a voice that you can hear.

Our books are designed to welcome you and then to engage, stimulate, and inspire. We judge our success not only by whether or not our books are beautiful and commercially successful, but by whether or not they make a difference in your life.

For your information and convenience, at the back of this book we have provided a list of other Jewish Lights books you might find interesting and useful. They cover all the categories of your life:

Bar/Bat Mitzvah	Life Cycle
Bible Study / Midrash	Meditation
Children's Books	Men's Interest
Congregation Resources	Parenting
Current Events / History	Prayer / Ritual / Sacred Practice
Ecology / Environment	Social Justice
Fiction: Mystery, Science Fiction	Spirituality
Grief / Healing	Theology / Philosophy
Holidays / Holy Days	Travel
Inspiration	12-Step
Kabbalah / Mysticism / Enneagram	Women's Interest

Stuart M. Matlins, Publisher

Or phone, fax, mail or e-mail to: **JEWISH LIGHTS Publishing**
Sunset Farm Offices, Route 4 • P.O. Box 237 • Woodstock, Vermont 05091
Tel: (802) 457-4000 • Fax: (802) 457-4004 • www.jewishlights.com
Credit card orders: **(800) 962-4544** (8:30AM–5:30PM ET Monday–Friday)
Generous discounts on quantity orders. SATISFACTION GUARANTEED. Prices subject to change.